ALSO BY SHEA SERRANO

Bun B's Rap Coloring and Activity Book

The Rap Year Book

Basketball (And Other Things)

Movies (And Other Things)

HIP-HOP (AND OTHER THINGS)

A COLLECTION OF QUESTIONS ASKED, ANSWERED, ILLUSTRATED

SHEA SERRANO

ILLUSTRATED BY ARTURO TORRES

NEW YORK BOSTON

Twelve

Hachette Book Group

1290 Avenue of the Americas, New York, NY 10104

twelvebooks.com

twitter.com/twelvebooks

First Edition: October 2021

Twelve is an imprint of Grand Central Publishing. The Twelve name and logo are trademarks of Hachette Book Group, Inc.

The publisher is not responsible for websites (or their content) that are not owned by the publisher.

The Hachette Speakers Bureau provides a wide range of authors for speaking events. To find out more, go to www.hachettespeakersbureau.com or call (866) 376-6591.

Print book interior design by Jarrod Taylor.

Library of Congress Cataloging-in-Publication Data has been applied for.

ISBNs: 978-1-5387-3022-5 (hardcover); 978-1-5387-0783-8 (signed edition); 978-1-5387-0784-5 (special signed edition); 978-1-5387-0785-2 (Black Friday signed edition); 978-1-5387-3021-8 (ebook)

Printed in the United States of America

WORZ

10 9 8 7 6 5 4 3 2 1

This book is dedicated to Larami, and to my sons.
They are all classic albums.

It's also dedicated to listening to rap while driving around in a car. Rap sounds better in cars. I don't know why that's true, I just know that it is.

CHAPTERS

FOREWORD by BUN B

I HAD A VERY MEAGER CHILDHOOD. My parents got divorced and after that my mom never really had a lot. There wasn't very much money in our house. One year, Christmas was coming around, and my mom was like, "You have twenty dollars. You can get one gift." I thought about it. And it didn't take long. I knew what I wanted. I asked her to take me to a record store because I wanted her to buy me a rap album as my one gift. The album I ended up getting was Slick Rick's *The Adventures of Slick Rick*. It changed everything for me. I'd heard rap before, but something about getting *that* album at *that* point in my life was different. It meant so much to me.

Slick Rick has this charisma to him; this purposeful charisma. It's very British in tone. It's posh. But it's ghetto posh. He would rap in this effortless and sophisticated way, and it felt like he was saying, "I'm trying to exhibit the best of social graces that I can within this environment, but don't fuck with me because I am still of this environment." It was like he was making a concerted effort to be the best version of himself, but also he could still reach into the worst version of himself if he needed to.

The Adventures of Slick Rick starts off with "Treat Her Like a Prostitute." That's literally the first song on it. But later on the album, you get "Hey Young World." It's an entire song to young children telling them to be good kids; telling them not to do what these other guys were doing, to stay in school, to get good grades, to listen to your parents. It was genius. He was able to do whatever he wanted. He was able to say whatever he wanted. And it all fit. It all made sense together. He planned for it.

Thinking back on getting that album, I realized afterward—this was *years* later—it wasn't a physical gift that my mom had given me. It wasn't just being able to open something with my hands and hold an album or a cassette. It went beyond that. It was bigger than that. She gave me something else. Something far more meaningful. She gave me art. She gave me access to this thing that lit up a new part of me. It's still lit up today.

•••••

Pimp C and I always loved rap. That was the only point of doing it. We were willing to sacrifice everything for it. And for a while, it didn't really seem as if it was going to work out. We weren't getting any traction. And then we got our deal. We signed a record deal with Jive. The day that I was told that I had a plane ticket to New York to go sign my record contract, I was like, "Yeah! We're making this shit work!" It was an incredible feeling.

But then, that's also one of the lowest points of my career as well, in that same moment. Because right after we signed the contract we saw KRS-One in the hallway of the building. And Pimp and I were excited. We were like, "Oh, shit! You're KRS-One! We're UGK. We came here to get signed. We came here to sign our deal." And his eyes got big and he grabbed our shoulders. He said, "Did you sign yet?" We were like, "Yeah! We just signed!" He was like, "Fuck. Good luck, then, man." He knew, because he'd already been through it. He knew the business part of it. And we were about to learn it.

•••••

Too Short gave me a piece of advice early in my career that I never forgot. "Don't stop rapping." Those were his words. That's what he said to me and Pimp. It was around 1996. We were in Cleveland for an outdoor concert and we were up onstage performing. Somebody started shooting. It happened somewhere in the crowd. And they ushered us off the stage. They took us in the back. When we were back there, Too Short came up to us. He said, "As soon as you can—as soon as they'll let you—go back out there and start rapping. You control the energy of the show. If you're like, 'Oh no, it's too dangerous,' then the crowd will panic. But if you get back up there and assure people that everything's okay, they'll get back into it. You'll be back in control." That's what he said to us.

But that advice was deeper than just that moment. Because the subtext there was like, "No matter what happens, don't stop rapping. I don't give a fuck what you're going through in life. Don't. Stop. Rapping. If you're in love, rap about being in love. If you're getting money, rap about getting money. If you're broke, rap about being broke. There's always going to be people that can relate to your station in life. You just have to not be afraid to tell them what that station is. Don't stop rapping. You need to keep going." That's really what he said to us.

•••••

The verse I've done that gets brought up most often is the one from "Murder." People always ask about that one. They wanna know if I knew when I recorded it that it was special. They wanna know if I went in there with the intention of doing something big, or if it just happened. And the truth is: it was half and half.

The entire time that we were recording music before that—if you look at *The Southern Way*, *Too Hard to Swallow*, *Super Tight*—the majority of that music is super slow. Pimp, he was the biggest Bun B supporter in the world. He was constantly telling people how good of a rapper he thought I was. But before "Murder," we never really had a song that allowed me to show it. The songs we were doing didn't call for me to do that. When he made the beat for "Murder," he was like, "Okay, this beat is where you can show everyone how good you can rap."

The day we recorded it, I was hungover. It was one of maybe five times in my life I've ever been hungover. I went into the studio and they were playing the beat. I wrote the rhyme and I went to sleep. I literally crawled under the board and went to sleep while they were tracking out the beat. They woke me up. Pimp went in to lay his verse. I went in to lay my verse. I immediately went back to sleep afterward. I didn't think anything of it.

But the more I listened to it, and the more other people listened to it—rappers in particular—the more I started hearing the same thing: "This is the hardest rhyme I ever heard anybody spit." That verse became my calling card. It legitimized me. People weren't just saying that I was a good rapper, or that I was a good emcee. They were saying that I was a good writer. And everybody that I considered my contemporary gave me my credit for that. That was really all I ever wanted. I wanted motherfuckers that could really rap to say, "Yo, you can really rap." And they did after the "Murder" verse.

•••••

The one Pimp C beat that sticks out to me clearly above everything else that Pimp did – and there are countless moments of sheer brilliance throughout his UGK and Pimp C solo discography – the one that sticks out is when he made "Quit Hatin' the South." And I'll tell you why.

That song was produced fully multiple times before anyone heard it. He produced it the first time when we were doing *Super Tight* in 1994. It had the same title and everything. He made that beat and he stepped back from it after he was done and said, "No, it's not time." And he cut it off. He erased it. He never saved it. It was gone. It didn't even exist. Then, seven years later in 2001, we were doing *Dirty Money*. And he made that beat again. He produced it again. He built it again from the ground up. From nothing. And he stepped back from it after he was done and he said, "Nope, it's not time. It's still not time." And he deletes it again. Then he catches his case, violates his probation, and goes to prison. He's gone. Then this whole Houston, Texas, and Southern Renaissance occurs. He gets out and he comes back home. We go in for the first UGK album after that. We're working on that. That was *Underground Kingz* in 2007. That's thirteen years after the first time he made it, and six years after the second time he made it. And he does it again. He builds it again. The whole thing. But that time, he stepped back from it after he was done and he said, "Now it's fucking time."

•••••

One of the things that make hip-hop special as an art form is that it can be replicated very easily in a public space without needing much. When I was a kid, we would take a milk crate and use that as a rim for basketball. Sometimes, if we didn't have that, we'd take the rim off a bicycle and use that as the rim. You can play a version of basketball anywhere with anything. Rap works the same way.

If you're in a band and you want to perform on the street corner, somebody's gotta at least have an amplifier. Even if you're an acoustic guy, you still gotta have a guitar. But if you're a rapper, you can just rap. When I first started, someone would just beatbox if we needed a beat, or we'd pound on a cafeteria table at school lunch. That's all we needed. At its purest – at its most base level – you don't need anything else. You don't need a recording studio. You don't need infrastructure. You don't need a facility. You just need passion.

AN INTRODUCTION, BY WAY OF TWELVE QUESTIONS

1. What is this book?

This is a book about rap—or, perhaps more accurately, this book is a celebration of rap, one of the three or four things I love the most in this world. There are very few things that can compete with that jolt of excitement you get when a song reaches out of a speaker and grabs ahold of you.

2. Does this book work the same as the other (And Other Things) books that you've written?

Yes. Thus far, I've written *Basketball (And Other Things)* and *Movies (And Other Things)*. In those books, each chapter was a different question that needed to be answered. That's what's happening here with *Hip-Hop (And Other Things)* as well. There are thirty-two chapters. Each of them is centered around a rap-related question that needs to be answered. There's also a bunch of art in the book, as well as a handful of charts, too.

3. Is that why you're doing the introduction like this? Is that why, rather than it just being a straightforward thing, it's set up around a bunch of questions?

Yes. I like themes. I like things when they all snap together neatly like that.

4. Okay. Well, that being the case, are there other themes throughout the book? Are there tiny little things and tricks in this book that people won't notice immediately?

Yes, there are themes throughout the book. And yes, there are tiny little things and tricks in the book that people won't notice immediately.

5. Will you just tell us all what those things are right now?

No.

6. Since all of the chapters are centered around their own questions, does that mean I can read the book in whatever order I want?

Yes. You can jump around as you see fit. You don't need to have read the Missy Elliott chapter to understand the Young Jeezy chapter, and you don't need to have read the Jay-Z chapter to understand the chapter about the best duos in rap. You can hit the chapters you want in whatever order you want.

7. I glanced through the book and noticed that art at the start of each chapter doesn't match the person the chapter is about. For example, the first chapter is about Jay-Z, but the first thing you see there is a picture of Pimp C in his white fur coat. Why'd you do it that way?

What I did was I put together a list of some of the most iconic outfits in the history of rap. It was stuff like Pimp C in his fur coat from the "International Players Anthem" video, or Lil' Kim's dress that she wore to the VMAs that one year, or 50 Cent's bulletproof vest, or Cardi B's checkerboard thing from the cover of *Invasion of Privacy*, or Biggie's Coogi sweater, on and on. Then I had Arturo draw them all. Then I placed them into the book at the start of each chapter. I just thought it looked cool, is all. The art within the chapters matches whatever's happening in the chapter. The art at the beginning, though, is more like a museum exhibit from the Rap Outfits Hall of Fame, were such a thing to exist.

8. I glanced at the table of contents and noticed that some of the questions for some of the chapters have a Part 1 and a Part 2. What does that mean?

Well, the quickest way to explain that is: Each chapter is usually somewhere around 3,000 words. In instances where I was writing about something that required more than 3,000 words, I'd break down the chapter into parts. So, for example, late in the book, you're going to find a chapter about the 1995 Source Awards, which, as you'll read when you get there, "remains the biggest, most historic, most impactful awards-show night in rap history." I needed about 6,000 words to talk about all the stuff from that night that I wanted to talk about, so that chapter became a two-parter. That happened a few times while I was writing the book. That's why you'll see some chapters that have a Part 1 and a Part 2 and so on.

9. Okay. Well, that leads me to another question then: Do I have to know about every rapper or song or album or music video or awards show mentioned in Hip-Hop (And Other Things) to enjoy it?

No. That's the point of the book, same as how you don't go into a movie already knowing the ending or how you don't go into listening to an album for the first time knowing every sound you're going to hear or every line the musician is going to say. The goal (for me, anyway) whenever you create something is to make it so that it's (a) accessible to everyone, while also being (b) interesting and compelling for people who are complete nerds over whatever that's being talked about. You didn't have to grow up in Compton to enjoy and love Kendrick Lamar's *Good Kid, M.A.A.D City*, and you didn't have to have previously been a member of the Fugees to enjoy Lauryn Hill's *The Miseducation of Lauryn Hill*, and you didn't have to get shot nine times to enjoy 50 Cent's *Get Rich or Die Tryin'*, you know what I'm saying?

10. Wait. Is this book as good as Kendrick Lamar's Good Kid, M.A.A.D City?

It definitely is not.

11. Would you be okay with getting shot nine times if it meant you got to be as rich and famous as 50 Cent was when he put out Get Rich or Die Tryin'?

A true story: One time, I called in sick to work because it was raining too hard outside. So, no, I would not be okay with getting shot nine times if it meant I got to be as rich and famous as 50 Cent was when he put out *Get Rich or Die Tryin'*. That's not an even trade in my eyes.

12. Is there someone you didn't get to talk about as much as you'd have liked to in this book?

Yes. A bunch of people, actually. The first one I think of is Busta Rhymes. I fucking loved Busta Rhymes in the mid-to-late '90s. He was a perfect rapper. He had, like, a six-month stretch or something where he put out videos for "Put Your Hands Where My Eyes Can See" and "Dangerous" and I just couldn't get enough of them, and of him. (In the videos, Busta re-created moments from *Coming to America*, *Lethal Weapon*, and *The Last Dragon*, all of which were movies that were very important to me.) He was all I wanted to talk about, and all I wanted to hear about. I wish I'd have had space for ten Busta Rhymes chapters in here. But I didn't. Because that's how these things work.

There's never enough room to talk about everything you want to talk about. But it makes sense, because that's not really the point. The point of these books isn't to talk about all of every single thing within a particular subject, be it basketball or movies or rap. The point of these books is to talk about some of the things in so specifically a way that someone can read them and go, "Oh, okay. I get it. I know exactly what he's talking about here. I cared about a different thing in the exact same way he cared about this thing." That's the point.

That's (hopefully) what this book is.

HIP-HOP (AND OTHER THINGS)

A COLLECTION OF QUESTIONS ASKED, ANSWERED, ILLUSTRATED

WHERE'D THOSE STRAY SHOTS THAT JAY-Z LET OFF LAND?

I DON'T KNOW WHAT ERIC BENÉT WAS DOING the night that Jay-Z's *4:44* album came out, but I do know what time it was when he felt compelled to respond to it.

Here's the logbook for that evening: *4:44* was released at twelve a.m. on June 30, 2017. And it was Jay-Z's thirteenth proper album, which was cause enough for high anticipation. But also there was extra pre-release buzz attached to it because it was rumored that *4:44* was Jay-Z's unofficial-but-official response to Beyoncé's *Lemonade*, a massively excellent multimedia album that, among other things, addressed Jay-Z's infidelity during their marriage. And so those two things together meant that a lot of people were ready for *4:44* and excited to listen to *4:44*. Which is why the name Eric Benét began trending on Twitter almost immediately after its release. Because what happened was this:

The very first song on *4:44* ("Kill Jay Z") had a part in it where Jay-Z began to approach an eventual apology to Beyoncé. He didn't come out and say it directly, though. Instead, he drew a line connecting himself to Eric Benét, who famously ruined his marriage to Halle Berry in the early 2000s by cheating on her. Here's the part from the song, which Jay rapped to himself: "You almost went Eric Benét / Let the baddest girl in the world get away / I don't even know what else to say / Never go Eric Benét."

People began sharing the line and making jokes about the line and discussing the line in relation to the Jay-Z/Beyoncé situation. And so that's how Eric Benét began trending on Twitter. Which is why Eric Benét sent the following tweet at exactly three a.m. EST[1] that night: "Hey yo #Jayz! Just so ya know, I got the baddest girl in the world as my wife . . . like right now! ✌"

Now, I'm not so interested in the various angles one could get into via Eric Benét's response, because that's not what this chapter is about. What I'm interested in is Jay-Z—or, more specifically, what I'm interested in are the numerous times that Jay-Z has let off a stray shot at someone similar to the way he did to Eric Benét. Because that's what this chapter is about.

AS A MATTER OF CLARIFICATION

A stray shot in a song (or in life, for that matter) is different from a subliminal diss. And a subliminal diss is different from a direct attack.

A direct attack is when one person calls another person out directly, either by name (like when Roxanne Shanté said "Now, KRS-One, you should go on vacation / With that name soundin' like a wack radio station"[2] on 1989's "Have a Nice Day") or by undeniable circumstance (like when 3rd Bass had a Vanilla Ice stand-in for their "Pop Goes the Weasel" video in 1991).

A subliminal diss is when someone pokes someone else in the eye via insinuation but maintains a level of plausible deniability (like when Kendrick Lamar said "I can dig rappin' / But a rapper with a ghostwriter? / What the fuck happened?" on 2015's "King Kunta" and everyone swore he was talking about Drake but it was impossible to tell if that was who Kendrick was talking about for sure).

And a stray shot is when a person who had nothing to do with a situation that's being discussed gets mentioned as a cautionary tale or through some kind

---

1. Three in the morning is an extremely Eric Benét time.
2. This is funny every single time.

of negative comparison (like when Freddie Gibbs said "Hoes get fucked and sent home early just like the Clippers" on "One Way Flight").[3]

That's what happened with Benét on "Kill Jay Z." It was a stray shot that hit him dead in his forehead.

AS ANOTHER MATTER OF CLARIFICATION

A stray shot – at least in the context it's being used here – does not refer to an actual bullet coming from an actual gun. It refers to a comment or a remark or a joke or whatever. Don't shoot people. Shooting people is bad.

•••••

Let's go through a few (but not all) of the stray shots that Jay-Z has let off.

> **The Stray Shot:** "I like my hoes on [ecstasy] like Eminem"
> **The Song It Appears On:** "Snoopy Track," from *Vol. 3 . . . Life and Times of S. Carter*

This one is in reference to how Eminem took ecstasy during early recording sessions with Dr. Dre.[4] (It was covered in a profile of Eminem that *Rolling Stone* ran in 1999. My favorite part of the story was when the writer[5] talked about how Eminem took a sip of ginger ale to help swallow the ecstasy.[6]) It feels like not that serious of a shot at all, really, which is why I began with it. If anything, this one is probably something that Eminem would remember or bring up in a What a Wild Time That Was kind of way, like when people brag about how drunk they would get in college, or when I look at old pictures of myself and see that I used to dye the tips of my hair a different color.[7]

Where'd This Stray Shot Metaphorically Hit Eminem? I'm going to say that this stray shot missed Eminem entirely. It was fired in his general direction, but it whizzed right past him. He's fine. He's safe. He's good. No damage. This one was less about Jay-Z being deadly and more about Jay-Z showing that he *could* be deadly if he wanted to be, something like the sniper training scene in *Clear and Present Danger* when the sniper sneaks all the way up to right in front of the practice station just to prove that he can.

> **The Stray Shot:** "Moral victories is for minor league coaches"
> **The Song It Appears On:** "So Appalled," from Kanye West's *My Beautiful Dark Twisted Fantasy*

Two things here:

1. Just so that it's on the record, I would like to say that I like moral victories. I'm a fan of them. They

---

3. This one is funny every single time, too, unless you're a Clippers fan, in which case I have to assume it is one of the five hundred worst things that have ever happened to you as a Clippers fan.
4. It also might be in reference to how Eminem rapped about women and drugs, or in reference to how part of Eminem's marketing involved various versions of pills. The only thing Jay-Z loves more than double entendres are triple entendres.
5. Anthony Bozza.
6. If three a.m. is an exceptionally Eric Benét time, then drinking ginger ale while taking ecstasy is an exceptionally 1999 Eminem thing.
7. Art Alexakis from Everclear is at least 40 percent responsible for this phase of my life.

make me feel good. I coached middle school basketball for several years before I was a full-time writer. During one of those seasons, we were last place in our zone in actual victories, but we were first place in our zone in moral victories. We were Moral-Victory League MVPs. It was great. Terrible basketball but good vibes.

2. Jay-Z has a song called "Smile" that appeared on *4:44*. On it, he says, "A loss ain't a loss, it's a lesson / Appreciate the pain, it's a blessing." It's the opposite energy that the "Moral victories is for minor league coaches" line has baked into it.

Where'd This Stray Shot Metaphorically Hit Minor League Coaches? It hit them right in their minor league hearts.

The Stray Shot: "Move weight like Oprah"
The Song It Appears On: "S. Carter," from *Vol. 3 . . . Life and Times of S. Carter*

Oprah has had—at least through the '90s and 2000s—a somewhat contentious relationship with rap, including disagreements with various rappers, featuring but not limited to Ice Cube, Ludacris, 50 Cent, and Snoop. So when Jay-Z appeared on her show in 2009 as part of his press run during the lead-up to *The Blueprint 3*, I assumed that at least part of the conversation would feel a little prickly or a little uncomfortable or a little icy. That never happened, though. Instead, what happened was what everyone should've known was going to happen: two of the most charming people on the planet sat down and talked to each other for an extended amount of time, and by the end of it they had both charmed each other and also everyone watching.

Oprah made her way so far into Jay-Z's heart, in fact, that he not only included a new lyric about her on *The Blueprint 3*,[8] but he also called into a radio show to tell her that he'd done so because of how meaningful it was that he'd been able to take her to visit where he'd grown up (they visited as part of a feature that ran in *O Magazine*). And Jay-Z made his way so far into Oprah's heart that following their interview, she started referring to him as her "new best friend."[9]

Where'd This Stray Shot Metaphorically Hit Oprah? This was a teeny, tiny nick. It scraped right past Oprah's shoulder, if that. Didn't even need stitches. Just one of them little Band-Aids.

The Stray Shot: "We stuck in *La La Land* / Even when we win, we gon' lose"
The Song It Appears On: "Moonlight," from *4:44*

I was watching live when the *MOONLIGHT* WINS BEST PICTURE BUT *LA LA LAND* GETS ANNOUNCED AS THE WINNER thing happened at the Oscars, and man, what a fucking wild ending that was. *Moonlight*, which featured Black actors in all of its primary roles, beating out *La La Land*, which featured white actors in all of its

8. "Meanwhile, I had Oprah chilling in the projects / Had her out in Bed-Stuy / Chilling on the steps"

9. Another example of how good Oprah is at disarming people: 50 Cent, an expert and unrelenting opponent in all beef matters, had a long-standing dislike of Oprah. (Part of his needling of Oprah included him announcing that he'd named his dog after her.) It lasted literal years. Then she invited him to appear on *Oprah's Next Chapter*. And he was helpless as soon as he sat down in a chair across from her. By the end of the show, he'd lovingly say, "This is a huge milestone for me—just being in your presence and on the show."

primary roles, but then *La La Land* still getting to celebrate as the winner was about as close as you can get to a perfect metaphor for America.

Where'd This Stray Shot Metaphorically Hit *La La Land*? I like Ryan Gosling a lot. The thing of it is, though, I like Emma Stone more. So rather than this stray shot hitting both of them here, I'm just gonna say that it hit Gosling twice instead. Remember the scene in *Shooter* when Mark Wahlberg has to meet with the bad guys up on the snowy mountains? And the bad guys are real scared about the meeting because Mark Wahlberg's character has, by that point, killed a bunch of dudes by shooting them in the head. So one of the bad guys, as a safety precaution, rigs up a contraption that keeps a gun pointed at the back of a hostage he's holding. And then, as a double safety precaution, he tapes the gun to his hand so that there's no way for him to be separated from it. But then Mark Wahlberg just shoots his thumb off from, like, a mile away. And then, just because this is the kind of movie that it is, Mark Wahlberg decides to just shoot his whole arm off, too. That's this situation. Two shots to Gosling.

> **The Stray Shot:** "If skills sold / Truth be told / I'd probably be lyrically Talib Kweli / Truthfully, I wanna rhyme like Common Sense / But I did five mil / I ain't been rhyming like Common since"
> **The Song It Appears On:** "Moment of Clarity," from *The Black Album*

This would (were such things measurable) likely be Jay-Z's most famous stray shot. It came as a way to address criticism that Jay, a masterful writer and rap tactician, had purposely dulled the blade of his sword a bit in pursuit of bigger successes and broader acclaim. (The five million that he's talking about refers to the number of copies that *Vol. 2 . . . Hard Knock Life* sold five years earlier, which was nearly four times as many copies as his album prior to that sold.)

There's a great interview that Dave Chappelle did on *The Tonight Show Starring Jimmy Fallon* in 2014 where he tells Fallon about the first time he met Kanye West. Part of the story includes how Chappelle was actually in a recording studio with Talib Kweli and Common the day that *The Black Album* came out. He said they were all listening to it together and they got to the Talib/Common line and Common responded, "Hey," with a beleaguered look on his face. "I'm not sure how I feel about that." That's probably exactly how I'd have felt, too.

Because on the one hand, it does seem like what Jay-Z is saying – that Talib Kweli and Common are both talented emcees who are capable of profound feats of wordplay – is a compliment.[10] But on the other hand, it also does seem like what Jay-Z is saying – that Talib Kweli and Common don't quite know how to translate their skill level into a commensurate level of success – is not a compliment.

Ultimately, I think it's one of those situations where it's a combination of the two; as a comment, it's 30 percent nice and 70 percent mean – like if someone told you that you're way too good looking to be dating the person that you're dating.

Where'd This Stray Shot Metaphorically Hit Talib Kweli and Common? This shot hurt a little bit,

---

10. Jay-Z went on to say nice things about both of them in his book *Decoded*.

for sure. And the fact that it has aged its way into a philosophical debate of sorts certainly does little to soothe the sting. Let's say the metaphorical bullet hit Kweli and Common in their metaphorical forearms. It left a metaphorical scar, but it never put either of them in any real danger.

The Stray Shot: "No, I'm not a Jonas Brother / I'm a grown-up / No, I'm not a virgin / I use my cojones"
The Song It Appears On: "On to the Next One," from *The Blueprint 3*

This song (obviously) is about how Jay-Z is in constant pursuit of whatever the next thing is. And for some reason, just right in the middle of it, he decides to bring up the Jonas Brothers, and also, he decides to imply that they're virgins. (This likely was because of the long-running story line that was baked into the Jonas Brothers' pop-culture arc about how they each wore a purity ring and were waiting until marriage to have sex.) Joe Jonas actually talked about the Jay-Z line during an appearance on *Hot Ones* with Sean Evans. He said of the line, "I thought that was awesome." Then he took a beat. Then he continued: "Little did Jay-Z know I used my cojones since before that, so joke's on you, Jay-Z. Fact-check your stuff." And it just really makes me happy to think about Jay-Z, sitting in a hot tub in a villa in Saint-Tropez, thinking up lyrics to use in songs, shouting to an assistant that he needs for them to find out if Joe Jonas has ever had sex before.

Where'd This Stray Shot Metaphorically Hit the Jonas Brothers? This was a good one. It took a decade before any of the Jonas Brothers ever got around to responding to it, and when Joe finally did on *Hot Ones*, it definitely looked like it was something that bothered him. And I already hate that this is where this has to go, but as far as placement goes, I think it's pretty clear that this stray shot hit each of the Jonas Brothers right in the dick. It was like one of those magic bullets from *JFK*.

The Stray Shot: "I lost thirty mil so I spent another thirty / 'Cause unlike Hammer, thirty million can't hurt me"
The Song It Appears On: "So Appalled," from Kanye West's *My Beautiful Dark Twisted Fantasy*

If I were 20 percent smarter, then right here I'd do a thing where I talked about how ironic (fitting?) it was that Jay-Z got into a small battle with MC Hammer, who was among the very first rappers to figure out how to reach mainstream commercial success at a massive level. I'm not 20 percent smarter, though. So instead of that, I'm going to say I cared a lot about MC Hammer when I was a kid. He made the exact kind of music that I wanted to listen to when I was eleven years old. I watched him go from "U Can't Touch This" to "2 Legit 2 Quit" (WHICH CAME WITH A VIDEO THAT FEATURED A CAMEO BY DAVID ROBINSON) to that song he did for the *Addams Family* movie, and best I could tell, he was the most talented and most important rapper who'd ever lived. But then he did that video for "Pumps and a Bump" where he was wearing boots, gloves, a leopard-print Speedo, and a whole lot of baby oil, and I was like, "Okay, maybe I misjudged that."

Where'd This Stray Shot Metaphorically Hit MC Hammer? I imagine this one hurt a bunch, mostly because it was rooted in the truth. (Let's say it hit Hammer in the chest.) Per *Forbes*, Hammer earned something near $33 million in 1990 alone. By 1996, he'd filed bankruptcy and he was $13 million in debt. I wish he'd have used at least some of that money to buy a stray-shot bulletproof vest.

The Stray Shot: "Why kill a puppet and leave Geppetto alive?"
The Song It Appears On: "Dig a Hole," from *Kingdom Come*

Three things here:

1. I know that this song was largely directed at Cam'ron, whom Jay-Z had softly warred with for several years before this point. And that being the case, that means this Geppetto line is more of a subliminal diss than it is a stray shot. HOWEVER, it's only a subliminal diss if you're talking about it as it pertains to Cam'ron. And that's not what I'm doing. I'm talking about it as it pertains to the actual Geppetto, as in the dad from the Pinocchio story who carved a marionette out of wood, which then came alive and eventually turned into a real human. Geppetto's the one who caught the stray shot here.
2. I wonder how Geppetto felt about the *Annabelle* horror movie franchise. I have to assume he hated it, if for no other reason than because of how detrimental it had to have been to the Creepy Wooden Dolls industry that Geppetto had dedicated his life to.
3. There was a period in 2014 when I was rewatching all of the animated movies that I could get my hands on because I wanted to compile a list of all the saddest animated movie characters. Geppetto was way high up in the sadness rankings.[11] Here's what I wrote about him: "A childless woodworker is so desperate for human companionship that he builds a marionette and then wishes for it to become a real child. Against all odds, life is blessed into the doll, only the little guy isn't fully a real boy, he's a puppet still, and he's stricken with an ultra-rare disease that causes his nose to grow each time he lies. The marionette is eventually kidnapped into a puppet show. He escapes from there, only to be tricked into going to an island where young boys are turned into donkeys (which I think is a metaphor for molestation, though I'm not quite sure). While there, the marionette develops a drinking and smoking problem. Geppetto, heartbroken at the thought of having lost his wooden son, sets out to find him. He gets eaten by a whale." That's a tough stretch of days for Geppetto.

So, Where'd This Stray Shot Metaphorically Hit Geppetto, Then? This one hit Geppetto square in the shoulder. He was just at home, minding his business, whittling a wooden girlfriend for himself or whatever, when he (probably) got a text message from Jiminy Cricket that (probably) said something like "Gee willikers, Geppetto. Jay-Z is talking a bunch of malarkey about you and Pinocc, says I."

11. He only got beat out by Marlin from *Finding Nemo* and Carl from *Up*.

HOW DO YOU TALK ABOUT MISSY ELLIOTT'S *SUPA DUPA FLY*?

THIS IS MY FAVORITE MISSY ELLIOTT ANECDOTE, and it's also a perfect explanation of how Missy Elliott became Missy Elliott, and possibly *why* Missy Elliott became Missy Elliott, though I don't mind telling you that the statements between the first comma in this sentence and the third comma in this sentence are impossible to verify for anyone who is not, as it were, Missy Elliott.

Early in her career, Missy wrote and produced a song called "That's What Little Girls Are Made Of." It was for Raven-Symoné, who was then a child rapper. The song included a brief feature from Missy. When the video was filmed for it, however, Missy was replaced with a thinner woman who had lighter skin (the woman lip-synced Missy's part). Missy explained in interviews later that she'd been told after the fact that, per the record label, she didn't have the right look to be included in the video. She recounted the event to the *Guardian* in 2001, saying, "They'd broken my heart. They said I could sing, I could write, but that I looked wrong. That was the lowest thing you could say. I didn't forget." That happened in 1993.

Four years later, Missy had parlayed her growing reputation as a songwriter and producer into a unique situation: Elektra Records offered her her own label, under the condition that she deliver for them a solo project of her own first.[1] So that's what she did. And that's how we got her 1997 debut, *Supa Dupa Fly*, an album so forward looking and borderless and futuristic that even today, more than two decades later, we've still not caught up to it. And that's how we get back to the thing about her being left out of the "That's What Little Girls Are Made Of" video.

The first video Missy chose to make for *Supa Dupa Fly* was for "The Rain (Supa Dupa Fly)." The opening shot in it (and then, later, the most iconic shot in it) is of Missy in an inflated-with-air black leather outfit, center picture, unmistakable, the magnified focus of a Hype Williams fish-eye lens. And so there Missy was, finally in full creative control of her career, and the first thing she chose to show everyone was an exaggerated version of the things she'd previously been told were bad about herself. And more than that, she did so while asserting, over and over again with a warm honey coo, that she was cool: "Me, I'm supa fly / supa dupa fly / supa dupa fly." She said it ten times in a row before finally making her way to the first verse. The whole thing – the imagery, the declaration, the unwavering confidence – was very clearly a FUCK YOU move. It was very clearly an I'M GOING TO DO THIS MY WAY move. It was very clearly an I'M THE ONLY PERSON ON THE PLANET WHO COULD'VE PUT THIS TOGETHER LIKE THIS move.

It was perfect and undeniable.

From that moment forward – from the first minute of the first video of her first album – everyone knew that Missy was something different, that Missy was something special, that Missy was going to change everything, in so many different ways.[2]

•••••

A very specific thing about Missy Elliott that is illustrative of a grander Missy Elliott effect: you don't write what you want to write about Missy Elliott if you're listening to Missy Elliott while you're writing. You just don't. You can

---

1. Her label is called the Goldmind Inc.
2. The least surprising Missy Elliott anecdote is that she had her IQ tested in school and her score registered her as an actual and literal genius.

THE COSMIC PULL OF MYSTERY, or: FOUR APT WORDS YOU CAN FORM FROM MISSY'S NAME			
MISSY ELLIOTT			
LIMITLESS	MISSILE	SIMILE	STYLE

try, sure. You can give it your very best effort, definitely. You can sit down with something in your head that you think might be good or clever or smart. But ultimately, you end up writing what she wants—or, more accurately, what her music wants.

It gets in your ears and then in your brain, and then, instantly and fully, all the parts inside your skull are soaked. Your frontal lobe is soaked, and your cerebellum is soaked (even if you don't really know where your cerebellum is),[3] and somehow even the edges of the backs of your eyes are soaked, like a sponge on a wet countertop. And then that's that. You're toast. You're no longer able to write what you want to write. Instead, you write what the music pushes you toward.

And so right now, I will tell you: it's a little after two a.m. as I write this sentence, and the robo-sex-funk of "Friendly Skies" has turned everything a soft orange hue, and I am compelled to write the following words: *Lynx. Crawl. Seduce. Helicopter. Idris Elba. Slip. Warmth. Fur. Exude.*

.....

"The Rain (Supa Dupa Fly)" is the best song on *Supa Dupa Fly.*[4] Here are eight other songs about rain, ordered by how enjoyable the rain sounds in each of them are:

1. **"Make It Rain" by Fat Joe featuring Lil Wayne:** This is the only song on this list where the rain isn't actually rain. In this case, it's money, which, if you're not a plant (which I am not), is typically way better. That's why it's first place.
2. **"Purple Rain" by Prince:** Prince performed this song at Super Bowl XLI while it was actually raining.

3. It's in the back, though I suspect a doctor would have a different description for its location than "It's in the back."

4. Excluding skits and interludes, the order goes (1) "The Rain (Supa Dupa Fly)," (2) "Sock It 2 Me," (3) "Friendly Skies," (4) "Beep Me 911," (5) "Hit Em wit da Hee," (6) "Best Friends," (7) "Izzy Izzy Ahh," (8) "Don't Be Commin' (In My Face)," (9) "Pass da Blunt," (10) "Why You Hurt Me," (11) "They Don't Wanna Fuck wit Me," (12) "Gettaway," (13) "I'm Talkin'."

There's a behind-the-scenes video about it that you can find online where Bruce Rodgers, the production designer for the halftime show that year, talks a little about the staff having to call Prince and tell him that it was going to be raining during his set. He said that they asked Prince if he was okay to perform in the rain, to which Prince said, "Can you make it rain harder?" That's the fucking funniest thing to me.

3. **"Through the Rain" by Mariah Carey:** The rain here is literal rain (as in, water from the sky) but also metaphorical rain (the video stars Bodie from *The Wire* and Meadow Soprano from *The Sopranos* as they deal with the fallout of being in an interracial relationship).
4. **"Walkin' in the Rain" by Marvin Gaye:** Beautiful rain. Healing rain.
5. **"November Rain" by Guns N' Roses:** Extremely dramatic rain. Perhaps the most dramatic rain. Rain so dramatic, in fact, that when it finally shows up in the video, everyone reacts like they've been caught in the middle of a drive-by.
6. **"Set Fire to the Rain" by Adele:** The second most dramatic rain. Rain so dramatic that Adele, otherwise a very measured and pleasant person, would like to set it on fire.
7. **"I Wish It Would Rain" by the Temptations:** Rain that you need because you want to hide how much you're crying. Real rain. Pain rain.
8. **"Prayers for Rain" by the Cure:** Muddy rain. Dirty rain. Rain that feels less like a restorative force and more like a destructive force. The kind of rain where, when you see it, you say to yourself, "Let me go on Facebook and leave some mean comments on photos of people I only barely know."

•••••

Supa Dupa Fly came out during the summer of 1997. Later that year, a movie called *Good Will Hunting* was released, too. In it, Matt Damon plays a reluctant genius who was orphaned as a child and then grows up to work construction in South Boston with Batman. There's a part in it where Damon's character, Will Hunting, recounts the abuse he suffered as a child to his therapist (Sean Maguire, played by Robin Williams).

He explains to Sean that sometimes his foster dad would place a wrench, a stick, and a belt on the table and then tell him to pick which of those three things he wanted to get beat with. Sean says that he'd have gone with the belt. Will responds immediately: "I used to go with the wrench," he says, looking off to the side, and you can tell he's replaying that exact moment in his head. He looks completely defeated. The amount of hurt that the memory still holds over him is obvious. Sean asks him why the wrench. Will blinks once, then looks up at Sean. His whole entire everything changes. He looks beyond defiant; he looks like he's made of titanium. "Because fuck him, that's why."

Nineteen ninety-seven was a strong year for geniuses telling people to fuck off.

•••••

LET'S READ WAY TOO FAR INTO THREE PARTS FROM THE BEGINNING OF *SUPA DUPA FLY*

1. The opening quarter of *Supa Dupa Fly* is as such: The first song ("Busta's Intro") is Busta Rhymes

talking shit and building momentum for about two minutes. You don't hear Missy say any words on it at all. The second song ("Hit Em wit da Hee") starts with a guest verse from Lil' Kim before Missy comes gliding in later. The third song ("Sock It 2 Me") starts with Missy, but then Da Brat comes in at the end to close things out. It's not until the fourth song of the album that we get Missy on a song entirely by herself.[5] **A way to read too far into that:** There's a progression through those first four songs where Missy seems to ease herself into the spotlight gradually. Maybe she did it that way on purpose. Maybe she did it as a way to glance at how her first instinct was to work in the background of things and she had to be coaxed into that version of stardom.

2. The first song that we hear Missy on in *Supa Dupa Fly* is "Hit Em wit da Hee." **A way to read too far into that:** The first time that Missy Elliott generated real heat as a rapper was when she showed up on the remix of Gina Thompson's "The Things That You Do" in 1996. Her verse was very normal to start – she was doing what rappers did whenever they popped up in R&B videos in the '90s, which is to say she was positioned in and around a car next to attractive people and doing lots of hand movements while she rapped. But then, a few seconds into it, she said the following line: "Hee-hee-hee-hee-how / Hee-hee-hee-hee-hee-how." Now, I don't know exactly what that line means (and, incidentally, neither does Missy[6]) but I do know that it's an incredible thing to say in a rap song, and also that everyone went fucking crazy about it. Maybe Missy choosing to make "Hit Em wit da Hee" the first proper song on *Supa Dupa Fly* was her way of looking back at how the "Hee-hee-hee-hee-how" changed everything for her.

3. The most memorable line from *Supa Dupa Fly* is on "The Rain" when Missy starts the second verse by saying, "Beep, beep / Who got the keys to the Jeep? / *Vroooooooooom.*"[7] **A way to read way too far into that:** Both Missy and Timbaland, her creative partner and also the sole producer for *Supa Dupa Fly*, are from Virginia. Maybe Missy choosing to include the Jeep/*Vroooooooooom* part in the song was her way of addressing that the music she and Timbaland were making was a product of Virginia, and if the rest of the rap world – by that point, largely broken up between the West Coast, the East Coast, and the South – wanted a piece of it, they were going to have to drive there and get it.[8]

•••••

It's fun to think about Missy Elliott's music in a spiritual sense, or a cosmic sense, or a philosophical sense. It's

---

5. And even then, technically that's not entirely true. "The Rain (Supa Dupa Fly)" samples 1973's "I Can't Stand the Rain" by Ann Peebles. Peebles is the other voice on the song.

6. On *Behind the Music* in 2011, Missy said, "I don't know where the hell 'Hee-hee-hee-hee-how' came from, but it worked. As soon as I said it, [Puff Daddy] was like, '*Ohhhhh!*' Puffy, he liked that line."

7. The second most memorable line is from "Sock It 2 Me," when Da Brat says that she and Missy "hit hard like penitentiary dick."

8. This one is absolutely ridiculous. A more likely explanation is that Missy put that Jeep/*Vroooooooooom* part in the song because (a) it sounds cool, (b) she is a fan of onomatopoeia, or (c) some combination of the two.

perfect for that exact thing, because she's the only person who has ever lived who can do the things she does in the way that she does them. You play a Missy Elliott song, and you hear the way she raps, and the things she says, and the manner in which she says them, and you combine that together with the beat, and there you go. It's a one of one situation.

It's also fun, though, to think about Missy Elliott in a very straightforward sense, or a pragmatic sense, or a direct sense. And it's fun to do it for that same exact reason: Missy Elliott makes music that only Missy Elliott can make. It's the single best argument to make for why she is one of the ten greatest rappers ever (and, incidentally, why she's one of my five favorite rappers ever).

I played in a Student vs. Teacher basketball game once that our technology teacher decided to videotape. I was very excited about it because I'd never played in a game before that I was able to watch later on. (My high school coach did not think it necessary to record our games, which should give you a pretty good idea of how good our team was.) So we went out there and the game started and I made a few shots and I was feeling real good. I couldn't wait for the game to be over so that I could watch myself on video. I really and honestly and truly felt during that game like I looked like Steph Curry or Diana Taurasi or Klay Thompson or Sabrina Ionescu whenever I shot the ball. I promise to you that I genuinely thought that. But then two days later I saw the video. And guess what? I extremely did not. They shoot the ball and it looks like poetry, or art. I shoot the ball and it looks like it weighs 20 pounds and is covered in oil.

Anyway, it's the same way with Missy Elliott and music. You could take 100,000 people and keep them in a recording studio for 100,000 hours and show them exactly what they needed to do to make a Missy Elliott song and they would never be able to make a Missy Elliott song. They would never be able to string together the correct combination of sounds and feelings that would cause other people to say, "Whoa. What is this? Is this a new Missy Elliott song?" At best, those 100,000 people would spend those 100,000 hours and make something that would cause other people to say, "Ewww. What is this? It sounds like someone trying to rip off Missy Elliott."

•••••

Talking about the arrival of *Supa Dupa Fly* means discussing not only the way that Missy Elliott expanded the borders of what rap music could be, but also the way that she forever advanced the position and cachet that women could hold in rap. Culture critic Candace McDuffie wrote a really sharp piece about that exact thing for *Vibe* in 2017, two highlights of which being these sections:

1. "When it comes to women who attempt to navigate hip-hop as artists – not sexual conquests or video vixens or reality television personalities – they tend to be placed into one of two categories: androgyny or hyper-sexualization. The former, in which female rappers have their worth and talent measured by their proximity to socially constructed ideals of masculinity (The Lady of Rage, Da Brat, Young M.A), stands in strong contrast to the latter in which hedonistic proclivities undeniably remain front and center (Lil' Kim, Trina, Nicki Minaj). What was so groundbreaking about *Supa Dupa Fly* was Elliott's refusal to be pigeonholed. Not only did she relish in her authenticity, she embraced the complexities inherent

with black womanhood and bravely magnified them for the sake of her art."

2. "Elliott's creative fearlessness, which has been her most revered trait since her introduction, shifted the imagination of hip-hop and made girls who refuse to adhere to the rules of a culture that was never made for us its focal point. *Supa Dupa Fly* is more than just a rap album; it is a celebration of the black female experience and the intricacies that are embedded in it."

What I find most fascinating about this part of Missy Elliott's legacy is the different levels at which it exists and at which it can be identified. And what I mean is oftentimes, when an artist is impactful in an undeniable way, that becomes the default way that that artist begins to be considered. Everything sort of springs out from (or toward) that same point. For example, if you and I were to spend several minutes talking about, say, Eazy-E, pretty much all of the main parts of that conversation would eventually (if not initially) include some version of the phrase "one of the godfathers of gangsta rap." That's his default setting.

But with Missy, whose impact is so omnipresent and encompassing, it can work differently. It's very easy to talk about one of the many ways in which she has been important – the iconography of her music videos; the Afrofuturism;[9] the above-mentioned ways she advanced rap and the place that women had in it; more, more, more – without ever making your way to the other things. It is, I would argue, the highest place at which an artist can exist; one where they are so overwhelmingly significant that there is no default, other than to say they are so overwhelmingly significant.

9. On *Say It Loud*, Hallease Narvaez said, "Using Afrofuturism as a lens to understand or categorize art is to point out Black folks have been underrepresented in speculative fiction as a whole, like sci-fi. In Missy Elliott's case, music videos helped close that gap."

THE EIGHTH SONG ON *GET RICH OR DIE TRYIN'*, 50 Cent's brilliant debut album, is called "If I Can't." And there are a lot of great parts in it, and some of those parts are even ones that I'm going to talk about later, but there's one specifically that I want to mention right now. It happens at the top of the second verse. It's a piece of advice that 50 Cent offers to current or prospective criminals who find themselves at serious odds with someone in their presence. He says, "You holding a strap / He might come back / So clap him."

50 is, in effect, saying to someone, "You have a gun. And this person that you're fighting with might come back later on and do something bad to you. So what you should do is kill him right now—that way you don't have to worry about him anymore." It's (obviously) not a moral thing that 50 Cent is arguing for, but it *is* a smart thing that 50 Cent is arguing for, at least with respect to gangsterdom. And a very straight-line example to cite here is *Carlito's Way.*

Carlito's Way came out in 1993. It's a gangster movie starring Al Pacino. He plays a felon named Carlito Brigante who is trying very hard to not be a felon anymore. Now, he ends up being really bad at this, of course—by the end of the movie, he has committed, among other things, several murders—but there's a scene early on where he actually does a good job of it.

What happens is this: Carlito is hanging out one evening at a nightclub. After a tiny scuffle breaks out at his table over a woman, he finds himself in a backroom argument with a guy named Benny Blanco, a young gangster who's trying to establish himself in the underworld. As they argue, Benny hisses at him, "You might as well fucking kill me now, because if I ever see you again, I swear to God I'm gonna fucking kill you!" The threat touches Carlito's spine, and before he can weigh all the parts of the situation, he pistol-whips Benny in the side of the head with a revolver, sending Benny tumbling down a flight of stairs toward the alley. Carlito considers killing him, and there's even a voice-over in the moment where we hear Carlito acknowledge that he knows he's supposed to kill Benny, but he decides against it. As Carlito walks away from the scene, we hear him in voice-over again: "Any other time, that punk would die. But I can't do that shit no more. Don't wanna burn nobody, even when I know I should. That ain't me now."

From there, Carlito bulldozes his way through the rest of the movie, trying to gather money so that he can retire to the Caribbean with his eventual girlfriend (Gail). All of everything eventually turns to shit in his hands, but he's able to survive an end-of-movie shootout and escape to a train with Gail, who has since become pregnant. Right before he boards the train, though, a previously unnoticed man in the scene, wearing a trench coat and a hat and glasses, says, "Hey, remember me?" Carlito looks at him, and terror spreads across his face: it's Benny Blanco.

Benny pulls out a concealed gun, shoots Carlito three times in the stomach, and that's that. Carlito dies before the paramedics can even get him out of the train station.

Now, I want to make sure that I say this clearly, because it definitely should be said: murdering someone is bad. Real bad. It's one of the worst things you can do, in fact. And you should for sure not do it. HOWEVER, clearly Carlito fucked up by not killing Benny earlier. And the way that turned out for Carlito is he died in front of the woman he loved, and Benny escaped into the night, free to chase down his ever-growing gangster legacy.

•••••

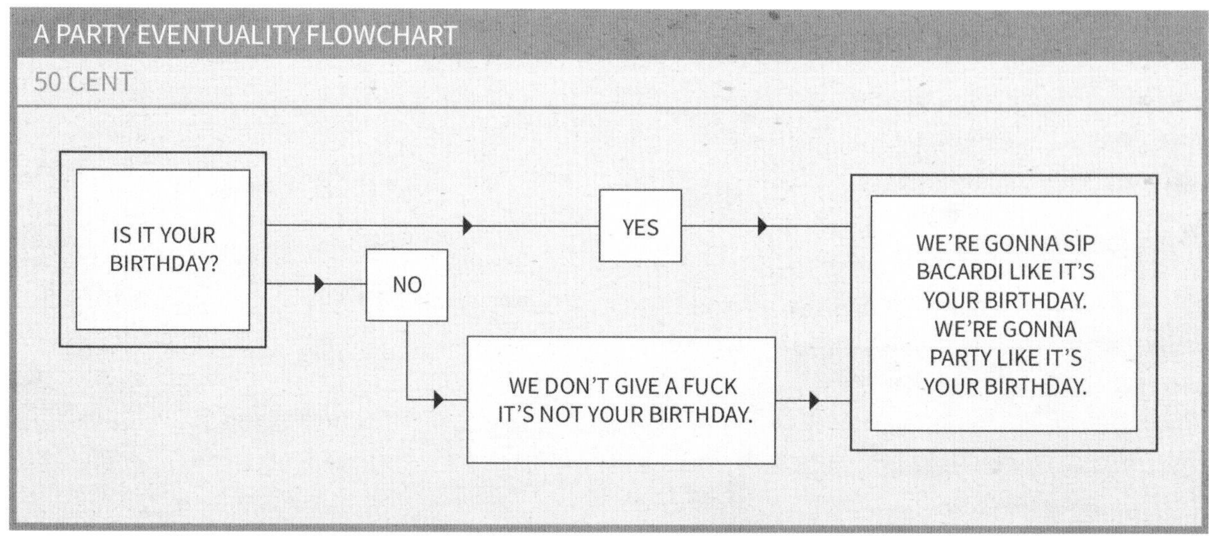

There's a lot of good advice on *Get Rich or Die Tryin'*. That's what this chapter and the next chapter are about. They're a collection of that advice.

The Advice: How to Not Incriminate Yourself
The Song: "What Up Gangsta"
The Line: "I try not to say nothing the DA might want to play in court"

Two things here:

1. This is smart advice. You should, in pretty much all instances, try not to say anything that someone might be able to use against you at a later time. That's why it's the first thing the police say to you when they're Mirandizing you during an arrest.
2. My favorite thing about this warning is that five songs later on this album, 50 Cent barks the following: "The DA can play this motherfucking tape in court: I'll kill you!" And lest you think 50 Cent is joking or speaking in hyperbole, he follows that up by saying, "I ain't playing" and "Catch you slipping, I'ma kill you."

The Advice: How to Be Honest About Your Abilities
The Song: "What Up Gangsta"
The Line: "They say I walk around like I got a *S* on my chest / Nah, that's a semiauto and a vest on my chest"

The implication here, with people telling 50 Cent that he walks around like he has an *S* on his chest, is that he moves through the world with the same kind of I Can't Be Hurt confidence that Superman has. 50 confirms that, yes, he is possessed of an abundance of confidence. *But*, he continues, it isn't because he's a superhero. It's because he's carrying a big fucking gun. And so the lesson here is simple: the best kind of confidence is rooted in something real.

When I was sixteen, I got a job at Chuck E. Cheese, which is a pizza franchise that has a rat for a mascot.[1] As part of my work duties, I was required to dress up in the Chuck E. Cheese costume for fifteen minutes every hour and walk around and wave at kids and give high fives and do things like that.

Prior to my suiting up for the first time, the manager told me that there were three rules everyone had to follow while dressed as Chuck E. Cheese. He said, number one, if you were wearing the suit, you weren't allowed to talk. And he said, number two, if you were wearing the suit, you weren't allowed to make lewd gestures. And he said, number three, if you were wearing the suit, you were not allowed to hold any babies or kids.

Now, those first two rules made perfect sense to me.

With the talking thing: Chuck E. Cheese has a very specific voice. And if you're a kid and you see Chuck E. Cheese walking around and you say hello to him and he says hello back to you, but he doesn't sound like Chuck E. Cheese, instead he sounds like a Mexican from the south side of San Antonio, I imagine that would lead to some difficult questions for that kid's parents. So I got that one.

And with the lewd-gesture thing: I mean . . . *obviously*. There's no situation where it's going to be good for anybody if Chuck E. Cheese is wandering around the restaurant dry-humping a Skee-Ball machine or doing that one thing where you make a circle with your thumb and index finger on one hand and then use your other index finger on your other hand to poke in and out of the hole. So I got that one, too.

But I was somewhat confused by the third one. I couldn't immediately think of a scenario in which a parent would ask a teenager dressed like a giant rat to hold their baby. And so I asked the manager, "Why would someone give me a baby to hold?" To which he replied with something close to "Just follow the rules, okay?" And then he sent me on my way.

So I got dressed up that first time, and I walked out into the restaurant, and I'm waving and high-fiving and making sure not to give anyone the middle finger, and things are going generally pretty okay for those first few minutes. And that's when I get a tap on the shoulder. I turn around, and it's a young mom and a young dad and their young son (he's maybe eighteen months old). The dad asked if I could take a picture with the mom and the baby, and so I nodded yes and got ready to pose. And right before the dad snapped the shot of us, the mom handed the baby toward me.

Now, listen: By that point in my life, I'd been around babies for longer than I could even remember. I was the oldest of four kids in my family, and I was the elder statesman to something like thirty cousins, too. Being handed a baby was something that had happened to me a lot.[2] And so when that mom handed her baby toward me, I reached for

1. This footnote area would have been a perfect spot for some sort of joke about how bad of an idea it was to pick a rat, generally regarded as one of the worst and trashiest animals, as a mascot for a chain of family restaurants. HOWEVER, when I searched around on the internet to learn about the history of Chuck E. Cheese, I found out something truly interesting, and so that's what I'm going to tell you right here instead. What I learned was Chuck E. Cheese was founded by Nolan Bushnell. He's the same guy who founded Atari. The reason he created Chuck E. Cheese was because he wanted to make arcade games something that more children were interested in. That's crazy, right? I had no idea.

2. Mexicans fucking love handing their baby to someone.

SMASH
POW
9000

him just as a natural reflex. And then guess what happened? I immediately dropped that baby on the floor.

When you get dressed up as Chuck E. Cheese, part of the costume includes these big gloves you have to wear over your human hands so they don't look like human hands, they look like cartoon rat hands. It's like if you were wearing a pair of soccer goalie gloves inside of a second pair of soccer goalie gloves. It's utterly impossible to hold anything while you have them on. It didn't matter that I'd held a ton of babies prior to that mom handing me hers on that day, because I'd never held a baby while dressed as Chuck E. Cheese before. I had confidence that I could do it, sure. But that confidence was an illusion. Unlike 50 Cent's gun-based confidence, my confidence was not rooted in anything real. And thus: a baby on the floor.

The Advice: How to Be Happy
The Song: "Patiently Waiting"
The Line: "I'm down to sell my records but not my soul"

I appreciate this sentiment a lot.

The Advice: How to Return Something
The Song: "Many Men"
The Line: "Go on and get your refund, motherfucker, I ain't dead"

This line is how 50 Cent ends a part of the song where he talks about some people putting a bounty on his head. It's funny to me to think about getting a refund from a failed assassination attempt. I wonder what the mechanics are behind a transaction like that. Like, is it an official transaction and you're issued a receipt when you book an assassination attempt in case things don't go as planned? Or is it something closer to, say, buying something off Craigslist, where both parties wordlessly acknowledge that no matter what, neither party will ever contact the other party again?

The Advice: How to Get People to Stop Trying to Rob You
The Song: "What Up Gangsta"
The Line: "Jux me, I'll have your mama picking out your casket"

The word "jux," at least in this context, is a synonym for "rob." And so 50 Cent is saying that if you rob him, he's going to kill you. And the life lesson tucked into that line is that wildly overreacting to something is a pretty good way to get people to stop doing stuff to you. It's like if you and I were hanging out, and just as a goof, you decided to sneak up behind me and flick me in the ear. If you did that, and then I responded by setting your house on fire or pushing you in front of a moving car or shooting you in the foot with a handgun, I'm pretty sure you'd never flick me in the ear again.

The Advice: How to Make White People Happy
The Song: "Patiently Waiting"
The Line: "Hey, Em. You know you're my favorite white boy, right?"

Four things here:

1. The "Em" that 50 Cent is talking about in this line is Eminem, who played an integral role in 50's ascent toward superstardom.
2. Eminem not only has a verse on this song (it's excellent, by the way) but also is an executive producer on *Get Rich or Die Tryin'*.
3. An enjoyable part of the 50 Cent–Eminem backstory is that before 50 Cent recorded "In da Club," which was his first big-budget single, he and Eminem met briefly. 50 Cent was so nervous, though, that he barely spoke to Eminem, who took that to mean that 50 Cent didn't like him. It was a replay of pretty much the exact same thing that had happened to Eminem a decade earlier, when he met Dr. Dre for the first time before recording "My Name Is," his own first big-budget single.
4. I don't know a lot about white people, but the one thing that I do know is that they really like it when someone who is not white says something to them along the lines of "You're my favorite white person."

The Advice: How to Not Get Beat Up
The Song: "Patiently Waiting"
The Line: "You know you shouldn't throw stones if you live in a glass house / And if you got a glass jaw, you should watch your mouth"

I have been in several fights in my life. One of the ones I remember most clearly happened when I was in the sixth grade. My friends and I were playing basketball one day, and I was talking shit to an older and bigger kid and I guess he got tired of it, so he shoved me. I wasn't expecting him to be as strong as he was, and so the force from his shove made me stumble in an awkward way. Everyone started laughing about it and I got embarrassed, so I picked up the basketball and threw it at his face as hard as I could.

It only ended up glancing off the edge of his head because my anger had corrupted my aiming software, but he got super fucking mad about it anyway and charged at me. I started punching as fast as I could, but he just walked right through them shits. He tackled me down into the grass, and from that point forward it was a wrap. He was just too big for me to do anything with. He pounded on me a bit, and then after five seconds or maybe two hours, a couple of my friends pulled him off of me. I stood up, dusted myself off a little, shouted "Fuck you, you food-stamps-using bitch!" at him, and then turned around and started to walk across the street toward my house.[3]

After I took a few steps, I threw up. Right there in the middle of the street. Just vomiting. And then as soon as I

3. Food stamps were how the government used to help poor families buy groceries. It's all done electronically now, but there were real, actual, literal food stamps before. They'd show up to your house once a month. It was a little booklet that had what looked like Monopoly money inside of it. I'm not sure why I thought "you food-stamps-using bitch" was a giant insult, given that everyone in our neighborhood used them. But that's what I went with. I guess it was one of those fog-of-war situations.

was done, I kept on walking like nothing had happened. And I'm not sure exactly how that story fits in here, or with 50 Cent, or with *Get Rich or Die Tryin'*, but I just kept thinking about it over and over again while I stared at the "And if you got a glass jaw, you should watch your mouth" line typed out in front of me.

The Advice: How to Win a Fight
The Song: "If I Can't"
The Line: "I don't fight fair"

This ties in with the story I just told. I know there's a certain celebration of integrity that shapes the rules of fighting. Something about valor and honor and righteousness and blah, blah, blah. It's things like, Weapons aren't allowed unless both people agree on it ahead of time. And fights should always be a one-on-one situation, or if there are multiple people involved, then there should be an equal number on both sides. And if someone goes limp, then the other person should stop the pummeling. So on and so forth.

But, I mean, that's just not me. If you and I get into a fight, and there's something nearby that I can easily pick up, I promise you that at some point during the fight, I'm going to try and crack you over the head with it. That's probably why I like Jackie Chan so much. Jackie Chan, for the past sixty or so years, has made better use of his environment during fights than any other fighter in history.[4] He's a master at it. If you and Jackie Chan square off and there's, say, a bucket anywhere within sight, the one thing I know for sure is that Jackie Chan is going to get that bucket on your head somehow.

The Advice: How to Know If You're Like 50 Cent or Not
The Song: "U Not Like Me"
The Line: "If you get shot and run to the cops, you not like me"

I am not like 50 Cent. If I get shot, I'm telling so fucking fast on whoever it was who shot me. I honestly might ask the ambulance driver to take me past the police station real quick on the way to the hospital so I can get an early start on my snitching. In fact, to take this a step further, let me say if I ever do get shot, it's extremely likely that I'll have been shot in the back, because as soon as I see you with a gun, I'm going to turn around and start running toward wherever the nearest precinct is to tell them I just saw a person with a gun.

4. A dark-horse pick here: Charlize Theron. She's really good at it, too. My favorite example is when she was fighting Will Smith in *Hancock*, which is a movie where it turns out they're both superheroes, and she hit him with a fucking eighteen-wheeler.

. . . **cont'd**

The Advice: How to Be a Bad Firefighter
The Song: "In da Club"
The Line: "If the roof on fire, let the motherfucker burn"

Four things here:

1. 50 Cent, who went from neighborhood hustler to centimillionaire,[1] is good at a lot of things, clearly. But he is a terrible, terrible fireman.
2. There's a more-than-three-decades-long history of roofs being on fire in rap. The very first roof fire to be ignored happened in a song called, as it were, "The Roof Is on Fire." It was by Rock Master Scott & the Dynamic Three, and it came out in 1984.
3. This is only partially related to roofs and fires, but whenever I hear the line "The roof, the roof, the roof is on fire," the first thing I think of is the part in Lil Wayne's song "Fireman" where he says that he's noticed that some women have begun wearing pants that show their butt crack as a style choice[2] but that his girls can't wear them, because he hides his stash in their butts.
4. There's also, by the way, a decades-long history of rappers mentioning people hiding things in their butt cracks in rap. 50 Cent even does it on *Get Rich or Die Tryin'*. To wit:

The Advice: How to Hide Drugs on Your Person
The Song: "Life's on the Line"
The Line: "They keep it on 'em, right there in they ass crack"

Honestly, I'm not sure if hiding something in your butt as part of your business practice is an example of exercising really good customer service or exercising really bad customer service. Either way, though, I think you have to respect the inherent level of dedication involved in the act.

The Advice: How to Be a Good Communicator
The Song: "What Up Gangsta"
The Line: "You getting money? I can't get none with ya, then fuck you"

Here is a dumb thing that my wife knows about me: I do not like to share a drink with her. I just don't. She's too aggressive in her beverage consumption for me to feel comfortable handing her my cup or bottle or whatever. She's a gulper, and I've been burned enough times in our relationship to know better now. So if we're out and picking up some fast food for me (she doesn't eat fast food), what always happens is I have to make sure that she has her own drink even though she's not eating anything. It's the Extra Drink Rule. That is a firm boundary and a clear expectation in our relationship. And I know that seems like a small thing, but it's actually a big thing. Because when you're in a relationship, knowing what's expected of

1. Per *Forbes*, 50 Cent was worth approximately $155 million in 2015.
2. This was in 2005.

you in whatever situation you happen to find yourself in is wildly important. It makes everything smoother for everyone. And that's what 50 Cent is doing here. It sounds like he's being a dick, and maybe he is, but also he's being a good communicator.

The Advice: How to Know When an Argument Is Over
The Song: "Many Men"
The Line: "Till I bust a clip in your face, pussy, this beef ain't over"

This bit of advice is a cousin to the *Carlito's Way* thing from the previous chapter. Oftentimes, it's difficult to know when a disagreement or a fight you're having with someone is over. However, if you simply shoot them in the face several times, then that pretty much clears everything up for you. Because a person cannot have a problem with you if that person does not have a face.

The Advice: How to Always Be Prepared
The Song: "Many Men"
The Line: "Every night I talk to God, but he don't say nothin' back / I know he protectin' me, but I still stay with my gat"

Two things here:

1. Contrary to the fireman thing from a moment ago, 50 Cent would make for a wonderful Boy Scout.
2. A version of this same line appears later on the album in a song called "U Not Like Me." In that song, 50 says, "Mama said everything that happened to us was part of God's plan / So at night when I talk to him, I got my gun in my hand." I hope that I die before 50 Cent dies so I can make sure and have a good seat in heaven for when 50 Cent gets there and finally gets to have his talk with God. I think it's genuinely going to be riveting.

The Advice: How to Follow Your Passions
The Song: "In da Club"
The Line: "And you should love it way more than you hate it"

This advice is very straightforward, so let me use this space to say this: I greatly enjoy the way 50 Cent sounds when he raps. It sounds like he's intentionally pressing his back molars all together, which sort of forces his words to slither out of his mouth between the tiny spaces in his front teeth. It's a very charming thing.

The Advice: How to Have a Healthy Understanding of Marketplace Competition
The Song: "High All the Time"
The Line: "There's no competition, it's just me"

One of my favorite rap stats is that no rap album that has come out since *Get Rich or Die Tryin'* has sold more albums than *Get Rich or Die Tryin'*.[3] 50 Cent was the exact right person (a new-era gangsta rapper with a massive pre-album mythology) at the exact right time (there was still a ton of CD burning that was already happening, which definitely chewed into his sales a little bit, but digital file sharing and the internet hadn't quite yet upended everything in music) with the exact right album (*GRODT* is beautiful and smart and vicious in the most likable way possible). He was an absolutely colossal force.

The Advice: How to Be Ambitious
The Song: "High All the Time"
The Line: "If David could go against Goliath with a stone / I could go at Nas and Jigga, both for the throne"

Regarding the massive pre-album mythology: There were two parts of it. The first part was how 50 Cent had been shot nine times at close range (INCLUDING ONCE IN THE FACE) and walked away a survivor. The second part was how part of his business model included bulldogging his way into prominence by picking fights with everyone all at once (his first big song, "How to Rob," was a four-minute-long diss track where he basically sprayed rap gunfire into the greenroom of an awards show). It was all just so very . . . I don't know . . . "Effective" seems like a good word to use here. I can't remember an artist arriving with more hype than 50 had when *Get Rich or Die Tryin'* finally showed up in record stores.

The Advice: How to Be Good at the Salem Witch Trials
The Song: "Back Down"
The Line: "Maybe I'm so disrespectful 'cause to me you're a mystery"

Over the course of fourteen months in the late 1600s, some two hundred or so people were accused of witchcraft in colonial Massachusetts. Of those two hundred or so people, thirty were found guilty[4] and twenty were killed.[5] And all of that started up[6] because someone did something that another person didn't understand, and so that person was like, "Hmm . . . I don't know what's happening here, and since I don't know what's happening, I'm going to assume that it's really bad, and thus, I must respond with a showing of ridiculous cruelty." And thus: the Salem witch trials.

The Advice: How to Accept (And, Subsequently, *Lean* into) What You Are
The Song: "Poor Lil Rich"
The Line: "See, I'm a liar, man, I really don't care"

3. It sold over eight million copies in the United States and over twelve million copies worldwide. Another good rap stat: you can add up all of 50 Cent's other album sales together in the United States, and the cumulative total is still less than *GRODT* sold.
4. I greatly want to know more about the lawyer who successfully defended the other 170 people.
5. Nineteen were hanged, and one man was, in effect, squished to death slowly over three days as authorities tried to get him to enter a plea of guilty or not guilty.
6. Probably started up.

A true story that happened to me once: During my senior year of high school, I went on a trip to the beach with the girl whom I was dating. While we were there, we rented one of those inner tubes to float around on the water in. At some point during our inner-tube play, she and I had managed to both get up on it and sit on opposing sides, facing each other. (She was sitting on one side of it with her feet in the water, and I was sitting on the other side of it with my feet in the water.)

While we were flirting (this consisted of her smiling and laughing at my jokes and me doing my best to accidentally flex every minor muscle in my stomach and chest), a terrible thing happened. A jellyfish somehow floated right up into the center doughnut hole where we had our feet in the water. When I saw it, I screamed "OH SHIT!" and then fell backward out of the inner tube and started swimming back to the shore. The girl screamed, too, but because I'd abandoned the inner tube in such a hasty manner, it ended up flipping her backward into the water, thus preventing her from swimming away as fast as she'd have liked.

Now, thankfully, the jellyfish didn't sting either of us. But that didn't even matter. She was real mad at me for not being more manly in that situation. She argued that I should've done something different there, that I should've tried somehow to protect her. And for a lot of weeks after that incident, I was bothered by the way I'd reacted. She was right. She had pinned me down perfectly. I had acted in a way that was incongruous with my general existence. Or so I thought. Because that was when I realized I wasn't a manly person who had acted cowardly. That would've been shameful. I was a coward who had acted cowardly. And that was totally to be expected. That's me. That's who I am. I'm not the guy who's going to run into the burning building. I'm the guy running the other way. You can't get mad at a prairie dog for not being a lion, you know what I'm saying?

Anyway, 50 Cent's line about knowing he's a liar and not caring: critical and accurate self-evaluations are good for your spirit.

The Advice: How to Be Good at Hanging Out
The Song: "High All the Time"
The Line: "Sit in the crib, sipping Guinness, watching *Menace*"

This—staying home, drinking a drink that you enjoy, watching a movie you enjoy—is one of the few times on *GRODT* where 50 Cent said something and I was like, "Yes. Yes, I know exactly what you're talking about here, 50."

The Advice: How to Be Clutch
The Song: "High All the Time"
The Line: "My team, they depend on me when it's crunch time"

When I was in college, my friends and I played in a basketball rec league. The season concluded with an eight-team tournament to determine who the rec-league champions were. In our second game, we were matched up against a team that was full of guys who were, on average, taller than us and more handsome than us and more athletic than us. But it didn't matter. I didn't care. Because what happened was during the pregame shootaround, I caught fire. I couldn't miss. I hit something like ten or twelve 3s in a row while we were all warming up. And as I made each shot, my confidence grew bigger and bigger and my mouth grew louder and louder.

"Aye, fuck these guys!" I shouted as I splashed in the sixth or seventh shot, making sure I said it loud enough that the other team could hear me. "Just give me the ball!" I shouted, another shot ripping through the net. "This shit is a wrap!" I shouted. "They don't have a single person who can shoot like me!" I shouted. "These motherfuckers don't stand a chance!" I shouted. *Swish, swish, swish.*

Then the game started. And I promptly went on to shoot 0 for 13.

> **The Advice:** How to Be Really Good at Hide-and-Seek
> **The Song:** "Heat"
> **The Line:** "If you was smart, you'd be shook of me / 'Cause I get tired of looking for ya / Spray ya mama crib and let yo' ass look for me"

Two things here:

1. Shooting at someone's mom's house as a way to get them to come find you because you're tired of trying to find them is a supremely fucked-up thing to do. It is also, I would guess, thoroughly effective.
2. My sons and I, like many fathers and sons, have played an uncountable number of games of hide-and-seek during our years together.[7] And I don't mind telling you they're super-duper good at it. The three of them have lithe vines for bodies and are able to fit themselves into spots that are otherwise untenable for most humans. As such, there have been times when we've played that, despite a maximum and genuine effort on my end, I just couldn't find them. And whenever that happens, if it lasts for more than a handful of minutes, what I do is stand in the living room and say very loudly, "*Come here, boys.*" I don't say it in my regular voice, though. I say it with the same pitch and tenor and seriousness that I use whenever they're in trouble.[8] And so what happens is, pretty much on reflex, one or two (or sometimes all three) of them will emerge from their hiding spots because they think they're in trouble. It's the G-rated version of the Shoot at Your Mama's House maneuver that 50 Cent talks about here.

> **The Advice:** How to Be a Good Manager
> **The Song:** "Heat"
> **The Line:** "I done made myself a millionaire by myself / Now shit changed, motherfucker, I can hire some help"

In the context of the song, 50 Cent is talking about how he doesn't have to do his criminal activities alone anymore.[9] And while perhaps an extremely small number of you all who are reading this may well be able to identify directly with that sentiment, I suspect the vast majority of y'all cannot. I suspect the vast majority of y'all are reading this book as you sit in a cozy

---

7. The twins got bored with regular hide-and-seek once they got to be around their teenage years. I wasn't ready to give up that part of our relationship just yet, though, so we modified things. We invented a game called *Halloween* Hide-and-Seek. The way it works is just like regular hide-and-seek, except (a) we play it only at night, (b) I turn on a YouTube video of the theme song from *Halloween* real loud on the TV, and (c) then I stalk around the house in a Michael Myers mask, holding a fake butcher knife. It makes things feel way more intense.

8. It's called Dad Voice.

9. Remember the song "How to Rob" that I mentioned earlier? There's a part in that song where he talks about how he has to do all of his criminal stuff by himself. I was glad to hear when I was listening to *Get Rich or Die Tryin'* after it came out that he had upgraded his lifestyle and had begun hiring criminal help.

spot in your home while wearing an outfit that you put on with the sole intention of relaxing. (There's a very high chance that you have had more than one conversation about this specific outfit in your adult life, during which you claimed it to have a unique level of comfort.) And that being the case, you (we) need to take a bird's-eye view of 50 Cent's message here. Because really what 50 Cent is talking about here is delegating work responsibilities. Really what 50 Cent is talking about is being a good manager. Good managers delegate.

The Advice: How Not to Get Shot
The Song: "Heat"
The Line: "If you don't wanna get shot, I suggest you don't go testing me"

Do you want to get shot? If yes, then test 50 Cent. If not, then do not test 50 Cent. This is a very easy flowchart to follow.

The Advice: How to Teach Lessons to Slow Learners
The Song: "If I Can't"
The Line: "I invented how to teach lessons to slow learners / Go ahead, act up, get smacked in the head with the burner"

I became a full-time writer in July of 2015. Prior to that, I was a middle school science teacher for nine years. And I feel like this piece of advice probably would not have translated that great to that particular profession. I mean, I remember one time early in my teaching career I got in trouble with my grade-level principal because she saw me giving candy out to one of my classes as a reward for an especially fruitful day of learning and participation. I have to imagine that's a less serious offense than if I'd chosen to bop a student in the side of the head with a pistol if they weren't paying attention to how to balance chemical equations.

The Advice: How to Be a Good Bargain Shopper
The Song: "P.I.M.P."
The Line: "I'm shoppin' for chinchillas in the summer, they're cheaper"

I greatly appreciate how 50 Cent is, at once, the type of person who (a) wants to own something as luxurious and unnecessary as a chinchilla coat but (b) prefers to purchase them out of season because he knows that that's when you can get a good deal on them. Investing prudently in things that are not prudent is a nice little lane to be in.

IS ACTION BRONSON A GOOD TRAVEL PARTNER?

ACTION BRONSON HAS TERRIBLE PLANE-PASSENGER ETIQUETTE.[1] On "Easy Rider," he demands that the pilot land the plane at a busy intersection, which is entirely unreasonable. On "Wolfpack," he talks about how he has so much lobster on the plane that the plane, struggling under the lobster weight, is unable to stay in the sky. (We're talking tens of thousands of lobsters needed to generate enough weight to keep a plane grounded.)

On "Dr. Kimble," as soon as the plane takes off, he starts smoking a pipe. (He doesn't specify what's in the pipe, but I suspect it's something illicit.) There are multiple instances where he's talked about making unscheduled jumps out of airplanes, none of which he was ever prepared for (on "Only in America," he says he does it while high on drugs; on "Swerve on Em," he says he does it completely naked; on "Marcus Aurelius," he says he does it while only wearing a hoodie, and for some reason it's funnier to me to picture him hurtling toward the ground naked from the waist down while wearing a hoodie than it is to picture him just completely naked). And there are at least two separate instances where he has talked about being on an airplane while aroused. (He says "Now I'm sitting in first class with a hard dick" on "Falconry," and he says "I'm on the plane to Russia with a hard dick and a tank top from Target" on "Tank.")

Thus, I say again, Action Bronson has terrible plane-passenger etiquette.

•••••

There's an anticipatory quality to Action Bronson's music that I find interesting. I know going into an album that he's going to say at least eight or nine things that will make an actual, real laugh come out of my actual, real mouth. As such, I listen to him differently than I listen to, say, ScHoolboy Q or Erykah Badu. With those two artists, their music feels more like one big brilliant piece, like everything is working together all at once; the production, the order of the songs on an album, the things each person is saying or not saying – it's built to be consumed as a whole, like, say, how the movie *No Country for Old Men* works the best when you measure up the entirety of its parts.

With Action Bronson, it's the opposite. I listen to his music in sections or pieces, always with the lyrics first and then everything else afterward. If we extend the movie metaphor from above, then Action Bronson makes music that functions the way the best slasher flicks function. I don't turn on *Friday the 13th* to learn some big idea about the world at large; I turn on *Friday the 13th* because I want to see a monster wearing a hockey mask punch a guy's head off his shoulders. That's Action Bronson. I don't turn on Action Bronson because I want him to say something in a way that reveals an unidentified feeling I have in my chest that I'd otherwise be unable to confront; I turn on Action Bronson because I want to hear him say a line like "My haircut is like Dominican folk art"[2] or "Came out the

1. A person should exist on an airplane the same way a ninja exists in the night, which is to say, they should be silent and odorless and always with their shoes on their feet.
2. "Irishman Freestyle."

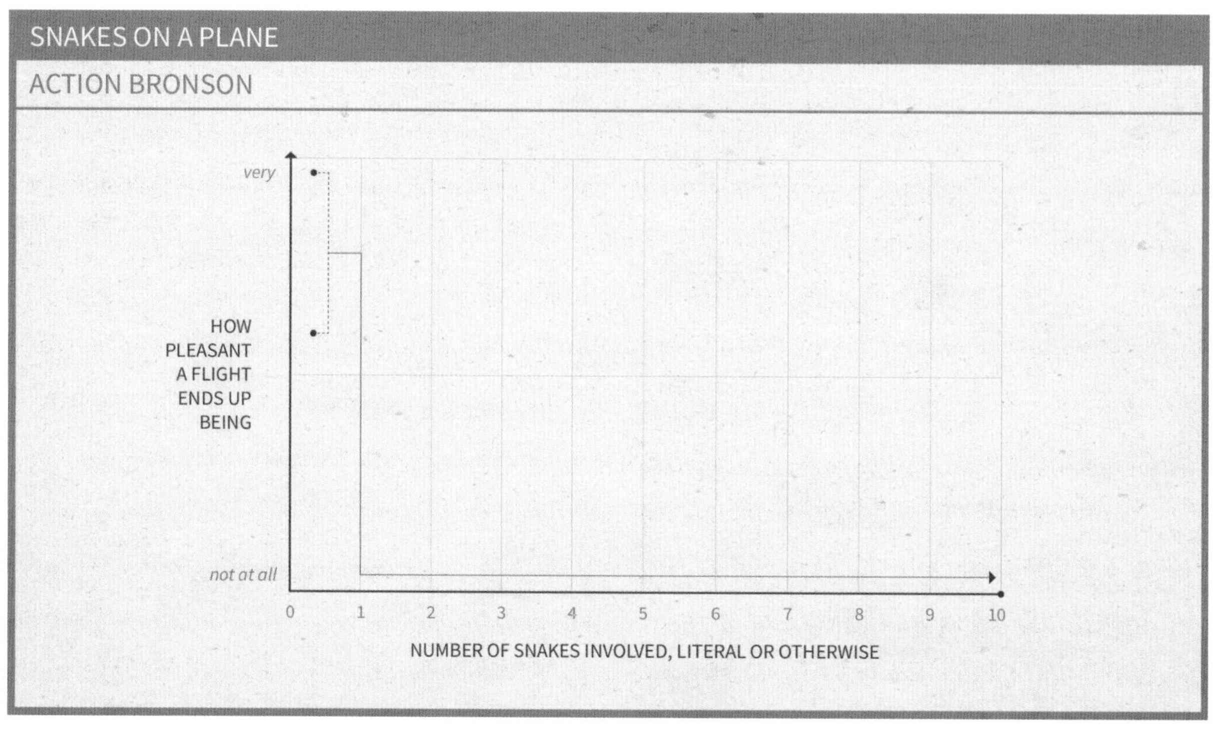

pussy wearing Timbs"[3] or "I'm in the corner with a hooker playing footsie."[4] It's a whole different thing.

•••••

TEN FAKE ACTION BRONSON LINES

- "Went to your mom's funeral and practiced karate in front of her casket"
- "Playing touch football with Mariah Carey and the Undertaker / Score a touchdown, then sing like Anita Baker"
- "I'm Joanna Gaines's role model"
- "Omelets made with bald eagle eggs / I float when I walk / I've never used my legs"
- "Gave your girl a ride home from the grocery store on the back of my bicycle"
- "Ran a hundred-yard dash in eight seconds flat / Usain Bolt asked me how I did that / I told him to eat a plate of Iberian ham, and if it ain't cooked to perfection, send it back"
- "Resurrected Whitney just to do a duet"
- "I got drafted in the first round by the Miami Heat / You come off the bench for your team in the church league"

3. "La Luna."
4. "The Madness."

- "Practicing archery on a yacht / I know all the nautical knots"
- "Pull up in an old Buick / The windows don't work but my dick does"

•••••

Is Action Bronson a good travel partner? That's the question that needs to be answered here. And so the way we get to an answer is we comb through all of the mixtapes, EPs, and albums he's put out over the past decade and grab any piece of evidence that serves as proof that he is either (a) a good travel partner or (b) a bad travel partner.

EVIDENCE THAT ACTION BRONSON IS A GOOD TRAVEL PARTNER

Here are the things Action Bronson has in favor of him being a good travel partner:

First, he mostly travels in nice cars or boats or planes. This one is important for obvious reasons. It's a Porsche ("Buddy Guy") or a limo ("The Rising") or a Mercedes ("Baby Blue") or a Lamborghini ("Tank") or an extended-size Rolls-Royce ("Brunch") or a yacht ("Brand New Car") or first class on an airplane ("A Light in the Addict"). And even in instances where he's traveling some way that is less swank (like when he mentions being on the 7 Train, which is part of the New York City Subway), he's often modifying it to make things better (he says he installed a Jacuzzi on the 7 Train to make the ride more enjoyable).

A sidebar: I've been to New York maybe twenty times in my life, for work-related events and meetings and whatnot. I have never ridden the subway once. I went down there and looked at it one time. That was as close as I got. It's just terrifying to me. Because for one, on a very fundamental level it is a metal tube powered by electricity traveling through the Earth, and that sounds way too much like the disaster plot of a science-fiction movie. And for two, I have, on numerous occasions, seen someone share a video on the internet of something happening on a subway train with a caption close to "This is so New York" or whatever. And it's never anything good. It's never, like, a young, spry person giving up their seat for an elderly man or woman. It's always, like, a baby girl in a stroller, and a rat has crawled into the carriage with her and is putting its nose in her mouth.

Second, he has excellent musical taste. If we limit his references to musicians he's name-dropped while traveling, there are three key ones that stand out. He has a song where he mentions listening to Janet Jackson in the car ("White Bronco") and a song where he mentions listening to Jimi Hendrix in the car ("Respect the Mustache") and a song where he mentions listening to Heavy D in the car ("Golden Eye"). That's a very great lineup because it offers you the opportunity to calibrate the listening experience to match whatever mood you might be in during a particular moment.

For example, if you find yourself on an open stretch of road in the middle of nowhere and want to punch your speed up to ninety-five or so miles per hour, then maybe cue up Heavy D's "Now That We Found Love." If it's late at night and you feel like theorizing about how perhaps there's a chance that someone could make a song so perfect or a dance routine so perfect that it would eventually

stamp out racism in America, then maybe cue up Janet's "Rhythm Nation."[5] If you feel like you want your car to lift right the fuck up off the pavement and drive into outer space, then maybe cue up Jimi's "The Wind Cries Mary." It's all in play. And it's all good.

And third, you're going to eat well on the trip. It's part of Action Bronson's whole thing. He's a former chef who still has chef tendencies. He talks about eating salmon on a cruise ship in "Miss Fordham Road ('86 '87 '88)." He gets out of a car and has steak and eggs for breakfast in "The Madness." He serves up veal in a Coupe DeVille in "Respect the Mustache." He even has just general snacks covered, too (he eats pretzels in a Tesla in "9-24-7000"). You're solid here.

•••••

TEN MORE FAKE ACTION BRONSON LINES

- "I'm in the passenger seat of an F-150 singing Brandy to the love of your life"
- "Swimming in the Adriatic Sea eating foods that are hard to spell"
- "I got William Faulkner and Edgar Allan Poe on a three-way call"
- "Catch me at the barbershop getting the same haircut as Dale Ellis"
- "The verdict came back / The jury said not guilty / I did a cartwheel out the room / Hollered at the victim's family: 'You can't stop me'"
- "I was born inside a tornado / They made your spine out of Play-Doh"
- "I showed up to my first job interview dressed like Crocodile Dundee / For the second interview, what'd I do? / Showed up dressed like Crocodile Dundee 2"
- "Stepped on the Harvard campus / The student body stopped and said the Pledge of Allegiance to my penis"
- "I'm the final clue on a treasure map / Someone tell Nic Cage to hit me back"
- "Squid ravioli in a lemongrass broth / All my plates look like the beginning of *American Psycho* / All your fates look like the end of *American Psycho*"

•••••

EVIDENCE THAT ACTION BRONSON IS A BAD TRAVEL PARTNER

The thing that happens is you go through the section from earlier outlining the ways in which Action Bronson is a good travel partner, and you start to feel like he is for sure a good travel partner. But then you get to this section, which outlines the ways in which he's a bad travel partner, and it feels a lot like that part in *The Karate Kid* where Daniel paints a section of the fence and he thinks he's done, but Mr. Miyagi is like, "Bitch, you thought,"[6] and then he shows him he's actually only finished about 10 percent of the work that needs to be done.

5. How crazy would it be if this ended up actually being a true thing? Like, a bunch of KKK members are gathered up for a meeting, and someone takes out their phone and tries to turn on a Johnny Rebel song but accidentally clicks Johnny Gill instead, and "My, My, My" comes on and everyone is like, "Well, hold on just a second. Maybe racism *is* wrong?"

6. It's likely that I'm misremembering this quote.

Here are the things Action Bronson has working against him being a good travel partner:

First, he has a suspended license. He talks about this one on "White Silk," which was part of the *Well-Done* album that he did with producer Statik Selektah in 2011. I asked a lawyer friend of mine what someone has to do to get their license suspended, and she said it can be the result of any number of things, ranging from Very Serious and Terrible (like getting popped for a DUI or getting into an accident that causes significant injury or death while being uninsured) to Not That Serious but Certainly Not Good (like getting a certain number of moving violations over a twelve-month or twenty-four-month period). It's hard to guess the cause for Bronson's suspension here, because he has one song where he says that he got a DUI after leaving a Trey Songz concert[7] and another song where he talks about doing a hundred miles per hour in a rental car in the rain[8] and another song where he says the cops are chasing him in an all-white Ford.[9] Either way, it's no good.

Second, there's the Hard Dick on the Airplane thing. As mentioned in the intro, he talks about this one on two separate occasions, first on 2015's *Mr. Wonderful* album and then on 2017's *Blue Chips 7000.* I've been on a plane a number of times in my adult life. I have never, in those situations, thought to myself, "You know what would make this flight better? You know what would be great right now? If this guy who I've never met before sitting next to me got a visible erection." I would rather sit next to Cillian Murphy's character from *Red Eye* than sit next to a stranger with a visible erection. And somewhat related to this point . . .

Third, he gets naked way too often on trips. He's naked in a Lamborghini in "Baby Blue." He's naked on a boat in "Splash." He's naked on an airplane in "Swerve on Em." That's too many times to get naked while traveling. The correct number of times to be naked while traveling somewhere with someone is zero, assuming the two of you are not sexually involved, in which case that number changes (as does the overall reputation of the airplane erection, I suspect).

Fourth, there's the drugs and guns thing. One time, a person whom I knew purchased a joint as a gift for his significant other. (This was in Texas, where marijuana is not yet legal.) He did so via text with a person who lived on the other side of the city. The person told him to meet up in the parking lot of a strip mall for the handoff. The guy did, and he got the joint, and it all went well. But then terror struck him. He realized that he was now going to have to drive back across the city – something like forty minutes – in possession of an illegal substance.

Now, in all likelihood, if this person did happen to get pulled over, and if the cop who pulled him over did happen to find the weed, the amount of weed was small enough that little to nothing truly serious would have happened. But that was not what he was thinking. What he was thinking was he had become Pablo Escobar mixed with Nino Brown mixed with Scarface. So, not wanting to

---

7. This shit makes me laugh every time. There's not one single sentence you can say that doesn't immediately become funnier if you add "after the Trey Songz concert" to the end of it. *I wasn't able to pay my rent after the Trey Songz concert. You and I need to have a serious talk after the Trey Songz concert. My little brother was sentenced to twenty-five years in prison after the Trey Songz concert.*

8. "The Rising."

9. "Actin Crazy."

end up like they did, he decided he needed to extremely hide the joint.

So he took it and he wrapped it inside of a plastic bag. Then he took that bag and placed it inside of another plastic bag. Then he took that double bag and stuffed it into a shoe. Then he took that shoe and he placed it in a backpack. Then he took that backpack and placed it in the trunk under every piece of junk he could find. Then he drove home several miles per hour under the speed limit with that same kind of manic panic that Ray Liotta was driving around with at the end of *Goodfellas.*

Anyhow, I say all of that to say: there are many, many, many instances where Action Bronson mentions being on the move with various drugs and various weaponry. Most people are not built to handle the kind of inherent stress that kind of situation causes. So the drugs and guns thing: very bad.

•••••

The verdict: While I understand the appeal of having (a) good food, (b) good music, and (c) good accommodations on a trip, I cannot, in good conscience, look past the guns and the drugs and the nakedness and the erections and just the general mayhem and law break-ery that a trip taken with Action Bronson includes. And so:

Action Bronson is not a good travel partner.

WHERE'S THE SECOND MOST IMPRACTICAL PLACE LUDACRIS MENTIONS HAVING SEX IN DURING "WHAT'S YOUR FANTASY"?

THE FIRST MOST IMPRACTICAL PLACE that Ludacris mentions having sex in during "What's Your Fantasy"—a song where he runs through a list of possible places someone might fantasize about having sex in—is the fifty-yard line of an NFL stadium. He says, "I wanna get you in the Georgia Dome on the fifty-yard line while the Dirty Birds kick for three."

And let me tell you something about that line: it's literally the first line of the first verse of the song. And let me tell you one more thing: "What's Your Fantasy" was Ludacris's first ever official single. That means there was a conversation that happened at some point before Ludacris was a star where someone said something like "Ludacris, you're a very talented and very likable rapper. We think you can have a big, successful career in the entertainment industry. We just have to be careful about how you're introduced to the American people. We want to cultivate the right kind of persona for you. What are you thinking for your first step into the spotlight?" To which Ludacris responded with something like "I want my first single to be about locations people have imagined having sex in. And I want the first line on it to be about fucking in the middle of the field after a drive by the Atlanta Falcons has stalled out and they have to kick a field goal." And then that's what he did.

Ludacris is awesome.

•••••

There are about twenty-five different places that Ludacris talks about having sex in (or on or at or around) in "What's Your Fantasy." So the goal of this chapter is to figure out which of those places is the second most impractical. First, though, a quick diversion to recognize an adjacent bit of brilliance:

Not so long after "What's Your Fantasy" proved to be a success (it was certified platinum, and it reached as high as number twenty-one on the *Billboard* Hot 100), a remix was announced. It featured verses from Trina, Shawnna (who provided the chorus for the original version), and Foxy Brown. Were we to arrange and rank the sexual-situation requests of the remix by impracticality, Foxy Brown would win in a blowout. And it's because of the line where she demands that her lover perform oral sex on her WHILE she has sex with him.[1]

Now, had I heard someone other than Foxy Brown make that particular request, I would've assumed it to be a physical impossibility, insofar as I understand the general structure and elasticity of the human body. But Foxy Brown says it with so much self-assured confidence that I am left to assume that it is not a physical impossibility and that the rest of us are simply just uncreative lovers.

•••••

Ludacris is always such an interesting artist to think about, particularly with regard to any of the larger rap conversations that take place. It feels like I never quite know where to place him or how best to measure his legacy. He's tricky to pin down. And probably the clearest example of that conundrum is to look at the list of the best-selling rappers of all time.

Ludacris typically sits somewhere between the thirteenth spot and the nineteenth spot on those lists (his

---

1. The line: "Then you gotta su-suck the pussy while I sit on your dick."

placement can fluctuate depending on how an individual list decides to count sales). And almost everyone else whose name is on that list with him (it's usually Eminem, 2Pac, Jay-Z, Drake, Beastie Boys, Nelly, Outkast, Biggie, MC Hammer, 50 Cent, Kanye, DMX, LL COOL J, Snoop, Will Smith, Wayne, Nas, Master P) can be used as an entry point into a discussion about the way rap began to shift in a certain direction at a certain point in time.

For example, 2Pac signaled, in a sense, the modernization of gangster rap. Outkast proudly and defiantly proclaimed that rappers in the South were aiming for the throne. Lil Wayne stretched and blurred the border between mixtapes and albums. MC Hammer stood at the forefront of the pop commercialism movement. Master P built an empire around his I'll Do It Myself business acumen. Those are all way-too-tidy explanations, of course, but you get the point I'm trying to make here: they all represent something.

But even all these years later and after all these millions of albums sold, I'm still not certain what to do with Ludacris. I'm not certain what entry point Ludacris represents. And I'm not sure if that makes him more meaningful than I'm imagining or less meaningful than I'm imagining. My guess is more, though.

•••••

The question: What's the second most impractical place Ludacris mentions having sex in during "What's Your Fantasy"?

The answer: Here are the non–Georgia Dome potential sex destinations that Ludacris mentions in "What's Your Fantasy": on the floor; in the DJ booth at a club; in the VIP section of a club; on a beach with black sand; on a tabletop; in various parts of Atlanta (no specific location is given, only areas of town); in a public bathroom; in the back of a classroom; up on the roof of whatever building it is that happens to be near; in a bathtub; onstage at a sold-out Ludacris concert; in the rain; in the library on top of a stack of books; at the White House; in a sauna; in a Jacuzzi; in the back row at the movies; on hay in the middle of a barn; on a bed with silk sheets covered in rose petals; in the back seat of a car; in a garden; somewhere where you are underpaid; in the sun or in the shade; on top of an Escalade; and on the ocean or in a boat.

A bunch of those are not altogether unreasonable and, as such, are not in contention for the Second Most Impractical Place to Have Sex title. So let's start by getting rid of them first. Let's get rid of . . .

- **Having sex on a bed with silk sheets covered in rose petals.** This one seems completely fine, assuming you have customary access to roses, which most of us do given that they're sold at most grocery stores.
- **Having sex on a tabletop.** Uncomfortable but not impractical.
- **Having sex in a Jacuzzi.** A small sidebar: Having sex in a Jacuzzi has never been appealing to me. It just doesn't sound sexy. It sounds gross. I think it has something to do with how most Jacuzzis are pretty much just public bathtubs. Even the word "Jacuzzi" is a little icky. Say it out loud to yourself right now. *Jacuzzi.* Gross. If you say it enough times, what happens is a thin gold chain will magically appear around your neck and you'll find yourself suddenly advocat-

ing for the return of those old Girls Gone Wild videos from the early 2000s.

- **Having sex on the floor, in the back seat of a car, in the sun, in the shade, in the rain, on the ocean or in a boat, and in various parts of Atlanta.** None of these are impractical. They're all out.

And just like that, we're down to only sixteen options left.

With the Georgia Dome scenario, it's important that you know that one isn't impractical because of how many people would be watching (it's over seventy-one thousand in person, by the way, and another several million via television). It's impractical because of the logistics involved. You'd have to not only run onto the field but also (a) make it to the fifty-yard line, (b) get undressed, (c) wait for the Falcons field-goal unit to line up, and then (d) start having sex right as the kicker kicks the ball, all before you got tasered by security or laid out by one of the players. That's why that one is so impractical. It has nothing to do with the exhibitionism of the situation. And that's why next we can get rid of . . .

- **Having sex in a public bathroom.** I would probably rather have sex in a public bathroom than in a Jacuzzi.
- **Having sex in the DJ booth at a club or in the VIP section at a club.** [*You're having sex in the DJ booth, and it's Funkmaster Flex who's working as the DJ that night, and rather than be mad at you for having sex in his booth, he just starts playing those Funkmaster Flex bomb sound effects to highlight how great of a job you're doing at sex.*]
- **Having sex onstage at a sold-out Ludacris concert.** [*You're having sex onstage at a sold-out Ludacris concert while Ludacris performs "Move Bitch."*]
- **Having sex in the back of a classroom.** I majored in psychology in college. And one of the classes you had to take at the time to complete your course load for that degree was Psychology of Sexuality. One day, the professor was clicking through a PowerPoint slideshow about various things related to the class. He would click his little button and then up on the screen would pop a picture of some old psychologist, whom he would then talk to us about for a minute or so. Or he would click his little button and then up on the screen would pop the name of some psychological theory, which he would then talk to us about for a minute or so. Or he would click his little button and then up on the screen would pop a graph, which he would then talk to us about for a minute or so. Anyway, one day he was doing that like normal, and then he clicked his little button and up on the screen popped a picture of a lion. Just a regular lion. Sitting there. Being a lion. And he said, "That's a lion." And then he clicked to the next slide. And he never explained anything about the lion or why the lion was included. I've thought about that day every day for the past seventeen years of my life.
- **Having sex up on the roof of whatever building it is that happens to be near.** Technically, this one would've also included either the sun, shade, or rain fantasy from earlier.
- **Having sex in a library on top of a stack of books, on top of an Escalade, somewhere where you're underpaid, or in the back row at the movies.** The second-worst movie to have sex to in the back row of a movie theater: *Midsommar*. The

first-worst movie to have sex to in the back row of a movie theater: *Peter Rabbit 2: The Runaway.*

And just like that, we're down to only six options left.

A sauna seems like it could be tricky, but I (probably) feel that way because I've never been in a sauna, and also because I don't even know where to go to find a sauna. All things measured, though, I suspect that it's not nearly as foreign a concept to most people, so I feel pretty safe eliminating it here. And that same logic applies to gardens (I don't know anyone who gardens, but I'm sure I could find one in a pinch), barns, and beaches with black sand (I've only ever seen pictures of black-sand beaches on the internet, but I imagine I could see one in person pretty easily if I wanted to, assuming that Southwest Airlines or Spirit Airlines flies to such destinations), so we can get rid of those ones, too.

And just like that, we're down to the final two options: in a bathtub and at the White House. And I know when you read these as the last two that are battling for the aforementioned Second Most Impractical Place to Have Sex title, you probably said something to yourself like "How is having sex in a bathtub impractical?" To which I invoke a centuries-old idiom: the devil is in the details.

The beginning of the bathtub line is regular—Ludacris says, "I wanna get you in the bathtub"—and if it ended there, it wouldn't be anywhere near impractical. But it doesn't end there. It keeps going. First, Ludacris tells you that the bathtub romp will take place among candlelight, and that's harmless enough. But then comes the catch: he says you're going to do it until the candles go out. And that's when things get tricky.

Per the National Candle Association, the most popular type of candle in America is a jar candle. And the average dimensions of a small jar candle are something close to 5.8 centimeters by 8.6 centimeters, with an average weight of about 104 grams. And a candle that size will burn for a little under fourteen hours.[2] If you move up to a medium jar candle (10.7 centimeters by 12.7 centimeters, with a weight of 411 grams), you're looking at nearly fifty-five hours of burn time. And a large jar candle (10.7 centimeters by 16.8 centimeters, with a weight of 623 grams) is gonna get you up to eighty-three hours. And so that's really what's at play here. Do you think it'd be easier to have sex somewhere at the White House, one of the most heavily guarded and secured tourist locations on the planet, or in a bathtub for, best-case scenario, fourteen hours or, worst-case scenario, more than three straight days? Which of those sounds more impractical?

It has to be the bathtub. There's no way you're surviving that. You would turn into the sex version of that guy who had to cut his own arm off after he got trapped in the slot canyon when the boulder fell on him and trapped him there for five days.

And so here's the official order for "What's Your Fantasy" impractical sex locations: The fifty-yard line of the Georgia Dome is the most impractical place that Ludacris mentions. Second place is in a bathtub for somewhere between fourteen and eighty-three hours. And third place is at the White House.

---

2. I learned way too much about candles and the candle industry while researching this chapter. Did you know that candle sales account for over $3 billion a year? And that more than one billion pounds of wax get used per year making candles? And that there are over ten thousand different candle smells available?

A LITTLE OVER SEVENTY YEARS AGO, Shirley Jackson wrote a short story called "The Lottery." It was unexpectedly controversial at the time of its publication but quickly grew its way into a position of admired art and brilliance. The plot mechanics are as such:

Once a year, a small town in America honors a tradition referred to as "the lottery." The way the lottery works is a bunch of smallish slips of paper are folded in half and placed inside of a wooden box. All of the papers are blank, save for one, which has a black dot scribbled on it. The heads of each of the families in the town come up in alphabetical order and pick one of the slips. Once they all have one, they open them and look at them. That's round one. If you're lucky enough to pick one of the blank slips, then awesome. You're good. You're safe. You're done until next year. If you happen to be the person who picks the one with the black dot on it, though, well, that means that shit is about to get real bad for you. Because what happens from there is round two. And round two fucking sucks. It's another drawing, except now it's among only the members of your family – mom, dad, teenagers, tiny children, whatever; everyone has to participate, regardless of age. And whoever in the family draws the slip with the black dot on it this time immediately gets stoned to death by everyone else in the town. That's the whole short story.

Now, technically, yes, "The Lottery" is about this one tradition in this one town. But really it's about other things, bigger things, grander ideas; it is, in effect, a massive indictment of some of the most rotten and insidious parts of human nature. That's why it's so great and so memorable, and why all of these decades later it feels like it has only become more essential. It's also why, as it were, we're leaning on a piece of it for this chapter and for the next two chapters to come.

•••••

What follows is a hypothetical. Please do not spend more than five seconds thinking about any of its parts. The whole thing is flimsy and will fall apart totally under even the slightest bit of duress. Just assume that everything you're about to read is infallible and undeniable. Thank you.

The Hypothetical: You've just been informed via text message that you have been selected at random by the United States government to fight someone in front of a very large audience.[1] (This government-sanctioned fight has happened every single year of your life since you were born, and for dozens and dozens of years before that, too. It's called, quite simply and unimaginatively, the Annual Fight. This is the first time anyone you know has ever been selected, and of course it was you who got picked out of all your friends and family, because that's the kind of luck you have.) There are no loopholes or trick exits for you to exploit. Your participation is inevitable. It is going to happen.

You are told that in twenty-four hours, an unmarked black van will pull up to wherever it is that you live, at which point you will climb inside of it and be driven to the fight destination by a man who will aggressively wear sunglasses and refuse to talk to you. Once there, you will meet your opponent. (This other person, same as you, has been selected at random.) Ten minutes after that, you

---

1. In addition to the live audience watching, it will also be streamed across various outlets on the internet, including whichever one it is that the person you hate the most prefers.

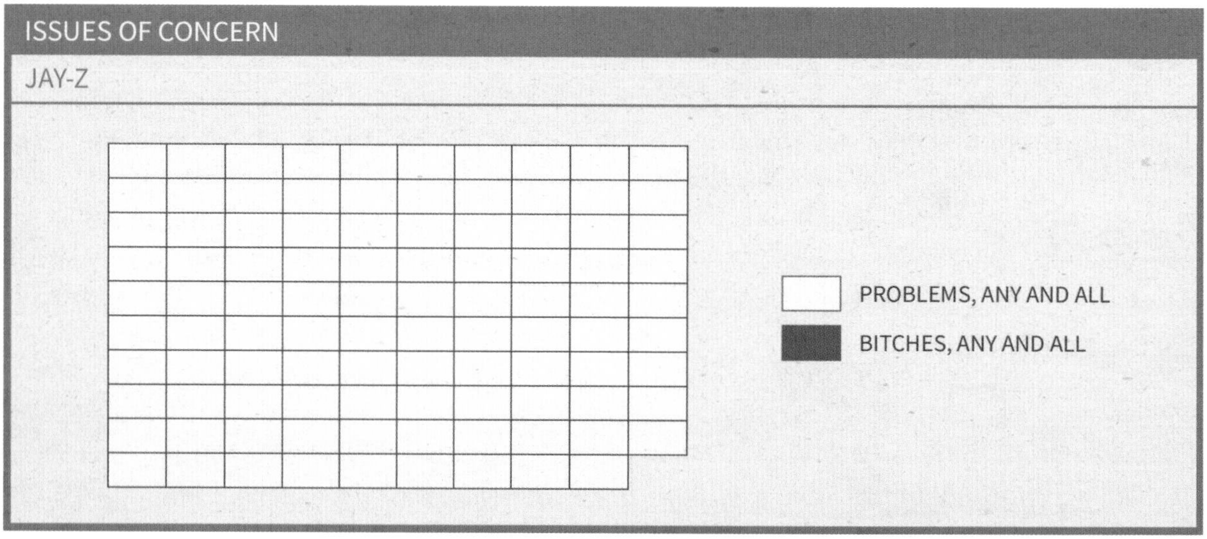

ISSUES OF CONCERN

JAY-Z

PROBLEMS, ANY AND ALL

BITCHES, ANY AND ALL

will both be walked into a large cage at the center of the arena, introduced to the crowd in a predetermined order, and then locked inside. You will fight until one of you is no longer breathing.

Your best hope, you decide on the van ride over, is that you get matched up with someone you have not only an at least passing interest in fighting but also a chance against (like, say, an extremely racist ten-year-old). But, again, because you are you and because your luck is your luck, that does not end up being the case. Instead, you walk into the pre-fight holding room and see that the person you are fighting is eight inches taller than you, has thirty more pounds of muscle than you, is approximately 40 percent more attractive than you,[2] and stalks around the space in a way that makes it very clear that this person has likely been kicked out of several mixed martial arts gyms for being too violent.

HOWEVER, there is a tiny bit of hope for you here. Because here's the thing: Several years ago, a very unctuous senator was able to get an amendment passed that affected the parameters of the Annual Fight in a potentially very significant way. A coin toss now takes place before every fight, and the winner of the coin toss gets to decide between one of two options. The winner can either (a) select the order in which the fighters will be introduced to the crowd, a wildly important option if you happen to be very superstitious about these sorts of things, or (b) choose to listen to any song they want to immediately before the fight, a wildly important option if you happen to be one of those people who can access some special reserve of strength or power or grit if you listen to a particular kind of song at a particular level of volume. The loser gets whatever option the winner doesn't choose.

2. Getting beaten to death by someone who is more attractive than you is unquestionably worse than getting beaten to death by someone who is uglier than you.

You (somehow) win the coin toss, and so you decide to go with Option B, hoping that you'll be able to find a song so aggressive, so massive, so visceral that it will, at least momentarily anyway, transform you into a more powerful version of yourself, something like the way the Super Star works in *Super Mario Bros.*, or the way cocaine worked for Scarface in *Scarface*.[3]

And so that's where we are: You're about to walk into an arena to fight someone you have no chance of beating. But you get to choose one song to listen to right before the fight as a sort of power-up. So: What song are you picking?

•••••

The setup for all of this is already pretty intricate, so let's make the actual selection process here as straightforward as possible. This is what we're going to do:

- We're going to make thirty picks here.
- We're going to pick thirty songs that would make for smart choices if you found yourself in a position like the one presented in the hypothetical above.
- Every rap song ever made is eligible to be chosen.
- We'll start in the thirtieth spot and then work our way up to the first spot.

That's it. That's what we're doing here. It's easy.

No. 30 Pick: "Pocket Full of Stones"
Artist: UGK
Best Line in the Song: "A fiend gon' be a fiend"

Admittedly, this is a controversial pick to start with, mostly because "Pocket Full of Stones" is not the kind of song you turn on when you want to hype yourself up for something. But my argument for including it here is twofold:

1. Anything this far back on the list of possible picks likely is not going to be a song with enough oomph in it anyway to energize someone into an extremely long-shot victory within the parameters that have been set forth. That being the case, I figured I'd slide something in here that would be a good final song to listen to before being beaten into oblivion. "Pocket Full of Stones" is really mellow and really beautiful and would becalm your spirit (I imagine) the same way breathing into a paper bag for a little bit becalms your body when you're nervous. It'd be a nice little respite, a beat of peace, really. So that's the first part of this. And the second part of this is ...
2. There's literally a line in Shirley Jackson's "The Lottery" where she describes one of the children in the town as having "already stuffed his pockets full of stones" in anticipation of the stoning. I feel like if I picked "Pocket Full of Stones" here as my song to listen to before the fight, eventually it would get out after I died that I'd chosen it, at which point someone would highlight how clever of a pick it was because of the way it reached back to hat-tip Shirley Jackson's story. "Shea's pick is a really interesting commentary on the dynamics of this whole corrupt system we have in place right now, and that's to say nothing of the way that it acknowledges the short story from whence the Annual Fight drew its inspiration," somebody whom I've never met would say online upon

3. It wasn't until this exact moment that I realized whoever it was who invented the Super Star for *Super Mario Bros.* was almost certainly inspired by cocaine.

learning about my song choice. "Sure," someone else whom I've never met would respond, "but we all know that UGK wasn't talking about literal stones in that song, right?" "Obviously," a third person whom I've never met would jump in to say, "but in a broader sense, neither was Shirley Jackson." And then those three people would all be proud of the conversation they'd just had and would never think about me again.

No. 29 Pick: "Pistol Grip Pump"
Artist: Volume 10
Best Line in the Song: "Rhyming is a cinch / Son of a bitch, I'm rich"

This is another unexpected pick, and I promise from here forward they will (mostly) be less disputable. But this song has to be on here simply as a matter of legacy. And what I mean is this:

The best example of the importance of matching a song to a moment happened in 1996. It was in a heist movie called *Set It Off*, which starred Queen Latifah, Jada Pinkett, Vivica A. Fox, and Kimberly Elise.

In the movie, the group commits three bank robberies together. Prior to each one, Latifah's character, Cleo, steals a car for the group to use during whatever robbery it is they're about to commit. And part of her car-stealing routine includes picking out an appropriate song to play before she drives off in the car she's just stolen.

The first time she steals a car, for example, she digs through the CDs inside of it, finds "I Ain't No Joke" by Eric B. and Rakim, turns it on, then says to herself, "Yeah, now that's what I ride to." Then she drives away.

The second time Cleo steals a car, she digs through the music again, but this time she doesn't find anything satisfactory. She tells Stony (Jada Pinkett's character) to give her a tape from her car (the other three members of the group are in Cleo's car and have pulled up alongside the car Cleo is stealing). After a bit of arguing, Stony tosses her a tape. It's Volume 10's "Pistol Grip Pump." Cleo puts it on, hears the opening thump of the song, then says to herself, "Yeah, that'll work." Then she drives away. (This robbery includes Cleo crashing an SUV into the bank to help the other members escape. She was super fucking hype after listening to "Pistol Grip Pump.")

The third time Cleo steals a car, she does the thing again where she looks for a CD or a tape to listen to that's already in the soon-to-be-stolen car. And same as the previous time, she doesn't find anything that she deems worthy to listen to. This time, though, Stony, who dropped off Cleo and Frankie (Fox) and T.T. (Elise), drives away before Cleo finishes looking through the music. Frankie, who has gotten into the passenger seat of the car, sees Cleo flipping through the CDs and asks what she's doing. "I'm trying to find some mood music," Cleo responds. Cleo looks up, sees that Stony has already left, and realizes there's nowhere for her to get any music she thinks is good enough to listen to, and so she says "Fuck it. *Radio*," and then turns on the radio and drives away.

And that's when things go bad.

Cleo had a very firm idea in her head of what she wanted to listen to after she'd stolen each of the cars. She knew the importance of matching a song to a moment, of allowing a song to get inside of her and activate that hidden reserve of strength or power or grit I talked about earlier.

She found an appropriate song the first time she stole a car, and that robbery was a success. She found an appropriate song the second time she stole a car, and that robbery was a success. She did not find an appropriate song the third time she stole a car, and that robbery ended with her dead, with Frankie dead, with T.T. dead, and with Stony on the run from federal agents.[4]

You have to match the song to the moment. It's important. Otherwise, everybody's ruined.

No. 28 Pick: "99 Problems"
Artist: Jay-Z
Best Line in the Song: That whole verse where Jay-Z has an argument with himself where he pretends to be a police officer

This is the first pick that's been made here with the intention of really honoring the purpose of the chapter. This is an exciting song and for sure one that carries a noticeable amount of punch to it. And yet still, really the main reason I grabbed it here was as a way to set up the twenty-sixth pick, which talks a little bit longer about the commingling of guitar riffs and rap songs.

No. 27 Pick: "Tear da Club Up '97"
Artist: Three 6 Mafia
Best Line in the Song: "They better call security / Bring them straitjackets and handcuffs"

Three things here:

1. Do you know how out of hand you and your friends have to be behaving not only for somebody to call security, but also for security to show up with some fucking straitjackets for everyone?
2. This song carried with it so much potent and uncontainable energy that clubs that were booking Three 6 Mafia for performances started putting it in the contract that Three 6 Mafia was not allowed to perform any version of "Tear da Club Up," because when they did, people quite literally tore the club up.[5]
3. One of my favorite Three 6 Mafia stats is that they made this song, which is an all-timer in the Turn the Fuck Up category, but they also made "Sippin' on Some Syrup," which is an all-timer in the Turn the Fuck Down category.

No. 26 Pick: "King of Rock"
Artist: Run-DMC
Best Line in the Song: "I'm the king of rock / There is none higher"

Run-DMC's relationship with guitars is always an interesting thing to think about, particularly with regard to three songs: 1984's "Rock Box," 1985's "King of Rock," and 1986's "Walk This Way." There's a progression to the way they used guitars in each of those songs that, if you squint, feels like it tells a much larger story.

With "Rock Box," Run-DMC connected rap and rock together in a meaningful way for the first time. And the

4. The song that was playing on the radio was "From Yo Blind Side" by X-Man, featuring H-Squad and Chocolate.
5. Despite agreeing to not perform "Tear da Club Up" ahead of time, Three 6 Mafia mostly did it anyway. DJ Paul explained the process during an interview on the podcast *Drink Champs*, saying, "We'd get all our money up front, talk 'em into it, do it last, and tear that motherfucker apart, man."

song was so good that it felt very much like mutualism, a feat unto itself given that at the time, white audiences considered rap to be second class. With "King of Rock," the guitar use was far more confrontational.[6] And if you somehow managed to miss the subtext in the song title or the song's lyrics, the video made it very clear. (It starts with a security guard at a pretend museum dedicated to rock and roll telling Run-DMC they don't belong there and ends with Run-DMC having desecrated several exhibits.) And then with "Walk This Way," which, per a 2015 *Guitar World* article, was responsible for helping to "raise Aerosmith's career from the toilet," it was like Run-DMC not only had conquered how best to use guitars in rap songs but had acquired the ability to weaponize guitars in whatever manner they felt.

No. 25 Pick: "Move Bitch"
Artist: Ludacris
Best Line in the Song: "And I been thinkin' of bustin' you upside your motherfucking forehead"

How about this: The video for "Move Bitch" opens with a reporter broadcasting from outside of a Ludacris concert. She asks into the camera where Ludacris is. Then we get a shot of Ludacris in a car on the road stuck in traffic. And that's when he starts the "Move, bitch, get out the way" thing. I think about that a lot. It's just really funny to me to think about the possibility that an all-time great Let's Get Hype song was made because Ludacris got stuck in bad traffic one day.

6. Eddie Martinez played the guitar for both songs, by the way.

. . . cont'd

No. 24 Pick: "Make 'Em Say Uhh!"
Artist: Master P, featuring Fiend, Silkk the Shocker, Mia X, and Mystikal
Best Line in the Song: "Stretch you out like elastic / Zip that ass up in plastic / Have your folks pickin' caskets"

Here are some (but not all of the) things that happen in the video for "Make 'Em Say Uhh!," which takes place on a basketball court:

- Master P participates in one of those T-shirt tosses where people throw shirts into the crowd. (This is the least outlandish thing that will get mentioned on this list. I'm including it, though, because despite the fact that I am an adult, and despite the fact that I have never found myself at a basketball game without a shirt on, I still 100 percent of the time stand up and wave my hands like a loon when I happen to be in a place where a T-shirt toss is happening.)
- Someone drives a gold-plated tank onto a basketball court DURING A GAME. (And just to be clear, this did not happen during a stoppage in a game, like with a time-out or at halftime or anything like that. The players were in the middle of bringing the ball up the court when the tank came out of the tunnel and drove up onto the court. The offense was one bad pass or bad dribble away from their point guard getting run over.)
- A gorilla wearing a basketball uniform for a team named Hustlers dunks it from what appears to be the three-point line.
- Shaquille O'Neal excitedly cheers as someone dunks it on an eight-foot goal.
- The aforementioned gold-plated tank fires a missile inside of a filled-to-capacity gym. (They don't show what they're shooting the missile at, but it seems pretty impossible that it went anywhere other than directly into a group of people watching the game.) (Catching a missile at a basketball game is decidedly less great than catching a T-shirt, I would guess.)

No. 23 Pick: "Made You Look"
Artist: Nas
Best Line in the Song: "BRAAAAAAAAAAAVEHEARRRRRRRT"

Nas has, since the very beginning of his career, been one of the smartest, most ambitious, most insightful writers in rap. He has been such an evocative writer, in fact, that a very common nice thing people say about him is some version of the "he paints pictures with words" compliment. Which is why my favorite Nas story is the one about how he was performing at an ancillary Art Basel Miami Beach event in 2011. He made a comment to the crowd about painting something, someone brought him some materials onstage, and so then he painted a literal picture while performing "Made You Look." He finished the painting and then finished the song and then auctioned the painting off right there onstage for $14,000 and then donated the money to a children's cancer nonprofit.

No. 22 Pick: "Superthug"
Artist: N.O.R.E.
Best Line in the Song: "What, what, what, what, what, what, what, what, wha–what"

This is probably a bad pick, but also it's possibly a great pick, and where you fall in that debate is likely aligned with how you feel about that period of rap where the Neptunes seemed to produce every other song on the radio.

No. 21 Pick: "B.O.B. (Bombs over Baghdad)"
Artist: Outkast
Best Line in the Song: "Don't pull the thang out unless you plan to bang"

I took a psychopharmacology class in college one year.[1] It was mostly very boring, save for one day a few weeks in when we started talking about methamphetamines. The professor was explaining the different effects that crystal meth has on people, and while doing so he told a story that a police officer had relayed to him. The officer, we were told, had been called to a motel because someone had said that a man who had possibly taken crystal meth was causing a giant ruckus. When the officer and his partner got there, they tried to subdue the man. The man wiggled free, then hauled ass up the stairs. The police gave chase, following him all the way to the fourth floor, which was the top level of that particular motel.

Once there, the man decided that it'd be better to jump over the ledge than to be captured by the cops. So that was what he did. He climbed over the ledge and then jumped right the fuck off, falling some four stories down to the ground. The police couldn't believe it. They were in shock. They ran to where the man had jumped from, and they looked over the handrail, expecting to see a completely obliterated human. That was not what they saw, though. What they saw was the man, perfectly fine, in a dead-on sprint running through the parking lot. The crystal meth in the man's body made him able to momentarily shake off having broken several bones in his body. That was what our professor told us as he wrapped up the story. It had filled the man with so much energy, with so much unhinged adrenaline, that it had basically turned him into a shirtless Captain America for a few minutes.

Anyway, "Bombs over Baghdad"[2] is the pick here.[3]

No. 20 Pick: "I Don't Like"
Artist: Chief Keef, featuring Lil Reese
Best Line in the Song: "Fredo in the cut / That's a scary sight"

A curious thing about "I Don't Like": because of the song's production, which is thundering and aggressive and swollen, it feels very much like the track is rooted in hate or in anger or in some other equally strong emotion.[4] The lyrics, however, suggest otherwise. The lyrics are mostly just Chief Keef telling you the things that he doesn't like, which suggests annoyance or possibly irritation or, at the most extreme, aggravation. (Bad weed? Chief Keef does

1. I failed a psychopharmacology class in college one year.

2. "Bombs over Baghdad" runs at 155 beats per minute. Some other songs that run near 155 bpm: Kenny Loggins's "Danger Zone," Bon Jovi's "Runaway," Queen's "Don't Stop Me Now," blink-182's "What's My Age Again?"

3. Similar to Ludacris's "Move Bitch," which briefly became tied to the nationwide protests happening in America in 2020, "Bombs over Baghdad" would later come to represent something that Outkast had not intended. In their case, it briefly became a pro-war statement for people eager to show their support of American troops during the Iraq War. Per the *Los Angeles Times*, this happened despite Big Boi being "strongly opposed to the U.S. invading Iraq without United Nations support."

4. That's why it made it up to the twentieth pick here.

not like it. Talking to the police? Chief Keef does not like it. Knockoffs of designer brands? Chief Keef does not like it.)[5]

It makes for an interesting dichotomy.[6] Because somewhere in that space between where the production takes you and where the lyrics take you is a good metaphor for the unexpected ways in which Chief Keef made himself an essential figure in contemporary rap.

No. 19 Pick: "Whoop That Trick"
Artist: DJay
Best Line in the Song: "Hoes telling me to calm down but I'm like fuck that shit"

This is one of the songs that they make during that movie *Hustle & Flow*, yes. But I don't care. It fucking rules. So I'm including it. And just because I'd like to spend a few seconds remembering other excellent songs from movies, here's a list:

1. "Whoop That Trick," from *Hustle & Flow*
2. "Remember Me," from *Coco*
3. "That Thing You Do!" from *That Thing You Do!*
4. "Grow Old with You," from *The Wedding Singer*
5. "Shallow," from *A Star Is Born*
6. "It's Hard Out Here for a Pimp," from *Hustle & Flow*
7. "We All Die Young," from *Rock Star*
8. "Ashley Wednesday," from *Popstar: Never Stop Never Stopping*
9. "I'm Black Y'all," from *CB4*
10. "Scotty Doesn't Know," from *EuroTrip*

No. 18 Pick: "Break Fool"
Artist: Rah Digga
Best Line in the Song: "Say 'fuck that' / Fuck that! / Fuck that / Fuck that!"

Rah Digga has a great rap voice. There's a back-of-the-throat wideness to it that is almost impossible to replicate. It makes it feel big and confrontational and like it's everywhere all at once, something like how it'd feel if you walked into a cloud of bees, or something like how it'd feel if you were driving a bulldozer that had its blade pressed down into the road. So you take her voice, and then you mix it together with the chaotic swell of the production on "Break Fool," and then you forge those two things into a pomegranate-sized container, and then you pull a detonating pin, and then you release the safety lever, and then you throw it at your enemies. That's a grenade. That's how grenades work.

No. 17 Pick: "Hit 'Em Up"
Artist: 2Pac, featuring the Outlawz
Best Line in the Song: "First off, fuck your bitch and the clique you claim"

"Hit 'Em Up" is the most vicious, most insulting, most unstoppably disrespectful diss song that has ever been recorded. It's a masterwork. Separate of everything else, here are some of the different ways that 2Pac uses a version of the word "fuck" in it:

- **"That's why I fucked your bitch, you fat motherfucker."** This is literally the first line of the song. And

5. These are all completely reasonable things to not like, by the way.
6. In a 2018 essay for the *Outline*, David Drake described the power of "I Don't Like" as such: "Our jarring experience of this music isn't to its 'nihilism,' but to [Chief Keef's] seemingly disproportionate, understated response to a life we think should prompt stronger reactions."

what's wild is it's not even part of the actual song. It's just 2Pac talking. He can barely even wait for the music to kick in before he starts setting fire to everything.

- **"First off, fuck your bitch and the clique you claim."** This is the first line of the first verse. It's as effective and encapsulating a thesis statement as has ever been written.
- **"Fuck peace."** War? Good. Peace? Fuck peace.
- **"You fuck around and have a seizure or a heart attack."** Immediately before this line, 2Pac brings up how someone in the Bad Boy orbit has sickle cell disease. He's talking about Prodigy, a member of the group Mobb Deep, who was tangentially connected to the Notorious B.I.G. and Puff Daddy. (Prodigy passed away from complications related to the disease in 2017.)
- **"Fuck you and your motherfucking mama."** I like the idea of 2Pac, later in the song, realizing that "Fuck your bitch and the clique you claim" didn't quite cover enough ground, and so he had to come back later with "Fuck you and your motherfucking mama."
- **"Motherfucker, my 4-4 make sure all y'all kids don't grow."** This one is super gnarly. He is, in effect, saying that if any of his enemies have children, those children will be shot to death, which is always a startling thing to hear on a song. This line always reminds me of the time that I was riding around in the car with my wife, Larami, in, I think, 2015 or so. We had just dropped our kids off at school and were headed to get breakfast together. I was the one who was driving, so I was the one who got to pick what music we listened to. I went with Maxo Kream, which lets you know that I must've been having a rough morning, because Maxo Kream makes music that is perfect when you want to soak in your own anger. Anyway, a song of his called "Trigga Maxo" came on, and there's a part where he talks about shooting at someone's car, and he says, "Aiming for the car seat, I'm a crazy motherfucker." He said that line, and Larami was like, "Okay, that's enough of that," and then she turned it off. And I was like, "Yeah, you're right. That's my bad. That's way too aggressive for a Tuesday morning."

Actually, you know what . . .

No. 16 Pick: "Trigga Maxo"
Artist: Maxo Kream
Best Line in the Song: "Aiming for the car seat, I'm a crazy motherfucker"

Originally, the no. 16 pick was supposed to be "Move That Dope" by Future. It's a fun song and a song that has an undeniable energy to it, and so I figured it might work well as a power-up here. But "Trigga Maxo" is going to swoop in and take its spot. It's more menacing and more vicious, and that might be a better state of mind to be in if you're headed toward participating in a bare-knuckle death match.

No. 15 Pick: "B.M.F."
Artist: Rick Ross, featuring Styles P
Best Line in the Song: "Self-made / You just affiliated / I built it ground up / You bought it renovated"

Were we to operate under the assumption that "Fy" = "Fuck Yes" and "Hfs" = "Holy Fucking Shit" and "L" = "Let's" and "F" = "Fucking" and "G" = "Go," then the chemical formula for this song would be as such: $Fy_4 + Hfs_2 + 3L_2F_2G_3$.

So that's four atoms of "Fuck Yes," two atoms of "Holy Fucking Shit," and three molecules of the "Let's Fucking Go" compound, which contains twenty-one total atoms.

No. 14 Pick: "I'm Bad"
Artist: LL COOL J
Best Line in the Song: "And even when I'm bragging / I'm being sincere"

This song is a testament to two things: First, it's a testament to its own production, which is rubbery and caustic and spirited in a way that still feels vital more than three decades later.[7] It feels alive and like it wants to escape, except that it can't because LL COOL J has put a saddle on it and is riding the fuck out of it. And that's the second thing the song is a testament to. It's a testament to LL COOL J's gravity as an all-caps COOL PERSON in 1987. He's so captivating in this moment and so compelling in this video that he's somehow able to talk about (a) jelly beans, (b) hats, (c) walkie-talkies, (d) eating cookies named after himself, and (e) peas, all while taking a firm anti-drugs stance. And he never once sounds like anything less than one of the five coolest people on the planet.

No. 13 Pick: "Down for My N's"
Artist: C-Murder, featuring Snoop Dogg and Magic
Best Line in the Song: "Make 'em bleed is the motto that I live by"

Four things here:

1. We had that song "Make 'Em Say Uhh!" by Master P at the start of this chapter. C-Murder is actually Master P's brother. And they're both brothers to Silkk the Shocker, who will get a mention later, in the final chapter of this countdown. The Miller family makes good music for very specific hypothetical situations.
2. I should've mentioned this earlier, but Master P actually created a "Make 'Em Say Uhh!" energy drink that was available for purchase for a short while. And that's only a surprising thing if you don't know that there are very few business angles that Master P, who was born into poverty and then flipped a $10,000 insurance settlement into an empire worth hundreds of millions, has not chased down, including but not limited to a travel agency, professional wrestling, and various food-related items.
3. C-Murder was convicted of second-degree murder in 2009. I took a psychology class in college one year.[8] We learned about something called labeling theory, which "posits that self-identity and the behavior of individuals may be determined or influenced by the terms used to describe or classify them."[9] I bet whoever thought of it read the news in heaven about C-Murder getting convicted of second-degree murder and was like, "I fucking told y'all."[10]
4. Some of the songs on this list lose a bit of steam after their openings. This one, though, does not. It feels just as frenetic and swarming in its final moments as it does from the get-go. Every song from here forward will, at minimum, have that same characteristic.

7. The production is built up from a mix of LL's "Rock the Bells," a Q2B siren, Rhythm Heritage's "Theme from S.W.A.T.," and, most crucially, an interpolation of the theme song from a cartoon from the 1960s called *Courageous Cat and Minute Mouse.*

8. I failed a psychology class in college one year.

9. Per *Wikipedia*, "Labeling Theory."

10. C-Murder has, for the duration of the time he's been associated with the crime, maintained his innocence. In 2018, two witnesses recanted their testimony identifying C-Murder as the murderer, saying that they were each pressured by authorities to testify against him.

No. 12 Pick: "Close Your Eyes (And Count to Fuck)"
Artist: Run the Jewels, featuring Zack de la Rocha
Best Line in the Song: "I'll bite into a cyanide molar before you whores win"

If the purpose of these three chapters is to work our way toward songs that would, in one way or another, help you survive in a literal fight for your life, then it would make sense to include "Close Your Eyes (And Count to Fuck)," the video for which is two people – a Black citizen, played by LaKeith Stanfield, and a white police officer, played by Shea Whigham – fighting each other in a way that makes it clear that they both believe their lives are at risk.

No. 11 Pick: "We Ready"
Artist: Archie Eversole, featuring Bubba Sparxxx
Best Line in the Song: "WeeeeEEEEeeeee readddddddddy / Forrrrrrrr y'alllllllllllllll"

This song came out when I was in college. It was one of those instances where something just became instantly popular within your cohort. It felt like one day it was nowhere, and then the next day it was everywhere all of the time. People would play it for everything. You would hear it while tailgating before football games. You would hear it at parties. You would hear it through your dorm walls or apartment walls when people who lived near you were getting ready in the morning for class or ready in the evening to go out. It was great.

My favorite personal memory attached to the song: I played on a flag-football team through a school rec league one year.[11] It was me and several of my dumb friends. Mostly, we just signed up because we thought it'd be fun to wear matching shirts and play catch with each other. It turned out, though, that we were kind of good. The success of the team was largely due to a player named Auggie, who had been a standout track runner in high school but soured on the experience his senior year and abandoned the sport. Any time we got into any trouble, we'd just give the ball to Auggie on a reverse, and he'd fucking Speedy Gonzales his way to the end zone. We played ten games that season, and we ended up winning seven of them, the last of which qualified us for the playoffs.

Prior to our first playoff game, a guy on the team named Oscar came up with what we felt like was an excellent (if not altogether obvious) idea. "We should play 'We Ready' real loud on a stereo when we come out on the field" is what he said. "That sounds awesome" is how the rest of us responded. And so that's what we did. We burned a copy of "We Ready" to a CD the day before the game, put it in a boom box that we carried to the field, then played it as loud as it would go when we came walking out. And I don't mind telling you it was incredible. We were so goddamn fired up. We could've chewed through leather, if you'd have asked us to. We could've ripped the transmission out of an F-150, if you'd have asked us to. We could've picked up an oak tree and thrown it an unreasonable distance, if you'd have asked us to. And then the game started. And we immediately got blown the fuck out. We were not, as it were, ready.

11. I think it was my junior year, though I'm not certain, because the number of years I had been in college stopped lining up with what my class rank was supposed to be once I learned about how you could just drop classes whenever you wanted.

WHAT'S THE ORDER OF THE LOTTERY SONG PICKS?

PART 3

. . . cont'd

> **No. 10 Pick:** "Queen Bitch"
> **Artist:** Lil' Kim
> **Best Line in the Song:** "Got buffoons eating my pussy while I watch cartoons"

There have been a few different moments of demarcation on this countdown so far. There was the first one, at the twenty-eighth spot, where, from there going forward, each song chosen had to be at least helpful in juicing your strength for your upcoming fight. There was the second one, at the thirteenth spot, where, from there going forward, each song chosen had to be able to maintain its energy from the start through the finish. And now there's this one, at the tenth spot: every song from here going forward, in addition to being a song that powers up your everything, is also a song that could function excellently as an Intimidating Ring Entrance song.

> **No. 9 Pick:** "Bia' Bia'" / "What U Gon' Do" / + 50 more
> **Artist:** Lil Jon & the East Side Boyz and more / Lil Jon & the East Side Boyz, featuring Lil Scrappy / + 50 more
> **Best Line in the Song:** "GOD DAMN IT, MOTHERFUCKER, WHERE YOU FROM?"

The truth is this: it would have been very easy to stuff these three chapters full of songs from the Lil Jon era of crunk music. It's music that, by its very design, is meant to make people feel excited and energetic and exhilarated and electrified and enraptured and a bunch of other adjectives that don't begin with an *e*.[1] But I didn't want to do that, because, same as how when you're building a basketball team, you don't just go with twelve power forwards or whatever, I wanted our final collection of songs to feel robust and interesting. So let me very quickly say the names of a few (but not all of the) other songs that philosophically would've fit in fine but ultimately were not selected because I was trying to avoid redundancy: "I Don't Give A . . . by Lil Jon & the East Side Boyz, featuring Mystikal and Krayzie Bone; "Damn!" by YoungBloodZ, featuring Lil Jon; "Get Low" by Lil Jon & the East Side Boyz; "Head Bussa" by Lil Scrappy, featuring Lil Jon; and "No Problem" by Lil Scrappy. There are a bunch, obviously.

(That said, there *are* a couple more songs ahead that fall into the crunk music category.)

> **No. 8 Pick:** "Bring da Ruckus"
> **Artist:** Wu-Tang Clan
> **Best Line in the Song:** "Yo, I'm more rugged than slave man boots / New recruits / I'm fuckin' up MC troops"

Any song from the Wu-Tang Clan is a natural pick for this type of exercise because the Wu-Tang Clan has, from its inception, aligned itself with martial arts movies and, more broadly speaking, martial arts ethos. It's always good music to listen to when you want to put your fist

---

1. Lil Jon had a great quote for *The Today Show* in 2004 when he was describing crunk music. He said, "The energy from these records, that's what makes crunk so popular. That's why it's winning. Because it makes you move a certain way. Like when you hear Aretha Franklin sing, it touches your soul. Crunk music, it makes you just wanna lose your mind, just be free and wild out."

through the back of someone's chest. I went specifically with "Bring da Ruckus," though, because of the following:

- **For one, it fucking rules.** It's chaotic and dusty and aggressive. It feels like a dark alley in a bad neighborhood, or like a knife on the ground with bloodstains on the blade. It has an inherent nefariousness to it.
- **For two, Ghostface Killah is so full of thunder that he barely makes it three lines before he starts hollering about an elephant tusk.** Physiologically, Ghostface Killah hollering about an elephant tusk is about the same as injecting heroin directly into your eyeballs or your genitals or probably anywhere in your body. I don't know. I have no actual direct knowledge of the way heroin works. I only know what I watched Jared Leto do in *Requiem for a Dream.*
- **For three, "Bring da Ruckus" is the very first song on the Wu-Tang Clan's iconic debut album *Enter the Wu-Tang (36 Chambers)*.** The RZA, who is the architect of the Wu-Tang Clan's brilliant business model, has always had a profound grasp on intentionality. Seemingly every move that the group made early on (or has continued to make through today) was not without a purpose, be it grand or small, easy to understand or impossible to understand. So I feel like them putting this song as the first on their first album was also absolutely not an accident.[2] There's a reason it's there. There's an all-caps REASON the very first thing anybody hears from any of the members of the Wu-Tang Clan on their debut album is the RZA full-mouthed yelling "Bring the motherfucking ruckus!" over and over again. Now, *I* can only guess at what that REASON is, but that's fine. I don't need to *know* the REASON to understand that it's there, same as I don't need to be able to see oxygen to know that it exists in our atmosphere, or the same as I don't need to have injected heroin into my penis to know that it's probably a pretty big kick to do so.

No. 7 Pick: "Slam"
Artist: Onyx
Best Line in the Song: Pretty much everything that Sticky Fingaz says

Sticky Fingaz has my favorite verse on this song, but Fredro Starr is my overall favorite member of Onyx. I suspect that's largely tied to his face, which is awesome,[3] and his temper, which is quick-fire,[4] and also to his acting career, which has put him on my TV screen during some of my favorite movies and TV shows. He played Bamboo in 1993's *Strapped* (this was a direct-to-TV movie that karate kicked you square in the throat near the end),[5] and

2. There's a Thai martial arts movie starring Tony Jaa called *Tom-Yum-Goong* (in America it's called *The Protector*). The RZA not only is in the sequel but also has a very solid fight scene with Tony Jaa. I mention it here because it's just interesting to me that Ghostface Killah mentions, of all things, an elephant in the first verse of "Bring da Ruckus," and then twenty years later the RZA fights Jaa's character, Kham, who plays "the last of a family line of guards who once watched over the King of Thailand's war elephants" (per *Wikipedia*).
3. I greatly appreciate how angular it is. His cheekbones are diamond cutters, and his eyes are razor blades.
4. He's like a stick of dynamite. I'm always drawn to people like that.
5. Bamboo and Diquan (played by Bokeem Woodbine) walk into a corner store. Bamboo gets into an argument with the clerk. The clerk tells him to get out of the store. Bamboo, already on edge, becomes fully enraged. He pulls out a gun and points it at the clerk. Right then, someone behind Bamboo makes a noise. He turns around and fires without looking. And then that's when we see: it was a five-year-old girl who made the noise. She was pushing a tiny stroller with a doll in it. And Bamboo accidentally shot her right in the chest. It's fucking wild. The face he makes when he sees what he's done is such a crusher.

he played Shorty in 1996's *Sunset Park*,[6] and he played Q on the TV series *Moesha* from 1996 to 2000, and he played Malakai in 2001's *Save the Last Dance*, and he played Bird for a few episodes of the TV series *The Wire*. It was a great run.

No. 6 Pick: "Neva Eva"
Artist: Trillville, featuring Lil Scrappy and Lil Jon
Best Line in the Song: "I knew you wasn't real 'cause all you do is chitchat"

There's a part in "Neva Eva" where Don Peezy says, "I knew you wasn't real 'cause all you do is chitchat." It hurt my feelings the first time I heard it, because I do like to chitchat in real life. That's always a funny thing to have happen to you. You're just sitting there, minding your business, enjoying a song, and then all of a sudden a couple stray bullets hit you dead in the center of your chest.

It happened to me on Drake's "Can't Have Everything" in 2017 when he said that it was embarrassing to stay at a Sheraton hotel (I've stayed at several Sheraton hotels, and I always found them to be enjoyable). And it happened to me on Trick Daddy's "Shut Up" in 2000 when he got offended that someone thought his Polo jeans were Bugle Boys (Bugle Boy jeans were like Versace when you grew up paying for shit with food stamps, lol). And, most devastatingly, it happened to me in 2018 when, literally while I was on a flight on Spirit Airlines with my wife for a vacation, Bhad Bhabie rapped into the headphones in my ears, "I ain't worried 'bout no basic bitches / All y'all look like you still fly Spirit." What a fucking kill shot that was.[7]

No. 5 Pick: "Never Scared"
Artist: Bone Crusher, featuring Killer Mike and T.I.
Best Line in the Song: "Like, hope for the best / But I don't think he gon' make it / Not the way he was shiverin' and shakin' on the pavement"

We're into the top five now. We don't have room anymore to be clever with the selections. Any pick made from here going forward has to have, at a bare minimum, a guaranteed Hakeem Olajuwon level of success. And what I mean is: Michael Jordan, the greatest (or second greatest) basketball player who has ever lived, was selected third in the 1984 NBA draft. The two picks before him were Hakeem Olajuwon, who was chosen by the Houston Rockets in the number one spot,[8] and Sam Bowie, who was chosen by the Portland Trail Blazers in the number two spot. Nobody ever really says anything to Houston about going with Hakeem over Jordan, because Hakeem not only became one of the ten greatest players ever but also delivered two championships to the Rockets. With Portland, though, everyone still gives them shit about taking Bowie over Jordan, because Bowie, it turned out, had legs made of pencil lead.[9]

6. This is a thoroughly underappreciated basketball movie.

7. The song was on one of those Apple playlists that have a bunch of different songs on them.

8. He was Akeem Olajuwon at the time.

9. How's this for circularity: Jordan wore the number 23 for most of his career. In the 2007 draft, which was twenty-three years after Portland chose Bowie over Jordan, they chose yet another oft-injured big man (Greg Oden) over another generational talent (Kevin Durant).

I desperately do not want to have a Bowie situation happen here; that's why each of these final five picks are thoroughbreds. You might be able to argue that another song could've wiggled its way into the top five, but you won't be able to argue that any of these are bad picks. And we're starting, of course, with Bone Crusher's "Never Scared." It checks off all the major boxes:

- **Is the production on the song intimidating?** It sounds like rumbling madness or like pulsating anger or like something extremely aggressive aliens would play over a loudspeaker during an invasion. So yes. The production is intimidating.
- **Does the song have an intimidating title?** It's called "Never Scared." So yes. (A dumb thing: the meat of the chorus, which is Bone Crusher shouting, "I ain't never scared," is sung in a cadence that lines up perfectly with "Sometimes I get scared," which is how I would sing it if it were my song.)
- **Is the rapper's name intimidating?** His name is Bone Crusher. So yes. It's an intimidating name. I have many bones in my body. I would like to never have any of them disturbed in any way, let alone crushed.
- **Is the rapper's voice intimidating?** It's guttural, and it sounds almost like it's grinding its way out of his mouth. It doesn't quite sound painful, but it sounds like it could inflict pain if it wanted to. So yes.
- **Are the people on the song talking about intimidating things?** Bone Crusher starts his verse by talking about how he's going to shoot you in the head. Killer Mike's whole verse is about his gun and how she has a name (Bonita)[10] and how she's more effective at blood withdrawals than the Red Cross (she takes it out by the liter) and how she punishes people indiscriminately. And T.I.'s verse has a whole section in it about sending people to the intensive care unit. So yes. They're talking about intimidating things.

No. 4 Pick: "Hard in da Paint"
Artist: Waka Flocka Flame
Best Line in the Song: "Flocka / Waka, Waka, Waka, Waka Flocka / Waka, Waka, Waka Flocka / Flocka, Flocka, Flocka, Waka"

Earlier in this chapter I wrote about the Wu-Tang Clan's "Bring da Ruckus." That song has an especially memorable snare in it. It feels bigger than normal and broader than normal. It hit your ears less like a laser beam and more like a shotgun scatterblast. During a 2017 interview with Roli, the RZA explained that the way he got it to sound like that was he recorded it inside of an elevator shaft. I always think about that whenever I hear Waka Flocka's voice. Everything he says, particularly in this song, feels like it traveled through a titanium hallway before it got to you. It doesn't float into your ears inasmuch as it presses its way into your whole head. And so you take that, and then you add in the production, which is just as massive and just as hostile and just as antagonistic, and all of a sudden you look around the room and there's blood smeared on the walls and the furniture has all been destroyed and you're holding someone's arm. Or maybe it's someone's leg? I don't know. It's hard to say on account of how mangled it is.

10. He gives a really clever high five to A Tribe Called Quest right here. After he says that his gun's name is Bonita, he says, "Knock the apple off any bum with a hollow heatseeker," referencing ATCQ's brilliant 1990 song "Bonita Applebum."

No. 3 Pick: "Knuck If You Buck"
Artist: Crime Mob
Best Line in the Song: "Yeah, we knucking and bucking and ready to fight"

The pedigree of this song for this situation is unquestionable, and so let me talk about "Knuck If You Buck" in a different way. Because "Knuck If You Buck" can be whatever you need it to be, however you need it to be. It exists as a song that allows you entry into a bunch of interesting conversations. Here are just three of them:

1. **The Staying Power Conundrum.** Typically, when a song has the kind of staying power that "Knuck If You Buck" has, it gets assigned a certain kind of intellectual weight. For example, Mike Jones released "Still Tippin'" the same year that "Knuck If You Buck" came out. And those songs, at least in spirit, are cousins. They're regional rap songs that were so good and so undeniable that they eventually became beloved nationwide rap songs. But "Still Tippin'" has aged its way into becoming the marker point for when Houston rap momentarily became the center of the rap universe. "Knuck If You Buck," which is probably more timeless than "Still Tippin'," feels like it has not yet become a proper marker point for anything.[11]
2. **The Subversion Angle.** The members of Crime Mob were real young when they made "Knuck If You Buck." (Diamond, who has gone on to become the most well-known member of the group, was just fifteen years old when "Knuck" received its official release.) As such, it's fun to consider the angle that a lot of the early listeners were also real young, which means "Knuck If You Buck" was maybe the first real example of something subversive that a generation of kids experienced. And to expand tangentially on that point . . .
3. **The Angst Angle.** In 2018, a podcast producer named Wallace Mack put together an oral history of "Knuck If You Buck" for an episode of *The Nod* that worked its way through the formation of the song and the importance of the song. During the show, Mack made a really profound point, explaining, "When people talk about angst, they don't ever associate that as, like, a thing that Black kids have. And I feel like if there's any group of kids in America to have angst, it would certainly almost be us. . . . And I feel like what this song did was it really perfectly captured what I feel like a lot of Black kids who grew up in areas like mine were feeling at that time: trapped. You're feeling trapped, and I feel like to give kids . . . to give *me*, at that time in my life, that kind of power, was really important."

No. 2 Pick: "Simon Says"
Artist: Pharoahe Monch
Best Line in the Song: "Y'all know the name / Pharoahe fucking Monch / Ain't a damn thing changed"

11. The rap historian Dart Adams, who helped with research on various parts of this book, brought up a good point when I asked him about this. He said that the song was very popular during the Ringtone Era, and so maybe "Knuck If You Buck" works as a historical precursor to Soulja Boy's "Crank That (Soulja Boy)," which was the first song to take full advantage of the social sharing aspect of the internet. I think that's a smart idea.

The transition at the beginning of "Simon Says" when it goes from the sample (Akira Ifukube's "Gojira Tai Mosura") into the rap version of itself that serves as the spine of the rest of the song is, I would argue, one of the five or six most perfect transitions in all of rap. It's perfectly executed. Pharoahe Monch was eventually sued because he never got actual permission to use the sample, but, I mean, come on. You have to let that one slide if you're the judge. You have to be like, "Listen. Technically, yes, what Pharoahe Monch did was illegal. But this shit super bangs, so I'm ruling in favor of the defendant. Case closed."

No. 1 Pick: "Ante Up"
Artist: M.O.P.
Best Line in the Song: "Fool, what you want? Your life or your jewels?"

Let me give you a tiny peek behind the curtain here. When this list of songs for these three chapters started out, there were sixty-seven choices on there. And since there were only thirty spots available here, that means there were a lot of hard omissions that had to be made, particularly once I got down to the final thirty-six or so.[12] And even after I had the top thirty picks, there was still a lot of cutting and pasting, and a lot of moving things back and forth, and a lot of arguing about where one song should be versus where another song should be. It was a long, arduous process. It took, I would say, somewhere around four solid weeks to pin down all of the pieces and also to do all of the research needed to write through everything here, and even then I'm pretty sure I probably made a couple wrong decisions along the way.

And yet, despite the chaos of the situation and despite the uncertainty of the situation, the one thing that was never in question was that M.O.P.'s "Ante Up," a song so hostile and so beautifully belligerent that listening to it louder than at a whisper's volume feels like you're being robbed at gunpoint by a trigger-happy hurricane, was absolutely, unquestionably, indisputably, inarguably, irrefutably, incontestably going to end up as the no. 1 pick.

It just had to be.

It just *had* to be.

12. The most crushing cut was when I had to remove U.N.L.V.'s "Drag 'Em 'N' Tha River," a song I greatly love. The other two that hurt a lot were knocking DMX's "What's My Name?" and "Ruff Ryders' Anthem" off the list, but I figured it was fine since there's a whole DMX chapter later in this book.

WHAT'S LAURYN HILL'S CAREER
SHOOTING PERCENTAGE?

LAURYN HILL HAS THE MOST INDESCRIBABLE SINGING VOICE in music. I can think of words to describe most everyone else's. Aretha Franklin's singing voice, for example, is the most irrepressible.[1] Whitney Houston's is the most powerfully pristine.[2] Jennifer Hudson's is the most nuclear. Erykah Badu's is the most confidently delicate. So on and so forth. But I don't know what that word (or combination of words) is for Lauryn Hill. All that I know is that when she starts singing—when she starts pumping those big emotions out into the universe, it activates something in you; something inert, something hidden, something that feels like it aches but also, curiously, feels like it's gorgeous. It's really hard to explain or to write about, which, as you might imagine, is troublesome for someone who writes about things for a living.

The closest I've ever come to getting Lauryn Hill's voice right isn't even an actual sentence I thought of or said. It's just me referencing a three-second piece of a scene from the movie *Sister Act 2: Back in the Habit*. And I know how silly it might appear to discuss one of the most influential musicians in history by bringing up a movie about a lounge singer who goes undercover as a nun and uses music to save a school she attended as a child, but I promise you that we'll eventually land on solid footing here. Anyway, the three seconds are:

Lauryn Hill, who plays a Saint Francis Academy student named Rita who is having her singing dreams stifled by her very pragmatic mother, has snuck away to perform at a statewide singing competition with her choirmates. And they're excited about everything at first. But then things unravel.

The song Saint Francis is scheduled to perform is "Joyful, Joyful." And, in a bad turn of luck for them, the reigning three-time state champions (Grand High School) perform the same song just a few minutes before Saint Francis is supposed to go on. Several of the Saint Francis students watch in dread as the champs, who have a massive choir of about forty-five singers, waterfall their way through the opening stanza. "They're like an army," one of them remarks.

Rita and the rest of the team consider quitting. Sister Mary Clarence (their teacher, played by Whoopi Goldberg) gives them a big rah-rah speech about integrity and adversity and the responsibility they owe to each other and to the people who believed in them enough to risk their jobs to get them to the competition. She leaves the decision of whether or not to perform up to them. And after a few seconds of talking among themselves, they decide to give it a go.

Their performance, in stark contrast to the all-caps MAX VOLUME power approach Grand High School went with, opens with just Rita onstage. Someone is there in the background to interpret the lyrics via sign language, and another student is stationed at the piano to accompany. But as far as the singing goes, Rita is the show. It is, in effect, her voice versus the combined voices of the other school's forty-five singers. And she fucking obliterates them. She's so much more compelling and so much more tender and so much more moving. It's incredible. And beautiful. And perfect. And devastating.

---

1. My favorite description I've ever heard of her voice is when Larami and I were watching Aretha perform at the 2015 Kennedy Center Honors and Larami said, "Aretha Franklin's voice doesn't obey any laws."
2. My pick for the note-for-note, moment-for-moment, line-for-line greatest singer in the history of the planet.

As she sings, the camera cuts to one of the friars from Saint Francis who's come to support the students. He's standing up against a wall in the back of the auditorium, his full attention on Rita. And this is the three seconds of the scene that I mentioned earlier that best describe Lauryn Hill's voice. Because as he watches and listens, his eyes fill with tears. He does his very best to hold it together, but it's clear that her voice has traveled inside of his chest and filled him with an uncommon and overwhelming amount of emotion. He doesn't talk or move or even breathe. But in those three seconds, you can see him cycle through so many different feelings (and, were I to guess, so many different memories he'd long suppressed). He's not sure whether he wants to smile or cry, so he ends up doing a little bit of both, Lauryn Hill's voice volleying him back and forth between the two the way a god might juggle two planets out of boredom.

I love it. I love that moment. He looks EXACTLY how Lauryn Hill's voice makes me feel. After all these years of listening to her, it's still the only way I can think to describe it. All I can do is say, "Go to YouTube. Search for the 'Joyful, Joyful' performance from *Sister Act 2*. Wait until they show the guy in the straw hat who's watching Lauryn Hill sing. And there you go. That's Lauryn Hill's voice."

•••••

Calculating someone's shooting percentage is easy. All that you do is take the number of shots that were made and then divide it by the number of attempts. So, to use basketball here since that's where I got this stat from, when the Rockets beat the Knicks in the 1994 NBA Finals after John Starks went 2 for 18 from the field in Game 7, his shooting percentage was 11 percent.[3] Or, to use basketball here again, when the Spurs beat the Knicks in the 1999 NBA Finals after Larry Johnson went 3 for 10 in the deciding Game 5, his shooting percentage was 30 percent.[4]

Or, to bring this back around: Lauryn Hill was nominated for ten Grammys (!!!) after she released *The Miseducation of Lauryn Hill*, her gigantic debut album, in 1998. She ended up winning five of them, meaning her shooting percentage at the Grammys that night was 50 percent. Here's the thing, though: I don't want to know what her shooting percentage was that night. I want to know what her shooting percentage has been for her entire career. So that's what we're gonna do. We're gonna go through a bunch of substantial moments from Lauryn Hill's career and figure out her overall shooting percentage.

•••••

Two music things that are often debated: Is Lauryn Hill a rapper or a singer? And is *The Miseducation of Lauryn Hill* a rap album or an R&B album?

There's equal weight to both sides of both arguments. Because one side can point to, say, "Lost Ones," which is *The Miseducation of Lauryn Hill*'s first song past the intro, and go, "Obviously, this is a rap song. You can't hear it and not know that. That means she's a rapper and *Miseducation* is a rap album." Meanwhile, the other side

---

3. Apologies to Knicks fans for the stray shot. It's just that this whole book is basically about how incredible New York is for being the city where hip-hop was not only created but also nurtured into a powerhouse, so I figured I needed to balance things out.
4. One more soft jab to the chin just for fun.

can point to, say, "Ex-Factor," which immediately follows "Lost Ones" on *Miseducation*, and go, "Obviously, this is an R&B song. You can't hear it and not know that. That means she's a singer and *Miseducation* is an R&B album."

And one side can say, "Well, if she's a singer, then why did she win a Grammy for Best Rap Album in 1996[5] and get nominated for Best Rap Solo Performance in 1998?" To which the other side can say, "Well, if she's a rapper, then why did she win a Grammy for Best R&B Album in 1998[6] and win a Grammy for Best R&B Performance by a Duo or Group in 1996?"

And one side can say, "If *Miseducation* isn't a rap album, then why did *Rolling Stone* pick it as the greatest rap album of all time when they redid their 500 Greatest Albums of All Time list? Don't you remember that big ol' dustup on the internet about it?" To which the other side can say, "That's actually a misinterpretation of what happened. What really happened is *Rolling Stone* listed it as the tenth best album of all time, and someone grabbed that piece of information and said that it was an indirect declaration that it was the greatest rap album ever."

But the answer to both of those questions—is Lauryn Hill a singer or a rapper, and is *The Miseducation of Lauryn Hill* a rap album or an R&B album?—is, quite simply, "Yes." Hill had the best explanation for it when she spoke with the *Source* for a 1998 cover story, saying, "I know this sounds crazy, but sometimes I treat rapping like singing, and other times I treat singing like rapping. But still, it's all done within the context of hip-hop." So there you go. An answer that is both (a) absolute and (b) completely open to interpretation. Just like Lauryn Hill.

•••••

Let's go with nineteen career moments to determine Lauryn Hill's shooting percentage.

CAREER MOMENT NO. 1

Lauryn Hill's First Televised Performance

Lauryn Hill performed "Who's Lovin' You" in front of a live audience at a taping of Amateur Night at the Apollo in 1987. And it went bad almost instantly. Less than fifteen seconds into her singing, the crowd grew audibly restless. By twenty seconds in, the booing had started. And listen, because it's important that you know this: The first guy who started booing her wasn't booing softly. It wasn't even the kind of booing that happens at a basketball game when the road team is shooting free throws. This was past that. It was a full-throated, hundred-decibel, wilt-your-spirit booing; the kind of booing that feels like it's been soaking in a bucket filled with hate for a decade, the kind of booing that they used to do in medieval villages hundreds of years ago when someone had done something everyone felt was exceptionally shameful.

And here's where it gets really wild: Lauryn Hill was ONLY THIRTEEN YEARS OLD WHEN THIS HAPPENED. *THIRTEEN!* She was a baby. Onstage. In front of adults. Wearing a nice dress. Singing for them. And some of those adults decided to just start throwing axes at her.

But guess what she did. Because her response was entirely unexpected. She didn't quit. She didn't shrink.

5. She got that one for *The Score*, which was put out by the Fugees. She also won a Grammy for "Killing Me Softly" that year.
6. She got that one for *The Miseducation of Lauryn Hill*, which she put out as a solo album. She also won four more Grammys that night, including Album of the Year, the most prestigious award.

New Jersey University

She didn't walk off the stage in tears, like most everyone else would've done. No. Instead, she finished her song. She sang the full thing. And then she left. And then twelve years later she became the first woman ever to win five or more Grammys in a single night in the history of Earth. This was a made basket for Lauryn. She's 1 for 1 so far.

CAREER MOMENT NO. 2

When She Sang "His Eye Is on the Sparrow" in *Sister Act 2*

I already wrote about when she opened up the "Joyful, Joyful" performance at the end of *Sister Act 2*. This moment comes before that one. It's the first time we get to see her really sing in the movie. It's just her and Tanya Blount singing together in what they believe is an empty church sanctuary. (There's another member of the clergy there watching as they sing. Lauryn Hill singing white people to tears in *Sister Act 2* is way up there on my list of Extremely Specific Movie Tropes.) And it is all the way pure and all the way poignant and all the way graceful. It's a made basket. She's 2 for 2 so far.

CAREER MOMENT NO. 3

The Way She Says "Strumming My Pain with His Fingers" on "Killing Me Softly"

It sounds like the way I imagine it feels to ride a Tempur-Pedic mattress down the side of a mountain made of clouds and cotton balls and heartache. It's my single favorite Lauryn Hill line delivery ever. Made basket. She's 3 for 3 so far.

Some other great Lauryn Hill line deliveries, and I'm going to count each of these as a Career Moment:

- **The Way She Snaps the Word "Ready" out of Her Mouth at the Start of "Ready or Not":** It's a declaration and a heat-seeking missile. Made basket. 4 for 4.
- **The Way She Ad-Libs at the Start of Nas's "If I Ruled the World":** It's the perfect temperature. Made basket. 5 for 5.
- **The Way She Says "Now the Joy of My World Is in Zion!" on the Hook for "To Zion":** It's unfettered love. Made basket. 6 for 6.
- **The Way She Says "You Might Win Some but You Just Lost One" Over and Over Again on "Lost Ones":** Remember in *Godzilla vs. Kong* when Godzilla shoots that nuclear laser from his mouth all the way down into the center of the Earth? That's what Lauryn did on "Lost Ones" to Wyclef. Made basket. 7 for 7.
- **The Way She Pronounces "Tired" on "Superstar":** Made basket. 8 for 8.

CAREER MOMENTS NO. 9 AND NO. 10 AND NO. 11

The Score and *The Miseducation of Lauryn Hill* and the Transition She Had to Make Between the Two

The Score, which was a group album that felt firmly like it belonged in the rap section of the record store, sold over seven million copies in the United States alone and was universally acclaimed. Lauryn Hill stepped away from that situation—from a group that everyone was begging to please put out another album—and instead made *Miseducation*, which, among other things, she'd released as a way to attempt to erase the line that it felt like had been drawn around rap and hip-hop that roped it off from everything else.

Lenesha Randolph sang backing vocals on *Miseducation*. Here's a really great quote she gave to NPR's *All Things Considered* in 2010 about Lauryn Hill being anxious for how people were going to receive the album: "I remember her saying, 'I don't know what they're going to think about the album because, you know, I'm a rapper and nobody wants to hear rappers sing.' And I'm like, 'What are you talking about?' Like, when you hear her sing and then hear her speak, you just say to yourself, 'Wow, that's something to, you know, strive for, that kind of purity.'" Lauryn Hill being nervous about how one of the greatest and most successful[7] and most impactful albums ever was going to be received makes me feel like a real jackass for having been confident about anything in my life at any point ever.

CAREER MOMENT NO. 12

When She Showed Up at *Dave Chappelle's Block Party* in 2004[8]

It'd been six years since *Miseducation* had dropped, and it'd been seven years since the Fugees, who'd dissolved as a group in the spotlight of megastardom, had performed together. And the only Lauryn Hill information that we'd gotten during that empty time felt like some version of propaganda and wild rumor mushed into one. Even the music that she did release during that period—the recorded audio from an *MTV Unplugged No. 2.0* performance—felt mysterious and presented more questions than it answered. And yet there she was, and there they were: the Fugees as a full group again, up onstage, headlining *Dave Chappelle's Block Party.*

As Lauryn Hill finished "Killing Me Softly," she said to the crowd, "Where y'all been?" Everyone roared, except for someone off to the side, who shouted back at her, asking her where *she'd* been. She smiled and laughed and then glanced toward the back of the stage. "You see," she said, pointing back to where she'd just looked. "That's where I been." The camera scanned over and zoomed in on a child being held in someone's arms. The crowd roared again. And it was perfect. Made basket. 12 for 12.

Some other great Lauryn Hill pieces (and also one bad one), and I'm going to count each of these as a Career Moment:

- **Her Verse on "Fu-Gee-La":** Made basket. 13 for 13.
- **Her Verse on "Rumble in the Jungle":** Made basket. 14 for 14.
- **When She Taught Everyone What the Word "Reciprocity" Meant:** Made basket. 15 for 15.
- **When She Got Sentenced to Three Months Incarcerated for Failure to Pay Taxes:** This was a missed basket, even though it shouldn't have been. If you reel off two albums in a row as good as *The Score* and *Miseducation*, you shouldn't have to pay taxes. You should be treated like how they handled the team that went up into space to explode the asteroid in *Armageddon*. 15 for 16.

7. Less than 130 albums in the history of music have ever been certified diamond. *Miseducation* is one of them.
8. Released as a movie in 2006.

- **When She Performed "Lost Ones" and "Everything Is Everything" at the 1999 MTV Video Music Awards:** Made basket. 16 for 17.
- **When She Started Crying at the End of "I Gotta Find Peace of Mind" on MTV Unplugged No. 2.0:** Made basket. 17 for 18. And I understand that this is a somewhat controversial made basket.[9] A lot of people did not like this performance at all, and part of that is because they did not like that Lauryn Hill decided to disappear herself from the public for a number of years. And that's fine. You can count that as a missed basket if you want. I don't want to, though. I feel like if you ever believe the best thing for you is to not be in a spot, then you are more than welcome to remove yourself from that spot.

CAREER MOMENT NO. 19

Lauryn Hill Returns to the Apollo

In the first Career Moment recap, I juxtaposed Lauryn Hill getting booed at the Apollo Theater as a child with her historic Grammy night some years later because I thought it to be a dramatic and fulfilling finish to the thought. But maybe a more appropriate moment to balance that one out is that nine years after getting booed at the Apollo, Lauryn Hill returned to the theater to perform as part of the Fugees. (This was when they had begun their ascension into the cosmos.) They did the song "How Many Mics." And halfway into the first verse, her groupmate Wyclef Jean stopped the set. "Hold on, hold on, hold on, hold on," he said, and she stopped rapping and the DJ stopped the music. He continued: "Yo. We got a problem. The crowd isn't moving. What's going on?" Lauryn hesitated: "Uhh-hhh." It seemed a lot like we were headed for catastrophe again. But then: magic.

Wyclef requested that she freestyle the next few bars, and so it was just Lauryn, the microphone, and an Apollo crowd again. And she started freestyling. And as she did, the DJ began dropping scratches into it as a way to accent her rhymes. And each time she hit the end of a line, she got louder and bigger and more animated, and so too did the DJ's scratches, and so too did the crowd. Ten seconds in, the whole fucking place was going nuts. It's an amazing clip, especially if you watch it immediately after watching her get booed as a child. I have to imagine that was an incredible moment for her, and if you squint hard enough, it foreshadowed everything that was going to happen from there going forward.

Made basket.

Lauryn finishes 18 for 19.

That's a career shooting percentage of 94.7 percent.

9. If you need a basketball analogy here, it'd be something like when Reggie Miller hit that buzzer beater during the 2002 Nets-Pacers series to send Game 5 into overtime. They showed the replay afterward and it was clear that he'd not gotten it off in time, but they didn't have the replay rule in place, so they couldn't overturn the call on the court.

WHAT'D THE CHICKENS HAVE TO SAY ABOUT PROJECT PAT'S "CHICKENHEAD"?

(ALSO: WHAT'S THE MOST IDENTIFIABLE FIRST SECOND OF A RAP SONG?)

THIS IS THE THING WHERE AN NBA PLAYER SITS AT A TABLE on a tiny stage in a room full of sports reporters after a big game and answers their questions, except it's not an NBA player; it's a chicken. (As in, an actual chicken, like what you find on a farm.) And it's not after a big game; it's twenty years after this particular chicken auditioned to make the chicken noises on Project Pat's 2001 hit "Chickenhead."

•••••

The chicken walks into the room. It considers sitting down in the seat at the press table but realizes that it won't be able to see the reporters if it does. Instead, the chicken jumps up on the table. It looks out into the room. All the reporters stare at it. The chicken clears its throat, then leans toward the microphone.

CHICKEN: Okay, let's get started.

REPORTER 1, speaking for the group: I think, first of all, before we start asking questions, we all just wanna thank you for taking the time to talk. I have to assume that you're very busy.

CHICKEN: No, not really. I'm just a chicken. So, I mean, mainly I'm just doing regular chicken stuff with my time. Pecking, scraping, jousting, et cetera. I'm no rock star. I'm just me. A chicken.

REPORTER 2: That's interesting. Because all of the chickens I've seen were always up to a bunch of wild shit.

CHICKEN: Really? Like what? What chickens are you talking about?

REPORTER 2, gesturing to the others: Probably the first chicken everyone in here thinks of is that one that Rocky was trying to catch in *Rocky II*.

Everyone in the room nods in agreement.

REPORTER 2, continuing: That chicken was clearly busy. Foghorn Leghorn was always up to some hijinks. And there was Chicken Little, who had that whole thing with the sky. There was that one chicken from *Moana*. All of the chickens from *Chicken Run* were extremely active.

REPORTER 3, who is Mexican: Don't forget Panchito Pistoles. He was another one.

REPORTER 1: Who?

CHICKEN: Yeah, I remember him. From a long time ago. The cartoon chicken with the guns.

REPORTER 3: Yes! That's him. Super racist—right up there with Speedy Gonzales and Slowpoke Rodriguez—but I loved him.

CHICKEN, to Reporter 2: I think I get the misunderstanding here, then. Because you're talking about pop-culture chickens—chickens from movies and TV and whatnot. I'm not that. I'm just like the other twenty-five billion or so other chickens out there who aren't helping train an eventual heavyweight boxing champion.

REPORTER 4: There are twenty-five billion chickens in the world?!

CHICKEN: Give or take, yeah. We're actually the most common bird on the planet, which a lot of people don't know. And we also outnumber humans by a count of about four to one. So . . .

REPORTER 2, jokingly, to the others: Careful, boys. We got a live one here.

The room laughs. The chicken would smile if chickens could smile.

REPORTER 1: That's wild. And what you said kind of ties back to why we're here—the pop-culture thing. Because you almost were a pop-culture chicken, right?

CHICKEN: Correct.

REPORTER 1: So let's start there. Walk us through the story—the "Chickenhead" story. Just give us whatever the details are that you think are important from that time.

CHICKEN: Well, there's really not much to tell. Here's what happened: There's this guy named Project Pat. He's a rapper from Memphis. And, as a matter of context and category: he's in that group of rappers who were regionally famous for a while and then had a quick moment where they were nationally famous and then went back to mostly being regionally famous. So he does this song in—I think it was 2001, but I might be wrong. He does this song called "Chickenhead." It's him and Three 6 Mafia and this other rapper named La Chat, who—she was really great. Not enough people mention her.

REPORTER 1: Right, right. I remember the song. It was wonderful.

CHICKEN: It really was. Especially the second verse when La Chat and Project Pat go back and forth making fun of each other. That's great writing right there—really, the whole song in general is just very exceptional. Which is why I was so excited about it.

REPORTER 1: How did the other chickens respond when you said you were auditioning for the part? Was there any blowback? I assume some chickens had to have been upset because the phrase "chickenhead" has a negative connotation attached to it in the song.

CHICKEN: I didn't get any real heat. Mostly, we in the chicken community were all just excited about finally being included.

REPORTER 3: That's exactly how it was with Panchito Pistoles for us Mexicans. Speedy and Slowpoke, too.

CHICKEN: Exactly. But so the song is coming together, and I get word that they're gonna include a chicken sound in the song.

REPORTER 2: You're talking about the "Bwok! Bwok!" that happens on the chorus, right?

CHICKEN: Correct. And what you hear on the song as it is now—that's a person who's making that noise. That's a human making a chicken sound. Which is fine. I get it. It came out great. But I auditioned for that part. I was in the studio and it was just me and an engineer, and I did a few takes and that was that. It was a good time. I was hopeful that they'd pick me for the song. It'd have been real cool to be on there making the chicken sound. But it didn't work out that way. They liked the human version better. Which, really, I can't blame them. Again: it came out great. Whoever that was in there making them noises, they nailed it. They were like . . . *[thinking]* Oh, do you know Andy Serkis?

REPORTER 2: The actor?

CHICKEN: Yeah. The one they always call in when they need someone to be a motion-capture gorilla in a movie or whatever. That guy. Whoever was making the chicken sounds on "Chickenhead," that person's the Andy Serkis of chicken sounds. Top level.

REPORTER 4: Were you disappointed that your recording didn't get chosen?

CHICKEN: A little at first, yeah. But only for a small amount of time. Because I found out later that they paid that person in money. And, you know, what am I gonna do with money? It's no good for me. I like grains, chicken feed; give me a good poultry pellet.

REPORTER 2: You could've gone to Walmart or whatever and used the money to buy that stuff, though.

CHICKEN: I'm a fucking chicken, dude. I can't just walk into a Walmart.

REPORTER 2: You're right. My bad. That's my fault.

REPORTER 3 raises his hand. The chicken nods in his direction.

REPORTER 3: If I can use a point you brought up earlier to get to another question, there's a part in "Chickenhead" where Pat mentions eating chicken wings. Did you have any reservations about participating in a song where the artist was advocating eating chickens? Is that a controversy in the . . . What'd you call it? . . . The chicken community?

CHICKEN: No. That's not a thing at all. We know what it is. We're delicious.

REPORTER 3: Y'all really are. Thank you for that. Thank you for your service.

CHICKEN: No problem. And to address your question: I kind of expected that I wasn't gonna get picked for the song. There have been a bunch of times in the past when a rapper chose a human making an animal noise over the animal making an animal noise for their song.

REPORTER 4: Really?

CHICKEN: Yeah. Like, think about all the people who have barked on a song. Or there's a rapper literally named Birdman who coos like a pigeon every chance he gets. There was this song "Buddah Lovaz" by a group named Bone Thugs-n-Harmony in the '90s that starts with one of the members howling like a wolf. I think it was Redman who was making orangutan and gorilla noises on "Let da Monkey Out." Wyclef caws like a crow on "The Beast." So there's a lot of that. Humans love pretending

to be animals. From the animals' side of things, it's honestly a little bit weird. Like, I mean, you know how to talk. So just talk.

REPORTER 1: Do you think that the "Bwok! Bwok!" from "Chickenhead" is the most identifiable, most memorable version of a human making animal sounds on a rap song?

CHICKEN: I'm probably a little biased here, but my vote is yes. Absolutely. If for no other reason than because as soon as you hear it, you know precisely what song you're listening to. If I played a DMX barking noise for you . . . Like . . . does anyone know how many songs DMX has?

REPORTER 3: If we're only counting his proper studio albums, then it's somewhere around 140 or so, I believe.

CHICKEN: Okay, so if I play the "Bwok! Bwok!" noise for you, you know exactly what song it is. If I play a DMX barking noise for you, then you got a 1 in 140 chance of guessing what it is. DMX is one of the greatest rappers ever, and in 1998 he was the best and most popular rapper on the planet. But I think the "Bwok! Bwok!" sound wins that particular contest.

REPORTER 1: The "Bwok! Bwok!" is certainly my favorite. It's just good energy. It's a little bit ridiculous but also extremely perfect. It's impossible for me to hear "Bwok! Bwok!" without my head automatically defaulting to La Chat saying, "Boy, please." I love the way she says that. It's soaked with condescension.

CHICKEN: You know who I'd really like to meet one day?

REPORTER 2: Who's that?

CHICKEN, excited, feathers ruffling: The elephant on Missy Elliott's "Work It." That's an actual elephant. And it's not just some throwaway sound either; it's actually incorporated into the song. It's a substantial piece of it. The animal kingdom was so fucking pumped when that song came out and we found out that a real elephant had been selected to be on that song with Missy. We're talking about an icon.

REPORTER 2, matching the chicken's excitement: Truly! Have you ever done the thing where you just read through her lyrics without playing the actual music? You read through them like you were reading a book. It's wild. She writes in waves. It's really neat.

CHICKEN: I mean, if I could read I would. But remember . . . [*he points to himself with his wing*] chicken.

REPORTER 2, sheepishly: That's right, that's right. I keep forgetting about that part.

REPORTER 1, interrupting: Okay, I have another question for you, and it's kind of tied in with what we were talking about earlier, except not really. You said that people would automatically be able to identify "Chickenhead" just by hearing the "Bwok! Bwok!" part. And that part is, what, maybe a second long? So off of that: What do you think is the most recognizable first second of a rap song? Like, you hear only the very first second, and you know immediately what song it is and who it's by.

CHICKEN: Oh, jeez. That's a tough one.

REPORTER 3: That *is* a tough one. Good question.

CHICKEN: There are so many candidates that jump into my head immediately. Those opening keys from Dr. Dre's "Still D.R.E." are definitely way up there.

REPORTER 1: For sure. That one might actually be my favorite rap needle drop in a movie.

CHICKEN: You're talking about when it happens in *Training Day*?

REPORTER 1: Yeah. With Denzel and Ethan Hawke. They're in Denzel's car and Ethan is just sort of taking everything in, and he asks where the office is, because Denzel's just told him they were gonna go to the office. And Denzel looks at him, gives him that Denzel Smile, then says, "You're in the office, baby," and then the opening keys from "Still D.R.E." come in as Denzel revs the car. It's art.

CHICKEN: Yeah, that one is definitely way up there. You hear those keys, and you know without a doubt what song it is. But, again, there are just so many. Remember that first key on Kanye's "Runaway"?

REPORTER 3: There's actually a great video on the internet of Kanye in concert, and he's just standing there at the little beat-machine thing. And he leans over and tinks that first note, and everyone hears it and goes bonkers. Do chickens have the internet?

CHICKEN: We do.

REPORTER 3: Neat.

CHICKEN: Ol' Dirty Bastard has a similar sound at the start of "Shimmy Shimmy Ya" that works the same way, just on a smaller scale. And that *tick, tick, tap* from the start of Mobb Deep's "Shook Ones, Pt. II" is in the conversation, too. So is the horn that kicks off House of Pain's "Jump Around." Another one—and this one doesn't come in the literal first second, but I think it should still be brought up—is that first *bwamp* at the beginning of the Pharcyde's "Passing Me By." And in that same group as the Pharcyde is the horn that shows up about four seconds into Queen Latifah's "U.N.I.T.Y."

REPORTER 2: That's a really good one. How about the start of "I Got 5 on It" by Luniz?

CHICKEN: Yep. Put it on the list.

REPORTER 1: What about the clinking bottles from Craig Mack's "Flava in Ya Ear" remix?

CHICKEN: Solid. Add it in.

REPORTER 2: That big hum thing and whistle in Warren G and Nate Dogg's "Regulate"? Or that whistling teakettle noise from Public Enemy's "Rebel Without a Pause"?

CHICKEN: For sure. And that first second of Cardi B's "Bodak Yellow" and the first second of 50 Cent's "In da Club" and that first second of Clipse's "Grindin" and that first second of Snoop's "Gin and Juice" and that first second of LL COOL J's "I Need Love" and the first second of Lauryn Hill singing in "If I Ruled the World" and that first second of the Geto Boys' "Mind Playing Tricks on Me." I could go on and on and on.

REPORTER 4: The first second of Biggie's "Big Poppa" has to be the winner, though, right? Because within that one you get not only the music, which is unmistakable, but also you get Biggie giving his "Unhhh," which is also unmistakable.

REPORTER 1, to REPORTER 4: Yeah, I'm with you. That's the winner.

CHICKEN: It's actually not. It's something else.

REPORTER 4: Really? What's more recognizable than that first second of "Big Poppa"?

CHICKEN: Well, here's the thing. Because the answer that I'm gonna give you right now isn't, per se, *MORE* recognizable than that.

REPORTER 3, whispering to REPORTER 1: I never thought I'd hear a chicken say "per se."

CHICKEN: A lot of the ones that have been listed so far are as high up on the Can You Identify This Song by the Literal First Second chart as they can go, the Biggie one included. There's a definite top level here, songs that, regardless of circumstance, their first second might as well be ten minutes long. But, again, here's the thing: If a bunch of songs can do that—if a bunch of songs *are* that—then that means the winner has to be one that, in addition to doing that, can do something else as well. The winner has to be something that, beyond having an unmistakable first second, also has a bonus piece to go with it. It has to, for example, create a moment or an energy or a kind of instant momentum that the others can't. That's why the winner is one that y'all haven't even said yet. And I'm gonna tell you what it is right now.

The chicken pauses. He looks around the room. Every eyeball is on him.

CHICKEN: The most identifiable first single second of any rap song ever . . . the one that instantly materializes a real excitement and a real exhilaration and a real enthusiasm . . .

REPORTER 2, whispering to REPORTER 4: I'm fucking so excited to hear this answer.

CHICKEN: Is . . .

The chicken holds the moment. A second passes. Then two. Then five. Nobody breathes.

CHICKEN: Juvenile's "Back That Azz Up."

WHICH LINE ON *ILLMATIC* IS THE MOST NASIAN?

PART 1

NA·SI·AN

/na-zēan/

adjective

1. of or reminiscent of the works of Nas, especially in suggesting a level of empathy and insight with regard to a subsection of New York and rap and life

During the fall of 1995, a movie called *Powder* was released. Let me tell you a tiny bit about it: *Powder* starts with a pregnant woman getting struck by lightning. And she dies from the trauma, but the baby inside of her survives. Then things fast-forward a bit to when the baby is a teenager. And we find out that the lightning superpowered his brain.[1] He's now at a level of brilliance that has never existed on this Earth before. He's so advanced, in fact, that he can control electricity and create magnetic fields and read minds and do a bunch of other stuff, too.

There's one part where, after his grandfather passes away and he's been shipped off to a boys' home, he finds himself on an impromptu hunting trip with a group of other teenagers from the home. The person who's organized the trip (a sheriff's deputy named Harley) shoots a doe, and so he and the other boys are all gathered around it as it lies on the ground dying. Powder sees what they've done and is mortified. He walks over, kneels down next to the deer, puts his hand on it, then grabs ahold of Harley's wrist and squeezes it tight. When he does, he's able to momentarily place the panic and terror that the deer is experiencing inside of Harley. And it's such an overwhelming shock that, shortly thereafter, Harley explains to a coworker that he'll never be able to look at something down the barrel of a gun again because of it.

"I'm telling you," Harley says, and his voice is trembling because he can still feel the edges of the situation in his heart. "He took whatever was in that goddamn deer … and he put it right into me."

Powder used his megabrain to let Harley feel exactly what that deer was feeling. He connected them together in a way they otherwise never would've been.

Anyway, let's talk about Nas.

•••••

Here are seven stats for Nas and for *Illmatic*, his seminal debut album and also one of the great works of musical art of the past century:

- In 2012, the *Source* picked Nas as one of the two greatest lyricists to have ever lived.
- In 2015, *Billboard* picked Nas as one of the five greatest rappers to have ever lived.
- In 2006, MTV picked Nas as one of the five greatest rappers to have ever lived.
- In 2005, MTV picked *Illmatic* as the second greatest rap album ever.
- In 1994, the *Source* gave *Illmatic* an ultra-rare five-mic review upon its release.
- In 2013, *Pitchfork* gave *Illmatic* a perfect score when it reviewed the reissued version.

1. Or *something*.

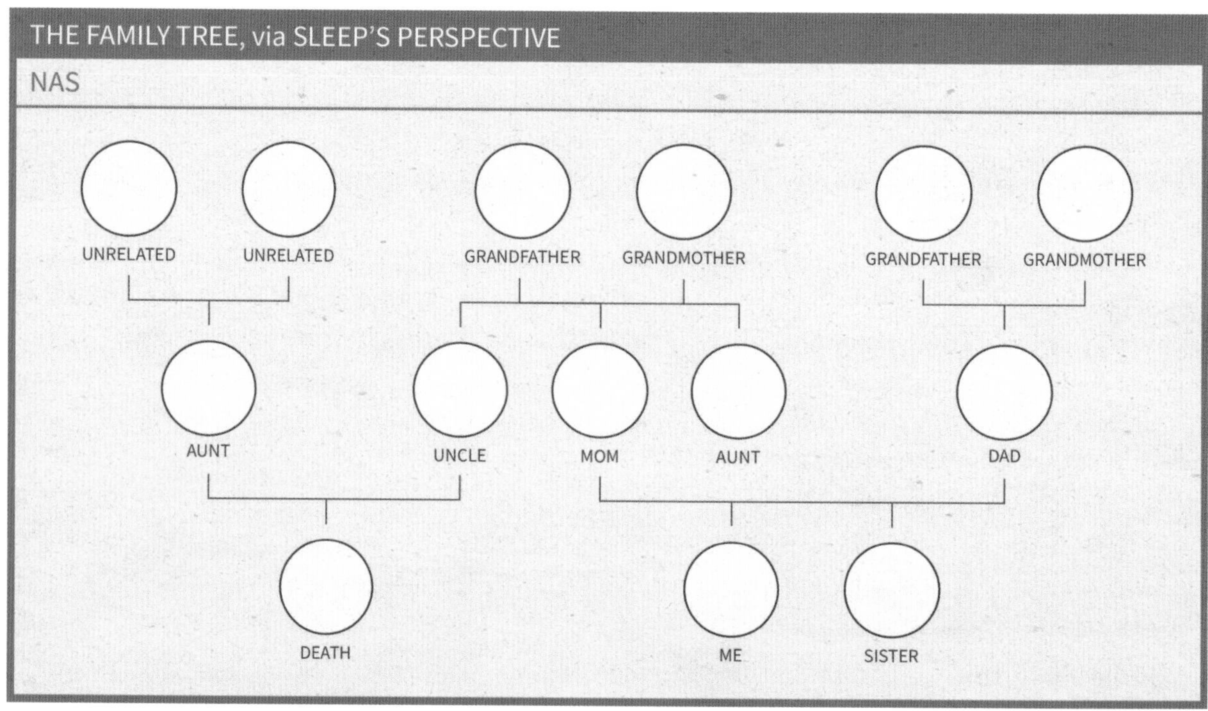

- In 2012, *Illmatic* was selected by the Library of Congress for preservation in the National Recording Registry.[2]

•••••

The most Nasian moment in a Nas interview happens during the back end of *Time Is Illmatic*, a documentary that recalls the setting and circumstances that led to the release of *Illmatic*. What's going on in that moment:

Nas, as "One Time 4 Your Mind" plays in the background, is talking about how his record label hired a photographer to do a photo shoot of him in Queensbridge. He discusses the event with a great joy and with a clear amount of pride. ("That day was a big day for me because we had made it. We were rolling out with an album. . . . To get to that point is the biggest day in your life, so we were celebrating.") As he does, we see photos captured from the shoot – shots of him and his friends, shots of potential album covers, shots of neighborhood kids gathered together smiling and playing for the camera. It's excellent. And it all feels very good.

Then the music fades out. And that's when his brother, Jungle, starts talking.

---

2. Only eight rap albums have ever been selected for this. They are Nas's *Illmatic*, Dr. Dre's *The Chronic*, Jay-Z's *The Blueprint*, Run-DMC's *Raising Hell*, N.W.A.'s *Straight Outta Compton*, De La Soul's *3 Feet High and Rising*, Public Enemy's *Fear of a Black Planet*, and Lauryn Hill's *The Miseducation of Lauryn Hill.*

Jungle tells his own version of the story, reiterating the good feelings Nas had expressed, talking about how excited everyone was and about how that excitement trumped whatever disagreements various people in the area might've had with one another. But then Jungle spins off of that into something more bleak. He holds up a picture taken during the photo shoot of seventeen people – grown men and children – sitting on a couple of benches together, Nas included. He points to one of the kids in the photo – he's maybe eight years old; he has a beanie on and a jacket that's big enough on him that his hands don't even reach out of the sleeves; he's adorable. Jungle says the kid, a grown man now, is currently serving fifteen years in prison. The kid next to him in the photo, he explains, is fighting a murder charge. The camera cuts to Nas, who, in a separate studio, is hearing his brother go person by person through the photo, saying what's happened to each one since then.

Jungle: "*He's* doing life in prison. . . . *He* just got locked up no bail. . . . *He* just did a shitload of time. . . . *He* do a bunch of fucking time in and out of jail. . . . This shit is real. It's the projects."

After a couple seconds of silence, Nas, who has absorbed all of the parts of everything he's just heard, finally speaks: "That's fucked up," he says. But he doesn't say it the way you or I say something is fucked up. When you or I say it, it's usually a throwaway comment; it's usually one of those responses where you're not really invested in what the person talking to you has just said but you don't want to be all the way rude about it. That's not how Nas says it here, though. You can see the weight of the moment pressing down on his spirit. You can see the toll it's taken on him. You can see how much he hurts. He keeps going:

"It's so fucked up just to see what happened, you know what I'm saying?"

The camera scans the picture of everyone as Nas continues his thought.

"Like, it makes me really realize, if it wasn't for music, you would've told a story about that kid, too, on the bench," he says, talking about himself. "That's not what I wanted to see happen to nobody in that picture, you know. I wanted . . . I wanted the best for my friends."

Nas is incredibly smart. And incredibly empathetic. And incredibly insightful. And, in his best moments, he's able to package those three things together when he's building a song. That's what makes his music so moving. That's what made (makes) *Illmatic* so special. Because for the entirety of it, he is so dialed in and so perfectly calibrated that he's able to act as a conduit for everyone and everything around him. He's able to plug himself into his surroundings, process all the pieces, and then say words in a way that sits pure in your chest.

•••••

This is the question: Which line on *Illmatic* is the most Nasian?

Or another way to say that: Which line on *Illmatic* is the best representation of all the things that make Nas *Nas*? Which line is it that only Nas could've come up with, only Nas could've written, only Nas could've summoned from the fucking dungeons of rap?

Rhyme is a disease. Meet the cure.

Let's go through a bunch of them. They're all organized here by how Nasian they are.

83 PERCENT NASIAN

"Verbal assassin, my architect pleases /
When I was twelve, I went to..."
–"The Genesis"

This is actually a line that Nas said on "Live at the Barbeque," which is a song from Main Source's 1991 album *Breaking Atoms*. The full line is "Verbal assassin, my architect pleases / When I was twelve, I went to hell for snuffin' Jesus." And that might seem like not that crazy of a thing to say today, but thirty years ago it was fucking outrageous. It was a thing where, after you heard it, you asked everybody you knew if they'd heard it yet. DJ Premier, who eventually produced three songs on *Illmatic*, said that hearing Nas say that was the first time he'd ever been shocked by something someone said on a rap song.

Nas choosing to include a piece of it as the opening line on the opening song of his debut album is a nod to how everything that Nas does is intentional and intricate and layered.

84 PERCENT NASIAN

"Writing in my book of rhymes, all the words
past the margin"
–"The World Is Yours"

This is a really good example of the way that Nas is able to grab a little piece of an observation and use it to insta-create whatever imagery it is that he wants in your head. In this case, as soon as he says this line, your brain automatically conjures up that notebook paper that we all used in school that had the little red lines on each side so you knew where to stop writing. It's a really powerful trick to be able to do, and Nas does it pretty much as his default setting. (I'm reminded here of the part in his famous five-mic review he got from the *Source* where the author, Shortie,[3] wrote, "Lyrically, the whole shit is on point. No cliched metaphors, no gimmicks.")

85 PERCENT NASIAN

"The smooth criminal on beat breaks / Never put
me in your box if your shit eats tapes"
–"N.Y. State of Mind"

There's a list of experiences that technology has preemptively stolen away from my sons that I'm sad about. Things like the following:

- My sons will never know what it's like to sit at the kitchen table, talking to a girl on the house phone, trying to be quiet enough that your parents don't hear you.
- My sons will never know what it's like to be arguing with your friends about something and not have the ability to just Google whatever information it is that you're arguing about. (I spent, maybe, a solid two weeks of my life in middle

3. "Shortie" was the pen name of journalist Minya Oh.

school believing that if a woman was on top during sex, then her egg could fall out of her and into the man's penis and the man could get pregnant, because one of my friends who'd had sex already said he knew someone that it'd happened to.)

- My sons will never know what it's like to listen to the radio and hear your favorite song come on and go absolutely nuts because you've been waiting to hear it all day. And, most applicable here:
- My sons will never know the heartbreak of a shoddy tape player eating your cassette, ruining whatever was on it forever.

86 PERCENT NASIAN

"I don't know how to start this shit"

–"N.Y. State of Mind"

That's what Nas says right before the first verse of "N.Y. State of Mind." And then he goes fucking bonkers on the song. It's a maximum-security prison's worth of bars. Do you remember that one episode of *The Fresh Prince of Bel-Air* where Will gets hustled in the pool hall and loses his car because he can't pay the hustler? And so Uncle Phil shows up to get back the car that Will lost? And the guy who hustled Will starts in on hustling Uncle Phil? But Uncle Phil starts talking about how he doesn't know how to play pool? But eventually the hustler talks him into it? And Uncle Phil slow-plays the situation, pretending like he has no idea what's happening? And as soon as the hustler decides to up the stakes to a hundred dollars per ball, Uncle Phil flips the switch, and it turns out he's the greatest pool player on Earth? Do you remember that episode?

Uncle Phil saying he's not going to bet on a game he's never played before is Nas saying he doesn't know how to start rapping at the beginning of "N.Y. State of Mind."

87 PERCENT NASIAN

"Aimin' guns in all my baby pictures"

–"The World Is Yours"

This is my second-favorite line on *Illmatic* that references what Nas was like as a baby. (The first one will appear in part 2 of this double chapter.) It's just really funny to me to picture, say, a two-year-old Nas at a department store with his mom, getting some annual pictures taken, and he's there in front of a pile of alphabet blocks waving a gun around.

88 PERCENT NASIAN

"I woke up early on my born day / I'm twenty / It's a blessin' / The essence of adolescence / Leaves my body / Now I'm fresh and …"

–"Life's a Bitch"

Here's what I want you to do: First, read this word out loud: "adolescence." Second, read this phrase out loud:

"Now I'm fresh and." And third, figure out how Nas got those two things to rhyme.[4]

89 PERCENT NASIAN

"You're still a soldier / I'm like Sly Stone in *Cobra*"
—"It Ain't Hard to Tell"

One of the things that makes Nas such an interesting lyricist to think about and talk about is the fact that (a) clearly he's a brilliant person and also (b) he's not above mentioning the fourteenth-best Sylvester Stallone movie in a song. And so you hear him compare himself to Stallone in *Cobra*[5] and because he's Nas and because he has consistently proven that he exists a few steps ahead of most everyone else, you can't help but start looking past the obvious stuff that connects him and *Cobra* (They're both cool! They both like sunglasses! They both were in a movie with LL COOL J!) and start trying to find whatever the fourth or fifth level of meaning is that Nas is making when he draws that comparison.

You're sitting there listening to *Illmatic*, and he says, "I'm like Sly Stone in *Cobra*," and you're like, "Wait, wait, wait! 'Cobra' has five letters in it and so does 'Nasir.' Is Nas using this line as an allusion to the Five Wounds of Jesus Christ referenced in Christianity???" Or you're like, "Wait, wait, wait! There's a shootout scene in *Cobra*, and also Nas would eventually go on to make a song called 'Shootouts' a few years later that mentions the movie franchise *Rambo*, which Stallone also starred in. Is Nas using the *Cobra* reference as a coded look at the way that America has historically abandoned its soldiers when they've returned home from war???" Or you're like, "Wait, wait, wait. Stallone kills a guy in a grocery store in *Cobra*, and so is Nas using this comparison here as a way to comment on both the theoretical and the practical implications of grocery gaps and food deserts that occur in socioeconomically disadvantaged areas???"

4. Kool Moe Dee had an especially good note about the way Nas bends his words together when he raps. It came in his 2003 book *There's a God on the Mic*. He said, "Before Nas, every MC focused on rhyming with a cadence that ultimately put the words that rhymed on beat with the snare drum. Nas created a style of rapping that was more conversational than ever."

5. Nas is so good in his songs that sometimes he'll say something completely wrong (in this case, he meant Sylvester Stallone and not Sly Stone), and everyone will just be like, "I know what you meant. Please continue."

. . . cont'd

> **90 PERCENT NASIAN**
>
> "Time is illmatic / Keep static like wool fabric / Pack a 4-matic to crack your whole cabbage"
>
> –"Life's a Bitch"

Nas has several different types of rhymes that he regularly dips in and out of. He has the thing where he says some extremely hard shit (like when he said "I'm wavin' automatic guns at nuns" on MC Serch's "Back to the Grill" in 1992). He has the thing where he points out some really small observation that instantly becomes gigantic as soon as it touches your ears (like when he said "Put my hat on my waves" on 1996's "Take It in Blood"). He has the thing where he makes some surprising pop-culture reference that becomes less surprising the more you think about it (like when he alluded to having watched Michael Mann's heist-movie masterpiece *Heat* on Mobb Deep's "It's Mine" in 1999). He has the thing where he turns himself into a novelist and says something you'd expect to find in a Herman Melville book (like when he said "I hear murder plans / From dope fiends with elephant hands" on Wu-Tang Clan's "Let My Niggas Live" in 2000).

He has the thing where he likens himself to some inanimate object that somehow conveys an entire ethos (like when he said "I was the project hallway" on the Beastie Boys' "Too Many Rappers" in 2009). He has the thing where he packages together some insight in a devastating way (like that verse on "Accident Murderers" where he talks about play wrestling with kids and then watching them grow up to be killers). And, like the line cited above from "Life's a Bitch," he has the thing where he creates a rhyming puzzle box that, if you listen to it enough times in a row, somehow begins to feel both impenetrable and completely accessible.

> **91 PERCENT NASIAN**
>
> "Thinkin' a word best describin' my life to name my daughter / My strength, my son, the star will be my resurrection"
>
> –"The World Is Yours"

A timeline of sorts: Nas, throughout his career, has referred to himself as Nastradamus, a play on the name Nostradamus, a French philosopher whom people often associate with telling the future.[1] → The lines listed above from "The World Is Yours" make four different predictions. → The first: Nas predicts that his first child will be a daughter. → The second: Nas predicts she will be named after a word to describe Nas's life. → The third: Nas predicts his second child will be a son. → The fourth: Nas predicts his son, in one way or another, will have something to do with stars. → Fifteen years later, all of those things had come true. → Nas had a daughter first.[2] → And she was named after a word that could be used to describe Nas's life (Destiny). → Then Nas had a son. → And his son had something to do with stars. (His son is named Knight, which is a homonym for "night," which is when stars come out. And if you read that sentence right now and said, "Okay, Shea. That's a little bit flimsy. You're

---

1. Nas even got around to making an entire album called *Nastradamus*, which, curiously, contained a surprising lack of predictions.
2. She was born just two months after *Illmatic* came out. He knew he was going to be a dad; he just didn't know if the baby was going to be a son or a daughter.

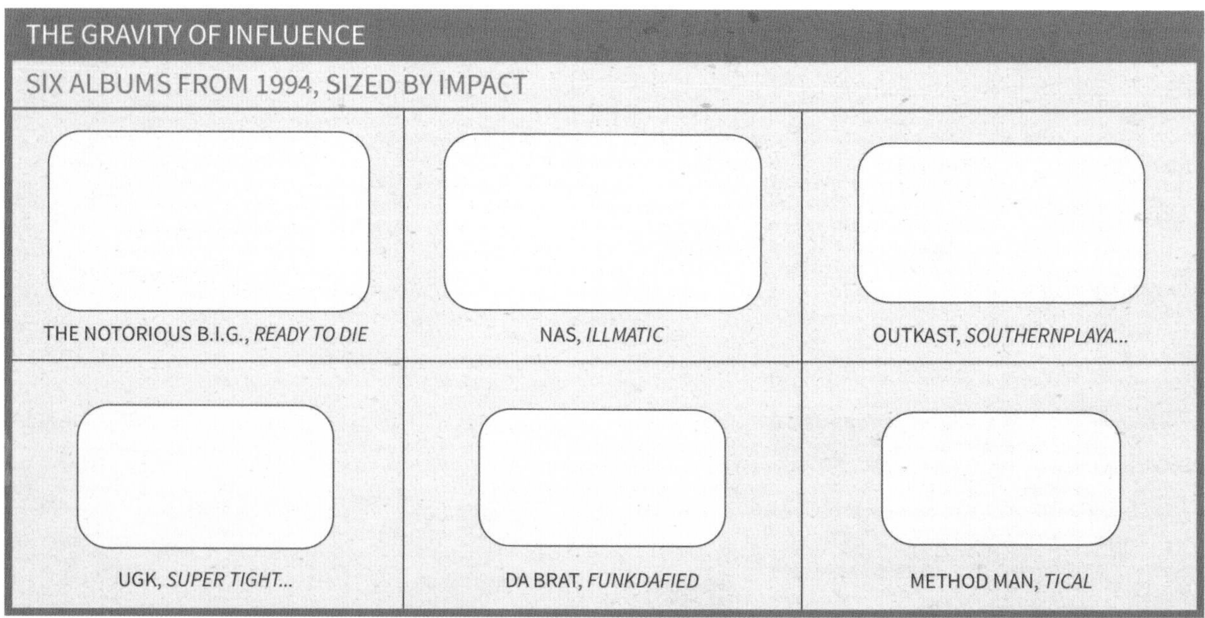

really reaching here," I'd like to point out that you bought a book about rap that has a chapter featuring a pretend interview with a chicken, so, I mean, come on.)

> **92 PERCENT NASIAN**
> "The mind activation / React like I'm facin' / Time like Pappy Mason / With pens I'm embracin'"
> –"The World Is Yours"

Two things here:

1. This is another one of those puzzle-box rhymes that Nas does. He's never been better at it in his career than he was on *Illmatic*, which is fucking wild to think about, because he was only twenty when it came out.[3]
2. This is my second-favorite mention of pens on *Illmatic*. The first-place mention happens on "One Time 4 Your Mind" when he says, "My pen rides the paper, it even has blinkers." Nas is funnier than he gets credit for. (Another line that he has on *Illmatic* that makes me smile is on "Halftime" when he says, "I wear chains that excite the Feds." Oftentimes, when I'm working on a chapter, I'll write a sentence or come across a turn of phrase that someone else has used, and I'll be like, "There it is. That's the one. That's what I'm gonna have Arturo draw as the art for this chapter." Hearing Nas say the chain line on "Halftime" was one of those moments. I said to myself, "There it is. That's the one. That's what I'm gonna have Arturo draw as the art for this chapter.

3. A line from *Illmatic* that I think is wonderful that's otherwise going to go unmentioned here: "Sentence begins indented / With formality" from "Memory Lane."

I'm gonna have him draw that scene from *The Wolf of Wall Street* where Kyle Chandler is talking to Leonardo DiCaprio on the boat, on account of Chandler playing a federal agent who was excited about the possibility of eventually seizing Leo's boat, except we're gonna replace Leo with Nas." Ultimately, we didn't end up doing that, though. We went with a different line. But I at least wanted to write out that description here so your brain could imagine what that art would've looked like.)

93 PERCENT NASIAN

"But I heard you blew a nigga with a
ox for the phone piece"
–"Halftime"

First, let me say, with regards to jail or prison, "ox" is slang for "razor blade."

Second, let me say, this type of reference here isn't something you can think up on your own. There has to be real-world experience behind it. Either you have sliced someone up with a razor blade because of a dispute over phone time while locked up, or you know somebody who's done it.

Third, let me say, there are times when I'm watching, say, a disaster movie of some sort—be it about an apocalyptic natural occurrence, or maybe a train that has a bomb on it, or maybe aliens that have begun to invade the planet, or maybe a big boat that is sinking, causing Leonardo DiCaprio and I, who are in love, to have to figure out how to survive together, et cetera—where I say to myself, "Okay, I could probably survive this. I think I could keep myself safe. I think, ultimately, this situation would turn out all right for me."

But I have never, ever felt that way about anything related to jail or prison or any sort of incarceration. It seems to me to be the worst, most treacherous place on the planet. I would be happier about being dropped off on the rim of an active volcano than I would about being dropped off at even the nicest, lowest-stakes city jail.

94 PERCENT NASIAN

"My window faces shootouts, drug overdoses"
–"Memory Lane"

A bunch of people have made a bunch of fuss about how Ernest Hemingway (*maybe*) wrote a flash story so stuffed fat with emotion and feeling and weight that, despite the fact that it was only six words, it was an unquestionable masterpiece. ("For sale: baby shoes, never worn.") I think this line here from Nas—*these* six words—is better, and more tightly wound, and more perfectly landed. There's only one instance in Nas's career where he was able to pack more into a space this small. (It'll show up soon here.)

95 PERCENT NASIAN

"Speak with criminal slang / Begin like a violin /
End like Leviathan / It's deep? / Well, let me try again /
Wisdom be leakin' out of my grapefruit, troop"
–"It Ain't Hard to Tell"

I'm not sure if this is a grand theory or a hot take or some combination of the two or something else entirely, but

SLEEP
RED
SLEEP MATTRESS
DEATH
mattress
TAG SALE

there is no best song on *Illmatic*. Not "N.Y. State of Mind," not "One Love," not "Represent," not "Life's a Bitch," not "It Ain't Hard to Tell," none of them. Because, opposite of the way that a lot of albums work (which is to say, as vehicles for eventual singles), *Illmatic* is meant to be consumed as an entire project. It's one big thing; it's one big artwork. You can't separate a piece from the others to highlight it, because then that compromises the integrity of the whole thing. It'd be like trying to find the best brushstroke in a painting, or like...You know what it's like? I'll tell you exactly what it's like:

There's a scene during season seven of *Mad Men* where Don Draper is talking to a computer engineer. Don makes a jokey kind of comment about companies that are working to replace humans. The computer engineer, who is used to having this exact conversation, tries to sway Don to his side by explaining the potential benefit of having a megacomputer in the office. "This machine is intimidating because it contains infinite quantities of information, and that's threatening because human existence is finite," he says. "But isn't it godlike that we've mastered the infinite? The IBM 360 can count more stars in a day than we can in a lifetime." The engineer is clearly proud of himself for stringing together such a coherent, convincing argument. And then Don Draper shreds it to ribbons exactly one second later: "But what man laid on his back counting stars and thought about a number?"

Trying to identify the best song on *Illmatic* misses the point of *Illmatic* entirely.

96 PERCENT NASIAN

"I hold a MAC-11 / And attack a reverend"
–"One Time 4 Your Mind"

To keep track, Nas had that one line I mentioned earlier from "Live at the Barbeque" where he said that he went to hell when he was twelve for killing Jesus. And then there was also that line he had about waving automatic guns at nuns on "Back to the Grill." And now there's this one about attacking a reverend with a submachine gun. And he also has another one on "Halftime" where he says, "'Cause when it's my time to go / I wait for God with the .44." Nas has a very rocky relationship with members of the clergy.

97 PERCENT NASIAN

"Deep like *The Shining* / Sparkle like a diamond / Sneak a Uzi on the island in my army-jacket lining"
–"It Ain't Hard to Tell"

Come on.

98 PERCENT NASIAN

"Y'all niggas was born / I shot my way out my mom dukes"
–"One Time 4 Your Mind"

Imagine this: Imagine you took a giant piece of titanium and put it in an even more giant piece of chromium. And then imagine you took that chromium with the titanium in it and put it in an even more giant piece of osmium. And then imagine you took that osmium with the chromium in it with the titanium in it and put it in an even more giant piece of steel. And then imagine you took that steel with the osmium in it with the chromium in it with the titanium in it and put it in an even more giant piece of iridium.

And then imagine you took that iridium with the steel in it with the osmium in it with the chromium in it with the titanium in it and put it in an even more giant piece of tungsten. And then imagine you took that tungsten with the iridium in it with the steel in it with the osmium in it with the chromium in it with the titanium in it and put it in an even more gigantic piece of vibranium. And then imagine you took that piece of vibranium with the tungsten in it with the iridium in it with the steel in it with the osmium in it with the chromium in it with the titanium in it and put it in an even more giant piece of adamantium. And then imagine you took that piece of adamantium with the vibranium in it with the tungsten in it with the iridium in it with the steel in it with the osmium in it with the chromium in it with the titanium in it and gave it to King Kong and told him to hold it in his hand as tight as he could. That's how hard the I Shot My Way Out My Mom line is from Nas.

99 PERCENT NASIAN

"What up, kid? I know shit is / Rough doin' your bid / When the cops came, you shoulda slid to my crib / Fuck it, black, no time for lookin' / Back, it's done"
–"One Love"

This is probably a surprise pick landing as high as it does, but not if you spend more than a few seconds thinking about it. Because Nas, separate from everything else, has always been an empath. And these lines here (this whole song, really) are the best display of that. He's checking in on someone he cares about, then commiserating with him, then reinforcing the idea that he'll always be there for him, and then he encourages him to let the past be the past and the future be the future. It's a beautiful sentiment and beautiful writing.

100 PERCENT NASIAN

"I never sleep, 'cause sleep is the cousin of death"
–"N.Y. State of Mind"

Three final thoughts here, one of which is small, one of which is medium-sized, and the last of which is (hopefully) meaningful:

The small one: Nas was clever enough to grab his Snuffin' Jesus line from "Live at the Barbeque" that everyone went crazy for and start *Illmatic* with it. He did the same trick again toward the start of his second album, *It Was Written*, using the Sleep Is the Cousin of Death line from "N.Y. State of Mind."[4]

The medium one: "I never sleep, 'cause sleep is the cousin of death" is one of those lines that you hear one time and you never, ever, EVER forget.[5] It's just so sharp and so insightful. And more than that: it's so efficient. A lot of people can sound brilliant if you let them talk for long enough, but that number drops down to a way, way lower percentage when you start asking people to be brilliant in ten or fewer words. And to that point …

4. It's part of the hook on "The Message," the album's second song. ("N.Y. State of Mind" was the second song on *Illmatic*, by the way.) (It feels like that's not a coincidence.) (The cover for *It Was Written* also mimicked the cover for *Illmatic*.) (That also feels like it's not a coincidence.)

5. This is actually a lift of a line from a 16th century poet named Thomas Sackville. That's how fucking deep Nas was on *Illmatic*. He was channeling Renaissance poets, and he was doing their lines in a more meaningful way than they'd done them.

The (hopefully) meaningful one: Nas has, for the entirety of his career, been celebrated for his ability to stitch together those puzzle-box rhyme schemes like the one chosen for the 95 PERCENT NASIAN level above. And for good reason: it's an incredible skill to have, and one that a very small number of rappers have ever possessed. Which is why this line being Nas's best, most representative, most exemplary rapping moment is so interesting and so impressive. It's like a music version of that one story about Giotto, the Florentine painter from the fourteenth century and also the guy recognized as the first genius of the Italian Renaissance. Here's the way the story goes:

By the start of the fourteenth century, word of Giotto's immense talent had spread far enough across Europe that it eventually reached Pope Benedict XI in Lombardy. The pope, wanting to see it for himself, sent a messenger to Florence to find Giotto and procure a piece of his art. He then instructed the messenger to grab works from some other masters as well so that he could see them in comparison with one another.

When the messenger returned, he laid out the pieces for inspection. All of the artists chosen to participate offered their most intricate, most complicated pieces. Giotto, however, did not. Instead, when he was asked for a piece of work that best displayed his mastery, he took a paintbrush, dipped it in red paint, drew a perfect circle by hand on the canvas, and then handed it to the messenger. The contest was never even a contest. It was a blowout, as was recognized by the pope and his courtiers. The other artists never stood a chance.

That's this. That's Nas's Cousin of Death line here.

SNOW
BEACH

KNOW THIS FIRST: *The Shawshank Redemption* is a movie about a man (Andy Dufresne, played by Tim Robbins) who is wrongfully imprisoned for double murder. He makes a best friend on the inside named Red (played by Morgan Freeman). And the two, generally speaking, are philosophically aligned on most things, save for one big idea: Andy believes the way to survive in prison – the way to maintain your humanity within an institution built to steal it away from you – is to keep a certain amount of hope in your heart. Red, who has been in prison twenty years longer than Andy, sees it differently. "Let me tell you something, my friend," he says to Andy one day. "Hope is a dangerous thing. Hope can drive a man insane. It's got no use on the inside. You better get used to that idea."

Now know this: About halfway into the movie, Andy, who has gained the trust of the guards because he's been a model inmate for seven years,[1] finds himself in a unique position – in the warden's office without the warden himself. He's there because he'd been writing letters to the state legislature requesting money to improve the prison's library. After six years of pestering, they finally sent him a bunch of books and albums and whatnot. He's supposed to take the stuff and move it down to the library before the warden returns. He doesn't do that, though. Instead, he does something magnificent.

After the guard who's keeping an eye on him steps into the restroom, Andy takes an opera album (Mozart's *Le nozze di Figaro*) and starts to play it on a record player. He locks the guard in the restroom, and then he locks the door to the office, too, so he can have a few more moments uninterrupted. Then, after a couple of seconds of measuring the weight of the consequences in his head, he walks over to the intercom system, turns on all the speakers, and then aims the microphone at the record player so all of the other prisoners can hear it, too. We get shot after shot of the inmates, each one stopped dead in whatever it was they were doing, staring up and out into the yard where the speakers are playing the music. And they are completely taken by what they're hearing. It's beautiful. And overwhelming. The music lifts everything it touches.

In voice-over, Red, because he is a perfect movie character, explains the impact of the moment perfectly: "I have no idea to this day what those two Italian ladies were singing about. Truth is, I don't wanna know. Some things are best left unsaid. I like to think they were singing about something so beautiful it can't be expressed in words and makes your heart ache because of it. I tell you, those voices soared higher and farther than anybody in a gray place dares to dream. It was like some beautiful bird flapped into our drab little cage and made those walls dissolve away, and for the briefest of moments, every last man at Shawshank felt free."

BECAUSE CONTEXT IS IMPORTANT, HERE'S SOME

By 2004, Atlanta had become the undisputable center of the hip-hop universe. There were just too many artists doing too many different things.

There was Outkast, who'd long been legends in the South but who'd officially crossed over into superstardom (they had both the number one and the number two song

1. And also because he's been helping the warden launder money.

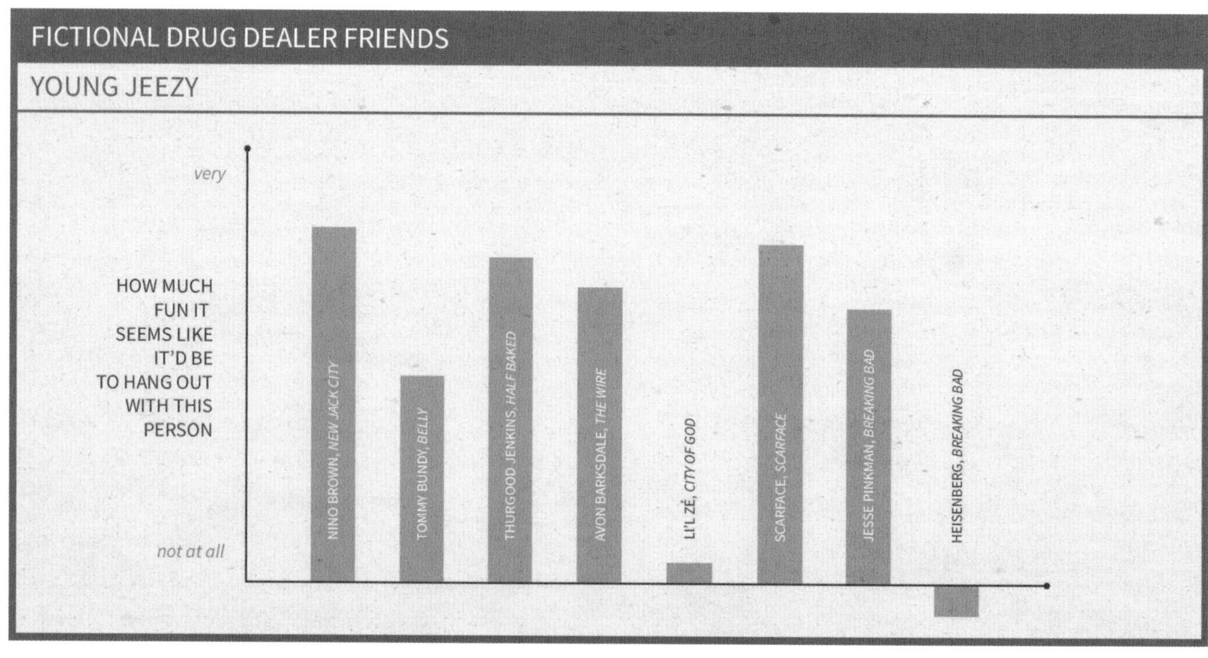

in America for eight straight weeks).[2] There was Ludacris, who put out a number one album in 2003 (*Chicken-n-Beer*) and then followed that up with a number one album in 2004 (*The Red Light District*).[3] There was T.I., who rode the momentum from 2003's platinum-selling *Trap Muzik* into 2004's platinum-selling *Urban Legend*. There was Usher (his *Confessions* album not only was the biggest album of 2004 and spawned the biggest song of the year[4] but would go on to become the second-best-selling album of the entire decade). And there were the last big moments of the crunk movement (*Trillville & Lil Scrappy* came out in February of 2004, and also we got Crime Mob's brilliant "Knuck If You Buck" that summer). And that's to say nothing about the stuff that was bubbling up underneath that top layer.[5]

All things measured, artists from Atlanta had the *Billboard* Hot 100 crown for forty-two weeks in 2004. As Rembert Browne noted in a 2015 article he wrote for *Grantland* about the *Thug Motivation 101* ten-year anniversary concert, "It was a complete takeover of the industry. Atlanta rap radio could play the biggest songs in the country and nearly all could be locally sourced." And that's when Young Jeezy showed up with his masterpiece album.

Jeezy had, of course, been making music before then—he had two independently released albums already

2. "Hey Ya!" and "The Way You Move," in that order. And then when "Hey Ya!" finally gave up the top position, it was "The Way You Move" that stepped into it.

3. And, just because personally it's important for me, he also showed up in *2 Fast 2 Furious*, the second installment of a movie franchise that would eventually go on to earn literally billions of dollars.

4. "Yeah!," featuring Lil Jon and Ludacris.

5. Gucci Mane, for example.

by that point, as well as two mixtapes, both of which were good but the second of which was wonderful.[6] He also had national exposure as part of Boyz n da Hood's "Dem Boyz" and Gucci Mane's "Icy." But *Thug Motivation 101* was his all-caps ARRIVAL, his big debut, his You Can't Have the Atlanta Rap Conversation Anymore Without Mentioning My Name moment. Looking back on things, *Fader* described the album by saying it was "widely accepted as the definitive album for trap music." *XXL* discussed the album's legacy by saying its "reputation and influence grows as each season slowly passes us by." *Complex* anointed Jeezy 2005's best rapper alive and also said that *TM101* was an "apotheosis—the moment when all of the energy on the streets and in clubs, the apocalyptic production of Shawty Redd and Drumma Boy, the totalizing rasp of Jeezy's voice became a region and generation's defining sound." It was massive. Jeezy was massive. He was rap's most exciting thing in rap's most exciting place.

•••••

The question that needs to be answered in this chapter is straightforward, and so let's get straight into it.

WHEN IS YOUNG JEEZY THE MOST MOTIVATING ON *THUG MOTIVATION 101*?

Is it when he posed for the album cover? The story goes that Young Jeezy was getting ready to pose for the photo that was going to be used for the cover of *TM101*. And it was supposed to be him in a chair surrounded by boxes of money that were stacked up on top of each other.[7] But when he got there and looked around, he noticed that the money that was being used was fake, the same as in all of those scenes in movies and TV shows where someone has a whole bunch of fake dollars in a duffel bag or safe or storage facility or whatever. And Jeezy, whose whole origin story is set around the authenticity of the things he raps about, objected. He said that the money in the picture needed to be real. And when the people overseeing the shoot said they had 2 million in fake dollars to use as the prop and that it was going to be impossible to get 2 million in real dollars there, Jeezy made a phone call. A short while later, a couple of unnamed people he knew pulled up with $1.8 million in cash. Wanting to match the original $2 million, Jeezy then dispatched someone to his car and had them grab the remaining $200,000 out of there. I love this story. I love the idea of having immediate access to millions of real dollars. It's very motivating.

Is this when he was the most motivating on *Thug Motivation 101*? It's really close, but this one isn't quite it.

•••••

Is it when he said he won Trapper of the Year four times in a row? I have a great, great time thinking about whatever award show it is that distributes the Trapper of the Year award. Like, what do you think it's

6. *Trap or Die.*

7. It was likely an homage to that scene in *Blow* where George and Diego run out of room to stack the money they've made selling and distributing cocaine. Jeezy has a line on "Let's Get It / Sky's the Limit" where he says, "Tryna get Boston George and Diego money / And stack it all up like Lego money."

called? Do you think it's something like the Trappies? Or maybe it's named after a famous big-time drug dealer, like the Pablos, or the Chapos, or the Blancos, or the Frankies? And who gets invited? Is it only real-life drug dealers who get invited? What about drug dealers from movies and TV shows? Do they get that call? Was Young Jeezy sitting at a table with Avon Barksdale and Scarface? And what about drug users? Do they get invited? You can't have the drug business without drug customers. They're probably the most important part of the equation.

And what are some of the other awards given out there? Is there a Trappies version of the Best New Artist award that the Grammys do? Is there a Trappies version of the Best Supporting Actor or Actress award that the Oscars do? And who do you think was also nominated for Trapper of the Year when Jeezy was? Do you think there's one person whom he just kept beating over and over, like how Walter White kept beating Don Draper at the Emmys?[8] I would be really excited to meet the Susan Lucci of the Trappies.

Is this when he was the most motivating on *Thug Motivation 101*? It's very impressive to win something four times in a row. It is, no question about it, very inspirational, and very motivating. But this isn't quite it either.

.....

Is it when Jeezy said he watched Animal Planet? This is a line from "Standing Ovation." And the argument for picking it as the most motivating moment on the album would be that Young Jeezy watches the same TV channel that a lot of us watch. And if he watches Animal Planet, and we watch Animal Planet, and he's worth tens of millions of dollars, then maybe one day we can all be worth tens of millions of dollars, too.

Is this when he was the most motivating on *Thug Motivation 101*? No. Turns out, he wasn't actually talking about the literal Animal Planet channel. It was a play on words to highlight how involved he used to be in the drug business. ("Infatuation with the birds / I watch Animal Planet")

.....

Is it when he spelled the phrase "trap star"? It happens on "Trap Star." It's part of the hook, actually. He spells it several times. Except he doesn't spell it normally. He doesn't say "t-r-a-p-s-t-a-r." Instead, one of two things happens. He either (a) combines the last two letters to make one sound ("t-r-a-p-s-t-ar") or (b) misspells it entirely ("t-r-a-p-s-t-r"). I hope that it's the second one, because it's just cooler to me to picture him writing the song, realizing that there's one too many letters in it for it to fit properly in the chorus, and then just being like, "Ah, fuck it. I'll just get rid of a vowel. It's close enough," like how people do when they create customized license plates. But I suspect that it's the first one. Either way, Young Jeezy deciding not to obey the traditional rules of spelling things is very motivating.

Is this when he was the most motivating on *Thug Motivation 101*? Not really, no. It's more motivat-

8. Bryan Cranston won the Outstanding Lead Actor in a Drama Series award for Walter White four times during his career. Each time he did, Jon Hamm was nominated as well. Jon Hamm didn't get his trophy for his portrayal of Don Draper until *Breaking Bad* ended.

ing than the Animal Planet thing but less motivating than all of the other options here.

.....

Is it when he [a whole bunch of options]? There are a ton of moments on *Thug Motivation 101* where Young Jeezy is very motivating. So many, in fact, that it'd be impossible to dedicate full sections here to each one. So I'm just gonna burn through a bunch right now.

- **Is it when he said, "Put my hands on the Bible and I solemnly swear / Leave the mall with more shoes than I could possibly wear"?** No. But I love this line.
- **Is it his ad-libs?** In most cases, it's hard to measure how valuable or effective or necessary a rapper's ad-libs are. Not with Jeezy, though. And that is no more evident than on the bridge of "And Then What" when everything drops out of the song except for Mannie Fresh's "boom, boom, clap" chant. That part should be a whole lot of nothing. It should be a bad real-estate investment in a failing strip center. But it's not. Jeezy, just by adding a few "ayyyyyyes" and "jjjyeaaahs" to the equation, turns it into beachfront property.
- **Is it when he said that he had a big gun in his car, which meant that he was "riding shotgun, literally"?** No. But I certainly do enjoy when Jeezy decides to get mean for a little bit. (His verse to open "Bang," the most menacing and ill-intentioned song on the album, is maybe the single most fun part of *TM101*.)
- **Is it when he said that other people look up in the sky and see clouds but that he looks up in the sky and sees opportunity?** No. But, again, I love this line. He's a far more clever writer than most people assume. To that fact . . .
- **Is it when he said, "I'm emotional / I hug the block / I'm so emotional / I love my Glock"?** No. But this is my second-favorite line on the entire album.
- **Is it when he made the snowman T-shirts that eventually got banned in schools?** A thing I find enjoyable is when the meaning of a thing travels slower than the thing itself. Dave Chappelle had this great bit on his *Chappelle's Show* series that ran in the early 2000s about how Lil Jon was using the word "skeet" in songs and that it had penetrated its way into the cultural lexicon before white people knew what it meant. The same thing happened with Young Jeezy's snowman T-shirts. He was using a snowman as his logo. It was, quite plainly, a reference to how he was a drug dealer.[9] But there was nothing else on the shirt that told you anything about anything. If you'd never heard of Young Jeezy and if you'd never seen him wearing the shirt in his videos or whatever, you wouldn't think anything of it. And so the shirts came out, and Jeezy got super popular super fast, which meant the shirts got super popular super fast. And then someone somewhere sent an email to a school administrator like "Hey, just a quick FYI: that snowman T-shirt that all the kids are

9. He explained it on "Icy," saying, "I got snow, man."

wearing is related to drugs and drug dealing." And then the shirts got banned from school.

- **Is it when he said, "I see you looking / With your looking ass"?** No. But, one last time, I love this line. It's never not funny.
- **Is it when he said, "These are more than words / This is more than rap / This is the streets / And I am the trap"?** We're real close now. This line would be, were I tasked with encapsulating such a thing, the most perfect distillation of Young Jeezy's thesis statement as a rapper. This is actually the second most motivating moment on the album. It's not the first one, though. The first one is...

.....

Is it when he said the "Patty cake / Patty cake / Microwave" line? Bang. This is it. This is the one. Two things here:

First, this is actually the first line of the first verse of the first single on Young Jeezy's first major-label album. That means this is how he introduced himself to every listener in America who had not heard of him before that moment: by saying "Patty cake / Patty cake / Microwave." And that makes me just so, so happy. Because there's no other way to interpret him choosing such a byzantine and insular opening than as an immediate and unmistakable declaration that he intended to only ever make music that felt good and important to him.

Second, I've been listening to *TM101* for over fifteen years now, and I've also listened to each subsequent album that Young Jeezy has put out. And I still have no idea what the line means. I would assume it has something to do with drug manufacturing or maybe drug dealing.[10] But that's just a guess. And you know what? That's all it'll ever be: a guess. I'm certain I could find out the answer if I really wanted to. But:

Truth is, I don't wanna know. Some things are best left unsaid. I like to think he was talking about something so beautiful it can't be expressed in words and makes your heart ache because of it. When Jeezy showed up and said, "Patty cake / Patty cake / Microwave," I tell you, his voice soared higher and farther than anybody in a gray place dares to dream. It was like some beautiful bird flapped into our drab little cage and made those walls dissolve away, and for the briefest of moments, every last one of us felt free.

Is this when he was the most motivating on *Thug Motivation 101*? Yes.

---

10. One of my aunts once told me when I was a kid that a good place to hide a small amount of drugs is under the glass tray in the microwave because the police never look there.

HERE'S WHAT WAS HAPPENING: I would sit down to work on this book – to brainstorm ideas or specific chapter angles or possible artwork subjects and so forth – and I kept finding myself in a similar space. I kept finding myself accidentally wandering back to music that I'd listened to heavily between 1994 and 2000.

I'd be like, "Oh, I know. I should figure out a way to write about Snoop's *Doggystyle*." Or "Oh, I know. I should figure out a way to write about Lil' Kim's *Hard Core*." Or "Oh, I know. I should figure out a way to listen to and discuss Ma$e's *Harlem World* or Juvenile's *400 Degreez* or Missy Elliott's *Supa Dupa Fly* or Biggie's *Ready to Die* or Lauryn Hill's *The Miseducation of Lauryn Hill* or 2Pac's *All Eyez on Me* or Bone Thugs-n-Harmony's *E. 1999 Eternal* . . ." I just kept landing somewhere in that same stretch of music over and over and over again.

Now, because I have an ego of a certain size, I initially thought to myself, "Well, obviously that makes sense, because my musical tastes are not *tastes* so much as they are *facts*. Every album I love and every artist I love is objectively good." But then I remembered how in 1998 after "It Ain't My Fault" came out, I spent, like, two weeks arguing with everybody that Silkk the Shocker was the best rapper on the planet, and I was like, "Okay, maybe there's something else at play here."[1] And so I went in search of answers. And that's how we ended up with this Magic Age Mixtape chapter.

Turns out, there's a very real connection in our bodies (or, more specifically, in our brains) to the music that we listened to as teenagers.

Morris B. Holbrook and Robert M. Schindler wrote an academic paper in 1989 that talked about this exact thing. They concluded that it is that period between late adolescence and early adulthood when we form our biggest, most substantial feelings toward music, saying, "Possible explanations include intrinsic components (e.g., a developmental period of maximum sensitivity analogous to the critical periods documented in ethological studies of imprinting) and extrinsic components (e.g., social pressures from one's peer group that reach peak intensity during a particular phase in one's life cycle)."

In 2020, cognitive neuropsychologist Dr. Catherine Loveday further explained the idea to the BBC by citing something called a "reminiscence bump," which is a phenomenon whereby older adults more fondly remember the events of their youth and the circumstances surrounding those events, particularly during the above-mentioned adolescence through early adulthood phase. (From the article: "Listening to our favourite music has a fundamental effect on the brain; there's a surge of activity in the reward pathways that increases the levels of dopamine and oxytocin in our brains – the same pathways that are triggered when we do anything pleasurable such as eating, drinking or dancing.")

It was Daniel J. Levitin, though, a professor of psychology and the former director of the Laboratory for Music Perception, Cognition and Expertise at McGill University, who used my favorite phrase when discussing all of this. He said to the *New York Times* in 2011: "Fourteen is a sort of magic age for the development of musical tastes. Pubertal growth hormones make everything we're experiencing, including music, seem very important. We're just reaching a point in our cognitive development

1. To be clear, I still believe that Silkk the Shocker's work during the late '90s absolutely rules.

when we're developing our own tastes. And music tastes become a badge of identity."

It was the "magic age" line that I liked the most when I read that article. It's fun to think about a time in your life when all of the stuff that people would eventually tell you wasn't very Big-Picture Important – the only stuff that really mattered – was music, movies, TV, playing pickup basketball at the park, whether or not you were able to do someone's fatality in *Mortal Kombat*, hanging out at the mall or the movie theater with your friends and lying about various sex-related things, et cetera. So that's what this chapter is: It's a mixtape of songs from that period for me. It's also, you'll see in a couple pages, a mixtape of songs from that period for you, too.

.....

THE MAGIC AGE MIXTAPE

What's the Time Period: 1994–2000

Pick a Song That Was Actually Exceptionally Popular: Picks for all of the categories past this one will be almost entirely subjective. This one, though, has to be at least a little bit rooted in real life. And so an easy way to do that is to just scroll through the list of rap songs that topped *Billboard*'s Hot Rap Songs chart, see who was up there the longest, and then grab something from that group.

During the 1994–2000 stretch, there were only nine songs that wore *Billboard*'s Hot Rap Songs crown for nine or more weeks. Missy's "Hot Boyz" was up there for eighteen (!!) weeks. Puff Daddy's "Can't Nobody Hold Me Down" was up there for twelve weeks. Da Brat's "Funkdafied" and Coolio's "Gangsta's Paradise" were each up there for eleven. Craig Mack's "Flava in Ya Ear" and Ma$e's "Lookin' at Me" were up there for ten. And Biggie's "One More Chance" was up there for nine.

That's an incredible lineup and one of those situations where no matter what you pick, you're going to be both right and wrong. For me, I think it has to be Da Brat's "Funkdafied." Half because g-funk is (probably) my note-for-note favorite subgenre of rap. And half because that song came out the same summer that I celebrated my thirteenth birthday, and there wasn't shit you could tell me when my mom bought me a shirt from the flea market that looked like the one Da Brat wore in the "Funkdafied" video.

Pick a Song That Made You Feel Like You Were Way More Grown Than You Actually Were: It was Adina Howard's "Freak Like Me." I was thirteen headed toward fourteen when it came out, but in my head I was thirty-three headed toward thirty-four. I was walking around telling people I needed a girl who was a freak, and I didn't even have all of my adult teeth yet.

Pick a Song That You Said You Loved Because All Your Friends Did but That Secretly You Kind of Didn't Like: This is a toss-up between two songs for me, and I'm already a little bit embarrassed that I have to say this, but it's either Ice Cube's "We Be Clubbin'," which came out in 1997 and was the lead single for his *Players Club* movie and just felt a little too much like something sharp rolling down the side of a hill, or Outkast's "Ms. Jackson," which came out in 2000 and was just a little too earwormy for my tastes. Of those two, I think I have to go with "Ms. Jackson" here. The same "Ms. Jackson" that sold over three million copies in the United States alone. The same "Ms. Jackson" that hit number one on *Billboard*'s Hot 100 chart and *Billboard*'s Hot R&B/Hip-Hop Songs chart. The same "Ms. Jackson" that won the BET Award for Video of the Year and the MTV Video Music Award for Best Hip-Hop Video. The same "Ms. Jackson" that won Outkast their first Grammy. The same "Ms. Jackson" that *Rolling Stone* picked as one of the 100 Best Songs of the 2000s and that *NME* picked as one of the 150 Best Tracks of the Past 15 Years in 2015. That one. That "Ms. Jackson." (I promise I'm going to make this up to Outkast later.)

Pick a Song That You Said You Didn't Like Because All Your Friends Hated It but That Secretly You Liked: I'm going to step outside of rap for this one. In fact, I'm going to step all the way outside of the country for this one. Because here's who I want for this category: I want Jimmy Ray, the English pop star who briefly flickered a bright light in America when he released "Are You Jimmy Ray?" I loved all of the parts I was seeing and hearing when he started popping up on MTV. I loved his cheekbones and the way his tall, tall body seemed to be made up entirely of arms and legs and neck. I loved his rockabilly outfits and that he described himself as "dangerous" while wearing a pair of jeans that kept getting the better of him anytime he tried to move in them. I loved the way his voice shot out from the back of his throat, and I loved that he spent pretty much all of his time in the video looking at the camera from up under his eyes. He was a lot of fun.

Pick a Song from the Soundtrack of a Movie That Came Out During This Time: The first two that I think of are (1) Warren G's "Regulate," featuring Nate Dogg, which was part of the *Above the Rim* soundtrack[2]; and (2) Will Smith's "Men in Black," featuring a dancing alien, which was part of the *Men in Black* soundtrack.[3] And since I already used up my g-funk pick earlier with Da Brat's "Funkdafied," I'm going with "Men in Black" here. I'm just a real sucker for Will Smith.

Pick a Song That Filled Your Body with Electricity: DMX's "Ruff Ryders' Anthem."

Pick a Song That Had a Video That You Went Nuts For: A thing that used to happen before the internet is you couldn't just watch a music video whenever you wanted; you had to wait around like an idiot and hope they played it on TV at some point. Which is why going to visit a cousin of mine who lived a block over was such a treat. Because he had one of those TVs that had a VCR built into it, and so he would fill up tape after tape after tape with videos. He had everybody in his collection, it seemed. He had Onyx's "Slam." He had 2Pac and Snoop's "2 of Amerikaz Most Wanted." He had Method Man's "Bring the Pain." He had Biggie's "Big Poppa" and 112's "Cupid" and Mary J. Blige's "I'm Goin' Down." More and more and more and more.[4] But the crown jewel of the bunch–the ONE video he recorded several times on several different tapes just to be absolutely sure that it was always available to be cued up: Lil' Kim's "Crush on You," an absolutely mes-

2. The single greatest movie soundtrack.

3. The single greatest movie soundtrack for a movie where Vincent D'Onofrio plays a space roach.

4. A curious inclusion: Babyface's "How Come, How Long," featuring Stevie Wonder, a very sad song about domestic violence that my cousin greatly enjoyed because the video featured a twist ending where it turned out that the woman killed the man who was beating her instead of the other way around.

merizing four minutes where Kim cycled her way through unforgettable outfits and wigs with the same confidence and regality that she cycled her way through metaphors and similes with. She's incredible on that song. Even listening to it today, more than a quarter century later, all of her words have so much snap to them and so much energy to them.

Pick a Song That You Don't Have to Explain – You Can Just Turn It On and Everyone Who You Grew Up with Is Gonna Hear It and Go "OHHHHHHHHH-HHHHH": Bone Thugs-n-Harmony's "Thuggish Ruggish Bone."

Pick a Song That Made You Feel Like You Knew What It Was Like to Be in Love: I'm going to cheat here. I'm picking two songs, but only because they feel connected in that Impossible to Describe Fully way that happens whenever you start scraping up against the top of Excellence Atmosphere. First, give me Method Man and Mary J. Blige's "I'll Be There for You / You're All I Need to Get By." And second, give me Busta Rhymes and Janet Jackson's "What's It Gonna Be?!" In both instances, it was two of the coolest and most talented people in existence just being cool and talented together.

A sidebar: Some other times this happened during that same period include when Nas and Lauryn Hill got together for "If I Ruled the World," when Mariah Carey and O.D.B. got together for the "Fantasy" remix,[5] and when Mýa and Silkk the Shocker got together for "Movin' On."[6]

Pick a Song That Had a Sound in It That You'd Never Heard Before: This is going to be at least a tiny bit ironic, because the sound I'd not heard before is actually a sample from a completely different song, but you know that howling, ominous hum from "Ready or Not" by the Fugees? That's what I'm going with here. Because that song fucking rules. And I can remember hearing it start – hearing that hum – and being like, "Oh shit. What is *this*?" It's a perfect noise. It's intimidating and assured and immediately sets the pace for the rest of the song.[7] It's also, I came to find out years later, a sample from a song called "Boadicea" by Enya.

Pick a Song That You Cared Deeply About Because It Reminded You of a Particular Moment: We were at a pep rally in high school one year. And the principal said that we were in luck, that she had okayed a special performance by a kid named Lupe and a kid named Randall, both of whom were in the uppermost tier of popularity at our school and both of whom I was in a one-way war with because I'd found out that a girl I was interested in liked both of them. Anyway, Lupe and Randall came walking out right as the opening to "I Got 5 on It" by Luniz started playing. The whole gym went fucking bonkers cheering for them. It was a horrible day for me.

---

5. There's a part on the song where Kelly Price sings, "Watcha gonna do when you get out of jail?" and Puff Daddy responds, "I'm gonna do a remix." It always makes me smile to think of Puff, king of the late '90s remixes, being so committed to the bit that making a remix to a song is the first thing he'd think to do after getting out of jail.

6. SILKK THE SHOCKER IS VERY UNDERAPPRECIATED.

7. A contemporary comparison would be that string that kicks off Beyoncé's "Formation."

Pick a Song That Allows You to Make a Very Bold Claim: Somewhere around my sixth or seventh year of being a teacher, I started carpooling to work with this guy who lived in the neighborhood near the townhome that my wife and kids and I were living in at the time. The guy—let's call him "K. O."—was this older dude (maybe sixty-two years old) who was super into music. He knew so many facts about so many songs. We'd get in the car, he'd put a song on, and then he'd be like, "Listen to this. Do you hear that sound in the background? That *tink-tink-tinking*. That's actually being played by Aretha Franklin. Yeah, she just so happened to be in the studio when Metallica was recording this song."[8] It was really great. I loved those trips to and from work with K. O.

Anyway, after several weeks of riding together, I asked K. O. if I could pick some stuff for us to listen to. And it took a little bit of haggling, but ultimately he said yes, that I could pick something, but that it was just going to be one song. And I knew from our previous conversations together that, while K. O. was obviously aware of rap as a genre and obviously he had heard rap music in passing, he had never sat down and intentionally listened to a rap song the way that he had with, say, rock or Americana or the blues or whatever. So I was fucking pumped. I felt like it was a really unique situation. I felt like I had been given the opportunity to play a rap song for a person who had never gotten to experience that unique jolt of joy that comes along when you hear rap that thumps you in your chest.

So I spent several hours one night trying to land on an exactly perfect rap song. I wanted something that touched on as many of the most fulfilling parts of rap as I could find. I wanted a song that had ambitious production, and a song that had ambitious writing, and a song that had ambitious voices, and a song that, even though we couldn't watch it, had an ambitious video. I wanted something that I could play and that he could hear and that, despite having no real history with rap at all, he would feel connected to. Which is why what I went with was "Elevators" by Outkast.

"What you're about to hear, K. O., is art" is what I said to him as I prepared to tap the song into existence with my phone. "Every single part of this is flawless. Every single moment is stuffed fat with creativity and exceptional brilliance. It somehow sounds like it's reaching backward in time and forward into the future simultaneously. It's the fucking DeLorean from *Back to the Future*. This is as perfect a song as there has ever been."[9] And then we sat there and listened to the whole thing in total silence, completely absorbing everything that Big Boi and André 3000 were offering up as they ice-skated across the beat.

When it was over, I unplugged my phone and looked at K. O. And I'll never forget this for the rest of my life: without taking his eyes off the road and without even a hint of a smile sneaking away from his mouth, he took a breath, paused for a second to gather his thoughts, and then finally spoke: "Not bad."

---

8. I'm making this connection up just as a way to show how obscure or interesting the stuff that K. O. would say was. I have no idea if Aretha Franklin liked Metallica, or if she had any thoughts at all on "Enter Sandman."

9. I'm certain that I didn't say it near as well as this in real life. It's more likely I said something closer to "This song is so good. Like, *really* good. *Really, really* good."

YOUR MAGIC AGE MIXTAPE

TEENAGE YOU

INSTRUCTIONS: FILL IN THE FOLLOWING TO CREATE YOUR OWN MAGIC AGE MIXTAPE. DON'T USE A PERMANENT MARKER BECAUSE IF YOU DO IT'LL FUCK UP THE PAGE BEHIND THIS ONE.	PICK A SONG THAT FILLED YOUR BODY WITH ELECTRICITY:
WHAT'S THE TIME PERIOD:	PICK A SONG THAT HAD A VIDEO THAT YOU WENT NUTS FOR:
PICK A SONG THAT WAS ACTUALLY EXCEPTIONALLY POPULAR:	PICK A SONG THAT YOU DON'T HAVE TO EXPLAIN ANYTHING FOR:
PICK A SONG THAT MADE YOU FEEL LIKE YOU WERE WAY MORE GROWN THAN YOU ACTUALLY WERE:	PICK A SONG THAT MADE YOU FEEL LIKE YOU KNEW WHAT IT WAS LIKE TO BE IN LOVE:
PICK A SONG THAT YOU SAID YOU LOVED BECAUSE ALL YOUR FRIENDS DID BUT YOU SECRETLY KIND OF DIDN'T LIKE:	PICK A SONG THAT HAD A SOUND IN IT THAT YOU'D NEVER HEARD BEFORE:
PICK A SONG THAT YOU SAID YOU DIDN'T LIKE BECAUSE ALL YOUR FRIENDS HATED IT BUT SECRETLY YOU LIKED:	PICK A SONG THAT YOU CARED DEEPLY ABOUT BECAUSE IT REMINDED YOU OF A PARTICULAR MOMENT:
PICK A SONG FROM THE SOUNDTRACK OF A MOVIE THAT CAME OUT DURING THIS TIME:	PICK A SONG THAT ALLOWS YOU TO MAKE A VERY BOLD CLAIM (AND LIST THE CLAIM):

ON OCCASION, A THING THAT I ENJOY DOING while writing a book is starting a chapter in some (hopefully) clever way that eventually reveals itself to (hopefully) be meaningful in an unexpected way. That's not what I'm doing here, though. Because there's too much ground to cover. And so instead, I'm going to just say Kendrick Lamar's major-label debut, *Good Kid, M.A.A.D City* (*GKMC*), is one of the two best albums of the 2010–2019 decade. Kanye West's *My Beautiful Dark Twisted Fantasy* (*MBDTF*) is the other one. This chapter is here to figure out which of those two is the tops.

Pick One: Better Legacy? The simplest explanation of each album's legacy is thus:

GKMC is Kendrick Lamar's major-label debut. It's all about a specific period of time spent in a specific part of the country, lived by a specific person specifically. You're supposed to listen to it and learn something about yourself and maybe about the world, too. As a project, it's a masterwork that (a) single-handedly reignited the conversation around the viability of concept albums in rap and (b) positioned Kendrick for an all-time run. Without the momentum from *GKMC*, we don't get 2015's *To Pimp a Butterfly*, which is (possibly) his most crucial work, and we don't get 2017's *DAMN.*, which won him a Pulitzer, and we probably don't even get 2016's *Untitled Unmastered.*, a wonderful collection of one-offs and loosies that he released as a stand-alone project in 2016.

MBDTF is Kanye West's fifth studio album. It's all about an interrogation of fame and the deification of celebrity by somebody who has been whipsawed around by exactly those things. You're supposed to listen to it and learn something about the world and maybe about yourself, too. As a project, it's a masterwork that Kanye put together as a kind of cultural apology following the backlash that accompanied his Taylor Swift debacle at the 2009 MTV Video Music Awards.[1] He had, by that point, already given us three obvious classics (*The College Dropout*, *Late Registration*, and *Graduation*) and one sleeper classic (*808s & Heartbreak*), and still, *MBDTF* was considered to be his greatest album almost immediately.

So that's what you have to choose between here: Are you more intrigued by an album that serves as someone's Superhero Origin Story, or are you more intrigued by an album that serves as someone's Superhero Returning from the Dead Story? I think I like that first experience better. I like the excitement bundled into it, and I like that very particular feeling you get when you realize that maybe you might be listening to your new favorite musician. Mark this category down as a win for *GKMC*. (1–0, *GKMC*)

Pick One: Better Performance by the Leading Man? *GKMC* and *MBDTF* have a lot of similarities. Both albums are sixty-eight minutes long.[2] Both albums feature arrangements from an assortment of producers as well as vocal contributions from an assortment of people (be they other rappers or singers or even non-musicians). Both albums have at least one song that is nine-or-more-minutes long. Both albums are now certified triple platinum in sales.

---

1. Taylor Swift, then still in the infancy of her stardom, won the MTV Video Music Award for Best Female Video. Kanye thought it should've gone to Beyoncé. So he went up onstage while Taylor was accepting the award, and he said as much. It was met with an instant and massive backlash. So much so, in fact, that Kanye went into exile for several months, eventually moving to Hawaii for half a year to make *My Beautiful Dark Twisted Fantasy*.
2. There's a deluxe version of *GKMC* available that's ninety-six minutes long.

THE COMPLETE FIRST SEASON

KENDRICK

Both albums have parts where a very popular television show is referenced. More, more, more. But Kanye and Kendrick do markedly different things as the leading man on each.

On *GKMC*, the spotlight is fully on Kendrick. There are other people on the tape, yes, but it's a Kendrick Lamar story that you're listening to, and he makes that clear before you hear even one single sound. To wit: There are four people on the cover of *GKMC*. It's Kendrick as a child, two of his uncles, and his grandfather. His uncles and his grandfather each have their eyes blacked out. Kendrick doesn't, though. His eyes are unblocked, and they're looking right at you. The symbolism is obvious. He explained the image as such in 2012: "That photo says so much about my life, and about how I was raised in Compton, and the things I've seen, just through them innocent eyes. You don't see nobody else's eyes, but you see my eyes are innocent and trying to figure out what's going on."

On *MBDTF*, Kanye is a symphony conductor, moving pieces and people in and out of moments as needed. He's the obvious star, obviously, but he's a star the way, say, LeBron James is a star, in that Kanye here proves he has the ability to pull something special out of somebody, and also he has the confidence and the wherewithal to know exactly how and when to do it. It's a skill that Kanye had shown flashes of before on other albums,[3] but it's something he perfected on *MBDTF*. Q-Tip, who worked on the album with Kanye, explained the situation in 2010: "I'd never worked the way Kanye was working in Hawaii. Everybody's opinions mattered and counted....It was like music by committee. I have my people that listen to my stuff—I think everybody does—but his thing is much more, like, if the delivery guy comes in the studio and Kanye likes him and they strike up a conversation, he'll go, 'Check this out. Tell me what you think.'"

Between these two options, I'm not sure which way to go. It's really close. It's *REALLY* close. But I think it has to be Kanye here. It's probably 1 percent tougher to do what he did on *MBDTF* than what Kendrick did on *GKMC*. Mark this one down as a win for *MBDTF*. (1–1)

Pick One: Better Mention of a TV Show? Kanye mentions *South Park* during "Gorgeous." Here's the line: "Choke a *South Park* writer with a fish stick." It's in reference to how the show spent an entire episode in 2009 making fun of him. (It started out with a cartoon version of Kanye not understanding a joke about how "fish sticks" sounds like "fish dicks" and then ended with him deciding to live in the ocean and become "a gay fish.") Kendrick mentions *Martin* in "Sherane a.k.a. Master Splinter's Daughter." Here's the line: "Soon as this episode of *Martin* go off / I'm tryna get off." It's in reference to how a girl wants him to come over, but he's gonna wait until he finishes the show before heading her way. *Martin* is a better show than *South Park*, so *GKMC* wins here. (2–1, *GKMC*)

Pick One: Better Guest Appearance? There are a number of Kevlar-tough guest verses on each album.

On the *GKMC* side, there's Dr. Dre on "Compton" (great). And there's Drake on "Poetic Justice" (excellent). And there's Anna Wise on "Real" and "Money Trees" (very excellent on both). And there's Jay Rock on "Money Trees"

3. Music critic Jeff Weiss had a great line about this exact thing when *808s & Heartbreak* came out in 2008. Speaking of Young Jeezy's guest verse on "Amazing," he wrote something close to "Kanye West knows how to utilize Young Jeezy better than Young Jeezy knows how to utilize Young Jeezy."

URKEL
0

(extremely excellent). The best, though, is when MC Eiht shows up on "M.A.A.D City."

On the *MBDTF* side, there's Cyhi the Prynce on "So Appalled" (great). And there's Raekwon on "Gorgeous" (excellent). And there's Pusha T on "So Appalled" and "Runaway" (very excellent on both). And there's Rick Ross on "Devil in a New Dress" (extremely excellent). The best, though, is when Nicki Minaj shows up on "Monster."

And so that's the contest here: it's MC Eiht on "M.A.A.D City" versus Nicki Minaj on "Monster." And it's a fun thing to think about as a debate prompt because of how far apart the two were in their careers for each of those verses.

With MC Eiht, it'd been six years since he'd put a tape out, and it'd been something closer to sixteen or seventeen years since he'd been a part of the national conversation in rap. When he popped up on "M.A.A.D City" in the Elder Gangster Statesman role, it was this great combination of nostalgia ("Oh shit! Is that MC Eiht?!") and reverence ("Oh shit! MC Eiht is still fucking excellent at this!"). It was like in *Jurassic World* when they went and got the original *Tyrannosaurus rex* from *Jurassic Park* to help fight the *Indominus rex* at the end of the movie.

With Nicki, she was at the very start of her career ("Monster" was released as a single in October of 2010; she didn't release her major-label debut, *Pink Friday*, until November). She was this new thing, this exciting promise of huge talent. And she'd earned herself a nice amount of buzz via mixtapes and guest verses in the lead-up to that moment, but there was a tiny amount of doubt in the air surrounding her because what was supposed to be the first single from her album ("Massive Attack") ended up not tracking at all. But then "Monster" came out. And nobody was asking any more questions.

She was a goddamn hurricane of chain saws and dynamite on it. She couldn't be contained. She bounced around between voices and personalities and cadences. It was an unquestionable triumph. *Spin* called it "the single best verse of the 2010s." *GQ* called it "one of hip-hop's most undeniable treasures." *Pitchfork* said, "Never has a female emcee inserted herself into the male-driven debate [of best rapper] with such force." A new-to-the-game Nicki Minaj got on a song with someone who was in the prime of his rapping abilities (Rick Ross) and someone everybody considered a genius (Kanye) and someone who was already being discussed as the greatest rapper ever (Jay-Z) and fucking ran them all off the court. She was the only part of the song anyone wanted to talk about. It was a career-defining moment and a legacy-defining moment.

Which is why, as enjoyable as MC Eiht is on "M.A.A.D City," Nicki wins this category. It's not only the best guest verse on either album, it's also the best overall verse on either album.[4] (2–2)

Pick One: Better Album Cover? I went over the *GKMC* cover earlier, so that part's already covered. The *MBDTF* cover was designed by an artist named George Condo. He actually made five different versions of the cover. And the primary one (a naked man lying down with a phoenix on top of him) has been picked a bunch of times by a bunch of different places as one of the best album covers ever. But I feel myself pulled to *GKMC*'s cover more.

---

4. Nicki explained in a 2018 interview with Rob Markman at Genius that Kanye told her he'd considered removing her verse from the song because he knew that people were going to say that it was the best verse on the album.

I don't know why; I just do. So that's the winner here. Because that's how art works. (3–2, *GKMC*)

Pick One: Better Short Film? I'm cheating a bit here. *GKMC* didn't have an actual short film attached to it. It was just part of the album's subtitle. (The full title on the cover reads "*Good Kid, M.A.A.D City: A Short Film by Kendrick Lamar.*") *MBDTF* definitely did have a short film attached to it, though. It was thirty-four minutes long, and it was all about Kanye spending time with a phoenix that he'd rescued after it crashed to Earth. (My favorite piece of it is the part where Kanye takes out a drum machine and makes the phoenix listen to him play it. It's the most Kanye West thing I can think of. He happens across this magical human-bird thing from Greek mythology and is like, "I know what I should do. I should tell her not to trust the news and then play her some of my music.")[5] *MBDTF* wins here. (3–3)

Pick One: The Most Confident Line? *MBDTF* is, in one way or another, directly connected to Kanye West's ego. You can't separate the two. Which is why it's so surprising that he loses this category. Because the most confident line across either album is when Kendrick Lamar talks about a girl he likes on "Backseat Freestyle" and says that she has a butt that is so big that (a) it makes him prematurely ejaculate and (b) he's not embarrassed about it. That's just a really incredibly confident thing to say in a song. Especially when you think back and remember that just twelve seconds earlier he was talking about how if you didn't respect his mind, then you'd die in a storm of bullets. He pretty much said, "Hey. Respect my mind, or you're gonna get shot a bunch of times. Oh, and by the way, I know a girl with a big butt who makes me have an orgasm way faster than normal." That's unfettered confidence. *GKMC* wins here. (4–3, *GKMC*)

Pick One: Better Production? Listen, as a personal preference, I like the production on *GKMC* more than I like the production on *MBDTF.* Both are obviously wonderful, but I just like the way *GKMC*'s production makes it feel like one long rap concerto. I'm a sucker for that kind of thing. That being said, this category has to go to *MBDTF.* Being a producer is kind of Kanye's whole thing. Mark this one down for *MBDTF.* (4–4)

A quick sidebar: In 2015, *LA Weekly* counted down the twenty best producers of all time. They put Kanye in the sixth spot. Three of the five people who finished ahead of him on the list (the RZA, Pete Rock, and DJ Premier) worked with Kanye at some point on *MBDTF.* Four of the best six producers ever put their fingerprints on *MBDTF.*

Pick One: Better Performance by Someone Who Wasn't a Musician? Let's hit six things to get us to the finish line:

1. The parents that you hear on *GKMC* who talk to Kendrick at various points are Kendrick's actual parents. That doesn't really have anything to do with anything here, because they haven't been chosen to compete in this category for the *GKMC* side, but it's just something I think is interesting. They're really good.
2. The two star figures competing here are Chris Rock and Maya Angelou.

---

5. Kendrick has a version of this, too. Kendrick resurrects 2Pac for 2015's *To Pimp a Butterfly* and then reads him some of his poetry.

3. Chris Rock is on *MBDTF*. He comes on at the end of "Blame Game" and plays a man who is grateful for the sexual enlightening that Kanye has led his girlfriend on. It's really funny. It's probably one of the five or six funniest rap skits of the new century. ("I was fucking parts of your pussy I never fucked before. I was in there like, 'Oh shit! I never been here before. I've never even seen this part of Pussy Town before.'")
4. Maya Angelou is on *GKMC*. She comes on at the end of "Sing About Me, I'm Dying of Thirst." She plays a kindly and tender old neighborhood soul who performs an impromptu baptism on Kendrick and his friends, offering them an alternative to the violence and chaos that surrounds them. It's beautiful. Even if you have zero experience with (or knowledge of) any of Maya Angelou's work, you listen to her talk on the album for ten seconds, and it's like, "I don't know who this woman is, but no stranger has ever made me feel more at ease than she's doing right now."[6]
5. Chris Rock and Maya Angelou are perfect in their roles. In each case, it feels like (a) their general presence makes sense within the context of the album, and (b) the album would be slightly less good without them.
6. As undeniably good as Chris Rock is on *MBDTF*, Maya Angelou is just a few paces better. She wins that contest, which means . . .

Good Kid, M.A.A.D City edges out *My Beautiful Dark Twisted Fantasy* by a score of five categories to four. *Good Kid, M.A.A.D City* is the best album of the 2010–2019 decade.

---

6. Maya Angelou has a long and storied relationship with rap. Probably the most famous story in that arena is the one where, after encountering an irate 2Pac on the set of *Poetic Justice*, she pulled him aside, allowed him to express his frustrations, and then explained to him how important he was. The encounter, according to Angelou, ended with 2Pac in tears.

FIRSTLY, I WAS NINE YEARS OLD when *Teenage Mutant Ninja Turtles II: The Secret of the Ooze* came out. Secondly, I'd not seen a trailer for the movie before I sat down to watch it with my parents. And thirdly, it was 1991 when all of this was happening, and 1991 was a markedly different time for movie consumption. It was wholly possible to watch something in a theater without knowing anything about it beyond whatever it was you saw on the poster when you lined up to get the tickets. Which was why I lost my motherfucking mind when Vanilla Ice popped up in a cameo role at the end of the movie.

I had no idea it was going to happen. I was just sitting there, watching what I considered to be potentially the best movie ever filmed, and then a fight scene carried the turtles into a crowded nightclub, and there he was. Vanilla Ice. My favorite rapper at the time.[1] Up on the screen, with Leonardo and Michelangelo and Donatello and Raphael. And he was scared at first (as he should've been, on account of having just learned about the existence of giant, mutated, talking turtles). But after a second, the music in the background caught his ear. And so he started dancing, and then he started rapping. And what's more, he was rapping *ABOUT* the Ninja Turtles – celebrating them, encouraging them, championing them. And then the turtles, after they'd defeated their enemies, started dancing, too. It was a perfect moment for nine-year-old me. I couldn't have asked for anything more. And that was when I knew that I was correct. That was when I knew I didn't have to add the "potentially" qualifier to the sentence anymore: I was watching the greatest movie ever filmed.

The song Vanilla Ice performed in the movie was called "Ninja Rap." And that's why this chapter is called "What's Your 'Ninja Rap' Moment?" Because here's what's happening:

I very much enjoy listening to people talk about stuff that they care about. As a practice, it's good for your spirit. And so I asked ten of my writer friends to each tell me about a "Ninja Rap" moment in their life. Here's the prompt I gave them: "Tell me about a time where you just really loved whatever rap thing it was that was happening in front of you. It can be from when you were a kid or when you were a teenager or when you were an adult. It doesn't matter. As long as it's something that you'll carry in your heart as a beautiful rap thing forever."

So that's what this chapter is.

KATHY IANDOLI, ON LIL' KIM'S SURPRISE APPEARANCE DURING THE BAD BOY REUNION SHOW IN 2015: My career in music journalism entered the double digits years ago, so I often wondered if I could have another fangirl moment. I had several in my preteen and teenage years – I mean, they're the reason why I even entered this industry of superlatives, word counts, and deadlines.

But in 2015, any semblance of jaded ol' me was thrown out the window during the BET Awards when Puff Daddy & the Family performed a montage of their biggest hits. They reached the "All About the Benjamins" portion, and before I even had a moment to emotionally prepare myself, Lil' Kim emerged from beneath the stage in her signature squatting pose. As she asked the infamous question "Wanna bumble with the bee, huh?" I couldn't even "buzz" back at her, because I was screaming and crying at my TV screen.

---

1. This was six months after the release of his debut album, *To the Extreme*. It felt like he and MC Hammer were personally battling each other for nine-year-old fandom.

I have always been a Lil' Kim fan, and just seeing her in that moment brought me back to 1996, when I first watched her shimmy down the escalator in the "No Time" video. When I later co-wrote her memoir, *The Queen Bee*, with her in 2021, I watched that performance every single day to hype me up. In fact, I'm watching it right now.

DART ADAMS, ON SEEING RAP ON TV FOR THE FIRST TIME IN 1981: Back on July 9, 1981, ABC News ran the first ever story about rap on *20/20*, called "Rappin' to the Beat." A reporter named Steve Fox decided to get to the bottom of the rap phenomenon after Blondie's "Rapture" became a hit. It was the first time I ever saw footage of Kurtis Blow performing "The Breaks" in front of a live audience, plus he was being interviewed on a mainstream outlet. My mind was blown. I saw the Sugarhill Gang, the Furious Five, Kurtis Blow, Funky 4 + 1, Mean Machine, etc. all on my television, as opposed to hearing them on the radio after the sun went down or on the records my older siblings and cousins bought from Skippy White's and Strawberries. I'll never forget the feeling I had as a rap-loving five-year-old that summer.

SEAN FENNESSEY, ON HEARING A HAT TIP TO ARRESTED DEVELOPMENT'S "TENNESSEE" WHILE PLAYING LITTLE LEAGUE BASEBALL: Bottom of the seventh. Two on base. A 2–2 count. Brian Crowe on the bump. We're losing, 5–4. Crowe is big, lithe, and powerful. He rears back: fastball. (We're ten years old. They're all fastballs.) I close my eyes and swing. Turn the wrists over, stay compact, and go with the pitch: contact—a skidding ground ball takes one hop, then two, and hits third base with a *thoomph*. The ball shoots to the sky, ricocheting toward the fence across the foul line. This is a base hit! A lucky one, but still. One runner in, the second rounding home. The left fielder recovers the ball and throws home. I'm pulling into second, slightly panicked and disoriented. Play at the plate. Safe. That's a game-winning hit. We won. Far off, I can hear it:

"Henn-eh-ssy!"

"Hennessy!"

"Henn-eh-ssy!"

This was a spirited, confusing celebration of my name, a distortion that referenced both the French cognac distillery—which we had never tasted but knew had alcohol in it and was thus cool—and a hit single by the Atlanta hip-hop collective Arrested Development. "Tennessee" is now a relic of a post-gangsta-rap inflection point in hip-hop history, released eight months before "Nuthin' but a 'G' Thang." This was before Outkast and T.I. and Migos, a larval stage in Atlanta rap.

And for me, too. When I got a hit in Little League baseball, my teammates started singing a song about a young man who had just lost his grandmother and his brother in a short period of time. "Lord, I've really been real stressed, down and out, losing ground," Speech, the group's leader, raps. "Although I am Black and proud, problems got me pessimistic."

Cognitive dissonance—it sounded like a celebration, and it was, in its way. An exorcism on the radio. "Tennessee" is a deep and unusual song that was dismissed as a "boho" curio. But it touched something that so much pop-crossover hip-hop accomplished in the '90s—it was a portal to a new city, a new way of life, a new perspective. It sank in.

CLOVER HOPE, ON HEARING MC LYTE'S VOICE AS A TEENAGER: In the year 2000, I was a newfound megafan of basketball—a moody sixteen-year-old who naively held out hope for a Knicks championship. As it happened, I was also becoming a fan of love. So imagine my glee when a movie called *Love & Basketball* arrived. I remember watching it on DVD in a friend's bedroom, a few of us girls sprawled out on the bed and the floor. The soundtrack was an absolute vision of dance, mush, and wistfulness, from Kool Moe Dee's "I Go to Work" to Chaka Khan and Rufus's "Sweet Thing." I was hooked. But the moment I heard MC Lyte's voice, that was it. "Lyte as a Rock" plays to open the movie's "Second Quarter," set in 1988, the year of the song's release. MC Lyte's unmistakably *hard* voice booms out over a black screen: "Do you understand the metaphoric phrase 'light as a rock'? It's explaining how *heavy* the young lady is." The song introduces the romantic lead, Monica (Sanaa Lathan), as a high school basketball star. It's a subtly powerful way to allude to the strength of a woman. On top of that, I was hearing a song that debated the definition of a simile versus a metaphor.

ROB MARKMAN, ON SEEING JAY-Z PERFORM IN THE BARCLAYS CENTER: If Biggie's "You never thought that hip-hop would take it this far" lyric was a person, it would be Shawn Carter. I remember thinking that walking into Brooklyn's Barclays Center for the very first time, when Jay-Z christened the arena with its very first event on September 28, 2012.

Before Hov took the stage, the lights went dim, and seventeen thousand people stood up as Roy Ayers Ubiquity's classic "We Live in Brooklyn, Baby" played like some sort of Brooklyn national anthem, except when Jay took the stage, he actually performed our borough's national anthem. I don't know if I ever rapped along to "Where I'm From" so hard.

But the big moment for me was when Jigga rapped his verse from "Do It Again (Put Ya Hands Up)": "Fuck the flow they jackin' our slang / I seen the same shit happen to Kane," he said coyly. Then the lights went down, we heard that classic "mmm, mmm, mmm," and Brooklyn's OG rap king, Big Daddy Kane, emerged to "Ain't No Half-Steppin'."

I still remember the way it felt like my body filled with electricity in that moment. I actually still can feel that excitement in me every time I watch the grainy footage on YouTube. Kane mentored Jay, and Hov built an arena in our hometown and shared the stage with the guy that inspired us all. It felt like the biggest celebration of our borough. It's a shame Biggie wasn't alive to share that moment.

But the way the whole arena rapped "Juicy" word for word, I know he felt that shit.

REMBERT BROWNE, ON WATCHING CAM'RON FREESTYLE ON *RAP CITY* WHILE HE COUNTED A STACK OF MONEY IN 2003: When I hear Cam'ron say "I'ma count cash money" over Scarface's "My Block" instrumental, I smile, because I know Jim Jones has just pushed Big Tigger out of the way to deliver his verse. I also smile because Jim is wearing a giant Priest Holmes jersey, because it's 2003.

And then there's Juelz Santana, in full 9/11 bars mode, his perfect bandanna tied across his forehead, in a 3XL Dolphins jersey. He says, "And thanks to Cam, I'm Harlem's new anchorman. Yes, chump, you should shake my hand," which is a perfect way to salute the freestyle's main attraction: Cam'ron rapping while counting a stack of money.

Cam's in the pink shirt, with the pink bucket, Dipset chain swinging, talking about some of everything. It's perfect Cam – confusing and lyrically dexterous while looking and sounding amazing.

Sure, this is a freestyle, but at its core this is Cam'ron doing a bit. He starts off talking about money, then he counts it in the background while his teammates rap, and then when it's his turn, he finishes counting and ends his

verse by addressing his stacks, saying, "Four mil from Def Jam and I ain't sell a record for 'em."

From albums to the *Rap City* freestyle to 2020's Kith commercial, Dipset will always be New York superheroes.

DANYEL SMITH, ON HEARING BUSTA RHYMES'S "PUT YOUR HANDS WHERE MY EYES COULD SEE" ON A YACHT FILLED WITH MUSIC-INDUSTRY TYPES: Too many moments to name. There's hearing, as a middle schooler, "Rapper's Delight" on the radio for the first time. There's dancing to Run-DMC's "Hard Times" at UC Berkeley's Pauley Ballroom—it was a fraternity dance that had balloons with dangling ribbons. There's seeing 3rd Bass open for Ice-T's Body Count in late-'80s San Francisco, at a packed and stinky club—MC Serch and Pete Nice wrecked our lives and stole the entire show. But what brings me joy for absolute ever are my memories of being on a yacht docked at Manhattan's Chelsea Piers. It was a celebration of Boyz II Men's *Evolution*. The lead single was "4 Seasons of Loneliness," the song that would go on to be their last number one pop hit.

This was August 1997. I had just been named editor in chief of *Vibe*. On the yacht, which was like straight out of a video shoot, the iconic Kid Capri was on the wheels, playing boss classics. Because it was, to be honest, a very music-industry and R&B crowd. Cool. Chill energy.

But then the Bronx's own Capri broke out Busta Rhymes's "Put Your Hands Where My Eyes Could See." The song was new. No one had heard it. Man, listen, we struck poses as curious as the animals in "When Doves Cry." Capri probably played "Put Your Hands" five times in a row. But in my memory? He brought it back over thirty times. "Gotta listen to how radio be playing us / Thirty time a day shit'll make you delirious / Damaging everything all up in your ear-ius." Ear-ius? This ninja said "ear-ius"? IT WAS TOO MUCH. We were blessed to be alive in that moment and to experience it together.

Back in those times, no one danced at industry parties. We were far too cool for that. But that evening? With the sun setting over the Hudson River? We screamed until we were hoarse. We shouted at Capri to "Bring it back!" That night a DJ changed my life. Busta Rhymes became a legend. We danced like that yacht was a studio called 54.

HUNTER HARRIS, ON DMX'S CAMEO IN *TOP FIVE*: Something about DMX always felt pleasantly enigmatic to me: I was too young to be a proper DMX fan, but I heard "Party Up (Up in Here)" on the radio all the time. I was five or six, but it was the funniest song I'd ever heard. I had no idea who this voice was or where it could've come from. And something about X's cameo in *Top Five* fit perfectly into whatever ideas I had about him: all of a sudden, this person—this *snarl*—just appears.

In the film, it's a micro-moment of surrealist cinema: the Chris Rock character, after relapsing, wakes up in jail to see that across the hallway is DMX. "What are you doing here?" he asks. DMX's reply is perfect; the rapper is delightfully incredulous: "*Really?* What am *I* doing here? I'm X, man—I live in this motherfucker!" For a moment, the men commiserate over being artists in industries that only want one thing from them. The Chris Rock character wants to trade his punch lines for serious dramas; DMX wants to sing, not rap. He belts out "Smile" and toward the end adds his own beat. It's such a perfect, absurdist moment. It's so special to me. After he died, I watched

Top Five again – basically none of that movie holds up. But that DMX scene: it's all heart, all humor.

VAN LATHAN, ON "NINJA RAP":[2] I'm sitting next to my father. He hates going to the movies. It's 1991. I'm eleven. For me, as a kid, the local cinema might as well have been Disneyland: a place you only go on special occasions but where lifelong memories are made every time. Anyway, we're watching *Teenage Mutant Ninja Turtles II: The Secret of the Ooze*. My mother had gone to see *Sleeping with the Enemy*, and my father wanted to see *Dances with Wolves*. But since I had to come, the turtles won.

I imagine the movie was unremarkable for him. He just kinda sat there as I got into it. Then something happened. Out of nowhere, the fearsome foursome ended up in a fight in a nightclub. One where the biggest hip-hop star in the world was performing. Make no mistake about it – in 1991 the biggest hip-hop star in the world was Vanilla Ice. I cringe now at how excited I was to see him. I LEAPT to my feet. (Fuck you. I was eleven and I regret nothing.) I remember something happening. My dad stood up. I was going so crazy he had to. "That white boy bad, ain't he?" He wasn't, it turns out. But it certainly seemed so at the time.

My dad was a certified old head. Cowboy hats and Johnnie Taylor on the radio. But he'd witnessed something. The turtles, whom I loved, hadn't gotten me to my feet. The music had. The energy of seeing hip-hop on the big screen, which I'd never seen before, had pulled me out of my seat. And it was contagious. My father had caught it, and it'd be about another four years before the world was fully infected. Robert Van Winkle's career wouldn't last, but he'd already served his purpose in my life. He'd shown my dad the energy. My dad had seen what hip-hop did to me – and still does, only now I have much, much better taste. Sometimes.

NADIRAH SIMMONS, ON THE WAY RAP, IN ITS BEST MOMENTS, CAN BRING YOU ALONG FOR THE RIDE: Anyone who knows me knows I live and breathe Roc-A-Fella Records. Its impact cannot be overstated, and not saying this out loud once a day is antithetical to my existence. So when Hov announced his 2015 B-Sides show and promised "special guests," I hoped some artists from the Roc's roster would be there.

What I hoped for came during the performance of "You, Me, Him and Her." Hov was joined onstage by Memphis Bleek, followed by Beanie Sigel, Young Chris, Neef Buck, and then Freeway a few seconds later for "What We Do." I had chills! The hair on the back of my neck stood up! Goose bumps covered my arms! My favorite rappers and idols were there onstage, together! The dopamine rush I got had me feeling like I was in the front row.

And that's what makes rap so beautiful to me. No matter who it is or where you are, the right rapper will make you feel like you're in the room with them. Feeling what they're feeling. Going through what they're going through. Enjoying what they're enjoying. And I get happy every time I feel like I'm in the room.

---

2. I've done a version of this chapter for each of the three (And Other Things) books. Each time, I start the chapter off with some personal anecdote about a thing, and then I turn that thing into a theme, and then I ask a handful of talented writers to write a memory connected to the theme. I've fielded a little over thirty entries this way. And this was the first time one of the people had the same angle on the theme that I did. It made me very happy to see. It's a testament to the overwhelming profoundness of a Vanilla Ice – soundtracked fight scene among mutant ninja animals in a twenty-one-and-up dance club.

HOW MANY TIMES DID LIL' KIM TELL THE FUTURE ON 1996'S *HARD CORE*?

THE SEATTLE SUPERSONICS EXISTED IN THE NBA FROM 1967 TO 2008. And they won a championship in 1979, yes, but it wasn't until the mid-'90s that they became truly special and truly important in a Pop-Culture Zeitgeist kind of way.

That version of the team was led by Gary Payton, a dynamo point guard with acid in his mouth and superglue on his hands, and Shawn Kemp, a deadly power forward with lightning in his feet and more lightning in his legs. And they fucking ruled. A lot.[1] They were cool and good and powerful. They won 357 games over a six-year stretch, and the way you know that was an incredible accomplishment is Michael Jordan and Scottie Pippen's Chicago Bulls, often considered one of the two or three best teams in the history of the NBA, were the only team in the league that won more games during that same period.[2]

Anyway, during the summer of 1996, the Sonics, who'd just come off of their most successful season in seventeen years,[3] signed an unheralded center named Jim McIlvaine to what was immediately recognized by everyone else as a goofily big contract (seven years, $33.6 million). And signings like that happen all the time, and it's usually not that big of a deal beyond a few headlines. But at that particular moment, Shawn Kemp had been wanting to restructure his contract so that his pay better reflected his status as one of the top players in the league. McIlvaine getting a big deal while Kemp was angling for one soured the relationship between Kemp and the Sonics. A year later, Kemp forced his way out of Seattle, and the Sonics never really mattered again.

And I mention all of that to say that right around the same time that Kemp and the Sonics were really beginning to fall apart, Lil' Kim released *Hard Core*, her brilliant debut album (this was November of 1996, just a few weeks after Kemp sat out the first five exhibition games of the 1996–1997 season). And she had a song on it called "M.A.F.I.A. Land" that contained the following line: "Damn / How could a deal for a couple mil / Result to such violence / And throw our whole shit off balance?" Now, obviously that line isn't actually in reference to the McIlvaine/Kemp situation, but my friends and I (because we were idiots) swore that it was when we heard it for the first time. The two things we cared about the most in that moment were rap and basketball, and it blew all of our fucking dumb little minds that Lil' Kim took a moment during a song about mafioso lifestyles to comment on the impending dissolution of one of the most exciting teams in the NBA. When Kemp eventually got traded to the Cleveland Cavaliers in September of 1997, it felt to us like Lil' Kim, in the midst of changing rap forever with *Hard Core*, had also somehow predicted that Shawn Kemp, a franchise cornerstone in Seattle, was going to get traded just fifteen months after taking the Sonics to the Finals.

And that's what this chapter is about. Sort of.

This chapter is about all of the other predictions that Lil' Kim made on *Hard Core*. Because there are a bunch. Really, though, this chapter is secretly supposed to be about how forward thinking and innovative Lil' Kim

---

1. This movie came out in 1994 called *Mi Vida Loca*. It was about these two Mexican teenage girls who were growing up in Echo Park. And the soundtrack had a song on it called "Run, Catch & Kill" by a rapper named Boss. In the video for it, a girl wears a Sonics jersey. It was a lot of my own personal boxes checked off at once.
2. They won 362 games.
3. They won sixty-four games and made it to the NBA Finals, eventually losing to the above-mentioned Bulls in six games.

was, and how rap was never the same after she arrived. Because she changed it a bunch.

FIVE THINGS ABOUT LIL' KIM

Number One: The first time it felt like everyone was talking about Lil' Kim all at once was after her verse on Junior M.A.F.I.A.'s "Get Money" in 1995. She showed up and started doing her Lil' Kim thing where she snaps off some words and elongates others,[4] and it was just like, "Wait. Whoa. Who the fuck is this? This is something special." Everybody knew immediately that she was headed toward a career as a solo artist.

Number Two: Lil' Kim released *Hard Core* in November of 1996. And it took all of two minutes to know that you were listening to something that would forever alter the rap landscape. The album opens with a man exiting a taxi. He's at a movie theater. You hear him ask for a ticket ("Can I have one for Lil' Kim, *Hard Core*?"), and then you hear him go inside. Softly in the background, you hear the woman who's just sold him the ticket say, "Fuckin' weirdo." Then you hear the man go to the concession stand and ask for "a small order of popcorn and a large order of butter and just, like, a lot of napkins." You hear the man walk into the theater. And then you hear moaning in the background. And that's when you realize he's at an X-rated theater. After a couple seconds, you hear him unzip his pants and begin masturbating (presumably using the popcorn butter he's just ordered), and then shortly after that you hear him climax while hollering Lil' Kim's name. And there are a lot of pieces wrapped up into opening an album like that, but critic Fullamusu Bangura summarized it all best in 2020 when she said, "Kim doesn't have to declare her power because the man is her proxy, hyping her up and demonstrating the lengths men will go to just for a sliver of access to her."

Number Three: *Hard Core* debuted at eleventh on the *Billboard* 200 chart. It was the highest-debuting rap album by a woman at the time. Its first two singles, "No Time" and "Crush on You," topped the *Billboard* Hot Rap Songs chart, making Lil' Kim the first female rapper to have two consecutive number one singles on the chart. *Hard Core* was eventually certified triple platinum and sold over five million copies worldwide.

Number Four: Nobody has ever been better at rapping raunchy lyrics than Lil' Kim. She's just always been able to access a different level than, say, Eazy-E or Too Short or Akinyele or 2 Live Crew or whoever, because she's a sharper rapper than everyone else who does it. And it becomes really obvious when you listen to her do other stuff on songs. (Her verse on Mobb Deep's "Quiet Storm" is a perfect example.) It's an underdiscussed part of her legacy.

Number Five: Lil' Kim, as a rap entity, was very much a new concept. Prior to her, female rappers challenged sexism in hip-hop by confronting it. Lil' Kim challenged sexism in hip-hop by exploiting it. It was a wildly important moment. It expanded rap. Writing for Revolt, KC Orcutt explained it as such: "While artists who came before her time, such as Roxanne Shanté, MC Lyte and Queen Latifah, are unequivocally heralded as pioneers for women in hip hop in their own right, Lil' Kim embraced her sexuality and femininity in a way that was a stark contrast at the time from other women artists who—for an array of reasons—leaned more

---

4. "You wanna be my main squeeeeeze, baby / Don't ya? / You wanna get between my kneeeeees, baby."

into a neutral or toned-down space when it came to such taboo topics. The relationship between gender and hip hop calls for a much more nuanced conversation, and as the subject of sexuality experiences a continued call for de-stigmatization and revolution, the work Lil' Kim put in must be considered and celebrated."

VARIOUS PREDICTIONS LIL' KIM MADE ON *HARD CORE*, SIX OF WHICH HAVE SOMETHING TO DO WITH A MOVIE OR A TV SHOW

The Line: "I used to be scared of the dick"
The Song: "Big Momma Thang"

Here's the thing: This lyric is a trick. People hear it and they assume it's "dick" with a lowercase *d*, as in a penis. But the truth is it's actually "Dick" with a capital *D*, as in the name Dick, as in the shortened version of the name Richard, similar to how Richard can become Rick or Ricky, which gets us to our prediction, which is about the movie *Rush Hour 2*, which was released in 2001.

Rush Hour 2's main villain is named Ricky Tan, an ex-cop turned ruthless businessman. He is a scheming, conniving, murdering madman. *Everyone* is afraid of him. Everyone. Even Jackie Chan's character, Yan Naing Lee, a veteran detective inspector in the Hong Kong Police Force and also a brilliant hand-to-hand combatant. And so "I used to be scared of the Dick" makes sense. But you'll notice in that line the use of the phrase "used to." That's because Agent Lee karate kicks Ricky Tan out of a window of an upper-level casino hotel room, sending him crashing to his death. That means Lil' Kim predicted (a) that there would be a movie called *Rush Hour* that would come out in 1998, (b) that it would do well enough in the theaters to spawn a sequel, (c) that the sequel would feature a villain named some derivation of the name Richard, (d) that the villain would be scary, and (e) that he would die, thus inspiring no more fear.

The Line: "I got land in Switzerland"
The Song: "Big Momma Thang"

Do you remember the massive housing-market crash that happened in America in 2007? A version of that same thing happened in Switzerland in the early '90s. There was this real-estate gold rush in the '80s, and then everything fell apart in the '90s. Dirk Drechsel and Anne Kathrin Funk recounted the events in an academic paper in 2017 titled "Time-Varying and Regional Dynamics in Swiss Housing Markets."

It took about ten years for Swiss housing prices to recover, but when they did, they experienced fifteen years straight of an increase in value. If Lil' Kim bought land in Switzerland around the release of this album, that means she got it when it was very cheap. And if she held it through the first decade of the 2000s, that means she made a lot of money. Lil' Kim predicted the resurgence of the Swiss housing market.

The Line: "One chick named Nick thought she was the shit"
The Song: "M.A.F.I.A. Land"

Most of these other predictions are silly, but this one is neat in a very practical way: Lil' Kim and Nicki Minaj

UNO

engaged in a years-long feud with each other over various slights and disrespects. Lil' Kim predicted it was gonna happen.

> **The Line:** "Never before have you seen such magnificence in the Black princess"
> **The Song:** "Drugs"

Lil' Kim predicted that Meghan Markle, who is biracial (her mother is Black and her father is white), would marry into the British royal family over two full decades before it happened.

> **The Line:** "You wanna steal the pussy like a thief"
> **The Song:** "We Don't Need It"

In 2016, a statue of a deceased internet-famous cat in Istanbul was stolen. Following a public online outcry, the statue was returned. Lil' Kim predicted that it was going to happen.

> **The Line:** "Chillin' in a Benz with my amigos"
> **The Song:** "No Time"

"Amigos" is how you say "friends" in Spanish. And there was an episode of the sitcom *Friends* in 2001 where you could see a Mercedes poster hanging up in Joey's room. So Lil' Kim predicted that Mercedes would score a product placement during an episode of a gigantic sitcom late in its run. Additionally, Matt LeBlanc, who played Joey on the show, appeared on *Conan* one time in 2012 and told a story about how his mom didn't approve of him quitting his carpentry job to move to New York and pursue acting when he was younger. Conan asked LeBlanc what she says now, given all of LeBlanc's success, to which LeBlanc replied that his mom now says, "Thanks for the Mercedes." So Lil' Kim also predicted that Matt LeBlanc would buy his mother a Mercedes using money he had from *Friends*.[5]

> **The Line:** "Hasta la vista / Bye-bye / Kiss your kids / It's the gangstresses"
> **The Song:** "Spend a Little Doe"

The "Hasta la vista" part here is a hat tip to Arnold Schwarzenegger's famous line from *Terminator 2: Judgment Day*. And the term "gangstress" means "a female gangster," which means that "gangstresses" means "multiple female gangsters." And that's important to know here because in October of 2019, the sixth film in the *Terminator* franchise, *Terminator: Dark Fate*, was released. The movie ends with three women – a cybernetically enhanced soldier named Grace (played by Mackenzie Davis), a haunted ex-mother who hunts terminators (Sarah Connor, played by Linda Hamilton), and the eventual savior of humankind (Dani Ramos, played by Natalia Reyes) – teaming up with Arnold Schwarzenegger's T-800 from *Judgment Day* to defeat the Rev-9, the most powerful terminator ever. So Lil' Kim predicted the ending of *Terminator: Dark Fate.*

---

5. Another prediction: The rap group Migos have a song called "WOA" where they talk about being in a Benz. Lil' Kim also predicted that.

Additionally, the part in the lyric where she says "Bye-bye / Kiss your kids" also offered a prediction for *Terminator: Dark Fate*. Because look: John Connor very famously survived the T-1000's assassination attempt in *Judgment Day*. And *Dark Fate*, which is a direct sequel to *Judgment Day*, opens with the childhood version of John Connor getting murdered.

So Lil' Kim predicted not only the way *Terminator: Dark Fate* would end but also the way it would begin.

The Line: "When in need, I lied for ya"
The Song: "Spend a Little Doe"

In 2005, Lil' Kim was sentenced to one year in prison for lying to a federal grand jury as part of an attempt to protect two associates who were involved in a gun shootout in 2001. Lil' Kim predicted it would happen.

The Line: "Blow you up to your girl like the army grenade"
The Song: "Crush on You" (Remix)

Three things here:

1. Lil' Kim doesn't have a verse on the original version of "Crush on You," which, incidentally, is the version on *Hard Core*. She didn't pop up on the song until a remixed version was released as a single seven months later. So she wasn't on this track for her album, but she was on the version that came out afterward. That's not a prediction; it's just something that's always been an interesting little tidbit to me.
2. 1996 was an incredible year for rap.[6] We got a big album from 2Pac (*All Eyez on Me*), we got a big album from UGK (*Ridin' Dirty*), we got a big album from Outkast (*ATLiens*), we got introduced to the Fugees via *The Score*, we got introduced to Jay-Z via *Reasonable Doubt*, we first heard Busta Rhymes as a solo artist via *The Coming*, and we met Lil' Kim via *Hard Core*. I gotta tell you, fifteen-year-old Shea was having an incredible time.
3. The prediction here: There's a scene in *Captain America: The First Avenger* where, as a way to prove a point about the toughness of one of the soldiers training to potentially become Captain America, Tommy Lee Jones throws a live grenade into the group of soldiers. They all scatter, save for Steve Rogers, who instinctively jumps on the grenade, offering to sacrifice himself to save the others. As he lies there waiting to die, Peggy Carter, a commanding officer and also his later-to-be-revealed love interest, runs over. "Get away," he yells at her, wanting to save her. "Get back!" Lil' Kim predicted this scene.

The Line: "Bloody bodies in the telly lobbies"
The Song: "Spend a Little Doe"

There's a scene in the sci-fi action masterpiece *The Matrix* where, as part of an attempt to rescue someone, two characters (Neo and Trinity) walk into the lobby of a building with one thousand guns. The security guards see the

6. It's either the third or the fourth best year ever, tangling with 1993 for that last podium spot, looking up only at 1994 and 1988.

guns and are like, "What the fuck?" Then Neo and Trinity shoot everyone there one billion times. Lil' Kim predicted one of the best scenes in the best action movie of 1999.

The Line: "And itchy-gitchy-yaya with the marmalade"
The Song: "Crush on You"

The line here is a play on a similar line from Labelle's 1974 song "Lady Marmalade." Lil' Kim was on the 2001 remix that was part of the *Moulin Rouge!* soundtrack. It was a massive hit. It was number one on the *Billboard* Hot 100 for five straight weeks, and, just for fun, it also secured Lil' Kim her first and only ever Grammy win. Lil' Kim predicted it was gonna happen.

The Line: "Bitches be lyin' about the clothes they be buyin'"
The Song: "Drugs"

For a couple of months in 1994, the most impressive pieces of clothing that you could own on the south side of San Antonio were (a) a pair of Girbaud jeans, (b) a Girbaud shirt, and (c) a Girbaud hoodie. Wearing one of those things was equal to walking into a room and throwing a stack of hundred-dollar bills into the air. Which was why I was so fucking out-of-my-mind excited when my mother returned home from a trip to the flea market with an extremely fake pair of knockoff Girbaud jeans and an extremely fake Girbaud hoodie.

It didn't matter to me that they were fake, and it didn't matter to me that they really weren't even the right size. All that mattered to me was that I was gonna walk into school that next day with the word "Girbaud" written across my chest and my crotch.[7] And that was why what actually ended up happening was so crushing.

What happened was I walked into school very much like how I imagine the Rock walks into any situation or location. I thought I was bulletproof. I was ready to be inundated with compliments and praise and teachers trying to make out with me. What happened instead, though, was a kid immediately recognized that the hoodie was from the flea market and started shouting to everyone about it. And listen: There's a Poor-Kid Code that almost everybody abides by when you're in high school. If you see someone who has on a knockoff item—be it a shirt, or shoes, or a hat, or anything—what you're supposed to do is just shut up. You don't say a word. You let that lie live uninterrupted. Because, at some point in the future, you're gonna be the kid with the knockoff thing, and you're gonna need to cash in that good karma for silence.

But this kid didn't abide by the Poor-Kid Code because this kid was an all-caps DICK. So, again: He started shouting to everyone about my flea market Girbaud hoodie as soon as he saw. And I lost my mind. I was in that hallway barely weighing 120 pounds talking about, "I'll fucking kill you if you don't shut up! I'll put you in the fucking dirt! This hoodie is from the mall!"

In that moment, I was, as Lil' Kim predicted, a bitch lying about the clothes I was buying.

7. The signature identifying mark of Girbaud jeans at the time was this little white stripe across the fly that had "Girbaud" written on it.

WHO GETS THE PHONE CALL?

(1977–1987)

DURING THE SONG "D.O.A. (Death of Auto-Tune)," which Jay-Z put out in the summer of 2009 as the first single for *The Blueprint 3*, Jay-Z says the following line: "I might send this to the mixtape Weezy."

He was referencing the fucking bananas run that Lil Wayne went on from late 2005 through 2008. Within that stretch, Wayne released four mixtapes (*The Dedication*, *Dedication 2*, *Da Drought 3*, and *Dedication 3*), three albums (*Tha Carter II*,[1] *Like Father, Like Son*,[2] and *Tha Carter III*[3]), and an almost uncountable number of guest features. By the time *Tha Carter III* arrived (June 2008), he'd not only become the most popular rapper on the planet but also put together a strong enough stretch that he had a legitimate claim to the Best Rapper Alive title. It was a wild, wild run.

Jay-Z mentioning it in the manner that he does is his way of acknowledging Wayne's unquestionable greatness during that period. He's basically saying, "Lil Wayne was so tough during that period that I would like to send this song backward in time so that that version of Lil Wayne could give me a guest verse." And, in a manner of speaking, that's what these next few chapters are about.

Here's what we're doing: Let's pretend that Jay-Z, because he is so rich and so powerful, actually does have the ability to reach back through time and grab a guest verse from anyone he might want to at any particular moment in the past or in the future. Let's pretend that he has, say, some sort of magic telephone that he can pick up, dial a number into, and then get ahold of, say, 2007 Lil Wayne or 1987 Rakim or 2017 Kendrick Lamar. Let's pretend that, if he really wanted to, he actually could get a guest verse from the mixtape-era version of Lil Wayne. Who else might he call? Who else might he want to get ahold of if he was hoping to get the best verse from the best rapper at a specific moment in time?

That's what we're doing.

CLARIFICATION, BY WAY OF THREE QUESTIONS

1. What's the objective?

The goal here is to put together a full list of whom Jay-Z might use his magic phone to reach out to at any given time in history. For example, let's say he wanted a verse from someone in 1979. And he's looking for the best one possible. Who would he call? Would he call Melle Mel? Grandmaster Flash? Kurtis Blow? Who gets that call? Or what about if he wanted someone from 1985? Or 1996? 2001? 2009? 2020? That's the answer we're after here.

2. How many different calls can we make in a given year? Can we dial up as many people as we want?

Let's set a cap on it. Let's say that you can't call more than two rappers in a single year. That'll be fun because it'll force some difficult decisions to be made when you end up in a year when a lot of people were putting out really top-level stuff. Because what do you do when you get to a year like 1994? We got incredibly great albums from Biggie, Nas, Da Brat, Scarface, Method Man,

1. Certified 2× platinum by the Recording Industry Association of America (RIAA).
2. A duo album he did with Birdman. It was certified gold by the RIAA.
3. Certified 6× (!!!) platinum.

Outkast, and a handful more. And you can only grab two of them. We're leaving a lot of talent on the shelf there.

And the opposite of that: Let's also say that, as a way to safeguard against holding on to the same artist for too long, you *have* to change picks regularly – at least once every eighteen months. Otherwise, you could get to, say, 2011 and be like, "I'm just gonna call Drake every year for a guest verse from here on out. He's got me covered."

3. What about picking the same person more than once? Is that okay? Can you call someone in 1996 and then call them again a few years later if they got hot again?

Sure. That's fine.

Let's get started.

.....

Time Period: Sometime in late 1977 to sometime in 1979
Who Gets the Call? Melle Mel
Who Do You Call If Melle Mel Doesn't Answer? DJ Kool Herc, Grandmaster Caz

In these earliest years, there's really no bad pick to make. Everyone who could be chosen is, in one way or another, one of the architects of rap, which is a pretty good thing to be as far as legacies are concerned. To wit: Melle Mel was, by most accounts, the first rapper to refer to himself as an MC. He was also the key figure in Grandmaster Flash and the Furious Five, which would go on to become the first rap group to be inducted into the Rock & Roll Hall of Fame. He was also one of the writers on "The Message," a profoundly important song in the history of the genre. So let's begin with him. Let's start off with Melle Mel, just like so many parts of rap seemed to. He gets the first phone call.

Time Period: Sometime late in 1979 to sometime early in 1981
Who Gets the Call? Grandmaster Caz
Who Do You Call If Grandmaster Caz Doesn't Answer? Kurtis Blow, Grandmaster Flash

Caz, same as Melle Mel, has a bunch of those The First to Do This Thing credits on his résumé, maybe the biggest of which being that he was the first person to have his lyrics stolen on a large scale.[4] But I'm giving him the nod here for a completely different reason.

In 2012, there was a documentary that came out called *Something from Nothing: The Art of Rap*. In it, Ice-T interviewed a whole bunch of rappers, talking to them mainly about what goes into creating a song and writing a song. As a way to punctuate certain segments in the doc, various rappers would perform an a cappella version of something they'd written directly into the camera. Q-Tip did one. Melle Mel did one. Mos Def did one. Eminem did one. MC Lyte did one. Kanye West did one. Snoop did one. There were a bunch. And after, say, the second or third one happened, everyone in the theater seemed to

4. Big Bank Hank, one of the rappers from the Sugarhill Gang, used Caz's lyrics on "Rapper's Delight."

realize that it was going to be a storytelling device that *Something from Nothing* was going to use regularly. It became something that I looked forward to and something that most of the rest of the audience seemed to look forward to as well.

And somewhere in that mix of rappers who were doing the a cappella performances – somewhere between the Grammys that had been won and the mansions that had been built off big rap money – was Grandmaster Caz. He was wearing a dark brown hat and a dark brown hoodie and standing in what appeared to be a makeshift studio in a room with low ceilings and bad curtains and a smoke detector that needed a new battery. He didn't float across the screen the way that Snoop did or have a curious gravity the way that Q-Tip did. He didn't, by most measures, stand out in any way, really. But then he started rapping. And that shit was like . . . *I don't even know*. Remember those old cartoons where someone would swallow an explosive and it would go off inside of them? It was like that.

Every line he said felt bigger and bigger and more powerful than the last. You could see on his face as he was going that he knew he was in a groove and that he knew he was doing well and that he knew that anybody who watched the doc was going to remember his part above all other parts. It was incredible. He just built and Built and BUILT and **BUILT** on the momentum – unstoppable and uncontainable and un-everything-able. You could feel the energy in the theater rising as the audience got swept up in the moment.

After Caz delivered his final line, which he did with that kind of extra oomph that a gymnast gives when they stick a landing, and to which the directors added that first big thump from Afrika Bambaataa's "Planet Rock," everybody watching just went fucking crazy. People were clapping and yelling and whistling in their seats. It was incredible. It's one of the ten best moments I've ever had in a movie theater. It was so much fun to experience at the time, and it's so much fun to remember in my head all these years later. I've had a real big soft spot in my heart for Grandmaster Caz ever since then. I'd have loved to have seen him in the late '70s and early '80s, when he was at his most powerful. He gets the call here.

Time Period: From sometime early in 1981 to sometime late in 1982
Who Gets the Call? Kool Moe Dee
Who Do You Call If Kool Moe Dee Doesn't Answer? Kurtis Blow, Afrika Bambaataa, Spoonie Gee

One of my very favorite stories in rap is the one about how Kool Moe Dee helped turn battle rapping into a proper thing. The short version of the story is Kool Moe Dee was attending the Harlem World's Christmas Rappers Convention.[5] While there, he watched a rapper named Busy Bee Starski perform. During his performance, Busy Bee, who was widely regarded as one of the best in rap at interacting with the crowd, claimed himself to be superior to most other rappers.

Now, somewhere right around here, the different retellings of the story are split a little bit. Some say that Busy Bee called out Kool Moe Dee by name during his performance. Others say that Busy Bee was speaking in

5. Kurtis Blow was the first commercially successful rapper. One of his earliest songs was called "Christmas Rappin'." Early rappers fucking loved Christmas.

generalities but that someone in the audience pointed out Kool Moe Dee and said that Busy Bee couldn't beat him, a claim that Busy Bee shrugged off, which was enough of a slight to force Kool Moe Dee into action. Either way, everyone agrees on what happened next: annihilation.

Prior to that moment, any sort of combat rap between two people or two groups had mostly been characterized by each side taking turns trying to get the crowd as excited and hype as possible. Kool Moe Dee decided to go a different way.

He didn't bother engaging with the crowd at all. Instead, he took out an ax and swung it at Busy Bee's neck. He immediately started talking shit about him, making fun of the way that he rapped, saying he copied other people, laughing at the very thought of his general existence. It was ruinous. Poor Busy Bee, he never stood a chance. He was playing a whole different game. It was like one of those early MMA fights where a former boxer would sign up for a UFC match, get into the octagon, take a couple kicks to the legs and head, and then immediately realize he'd made a horrible mistake. Busy Bee wasn't ready for the level of violence that Kool Moe Dee was operating at. In truth, it wasn't even something he'd ever even considered, because it wasn't anything that anyone had ever considered. Kool Moe Dee invented it.

Time Period: Sometime late in 1982 to the summer of 1983
Who Gets the Call? Kurtis Blow
Who Do You Call If Kurtis Blow Doesn't Answer? Nobody. I wanted to slide Kurtis Blow in here somewhere because I kept having to step over him to make other picks earlier. I'm just gonna keep calling him until he answers.

Kurtis Blow's best and most important song ("The Breaks") came out in 1980. The thing of it was, though, for as much as I like Kurtis Blow, I couldn't talk myself into picking him over Kool Moe Dee for that stretch of time. Kool Moe Dee was just too...Pardon me here, but he was just too kool. Kurtis Blow's second best and second most important song, however, which was called "Basketball," came out sometime in 1984. So here we are. Grabbing Kurtis right before he gets around to writing that one. It's a good investment, like buying a house in a neighborhood right before the property value skyrockets.

Time Period: The summer of 1983 to the start of 1985
Who Gets the Call? All three guys from Run-DMC (Run, DMC, and Jam Master Jay)
Who Do You Call If Run-DMC Doesn't Answer? Schoolly D, the Fat Boys

Let's make this a rule right now since this is the first time we're getting to a spot where we've had to deal with this: as far as groups are concerned, the rule is we can grab a group in its entirety if we want it. It's just easier that way. And in this case, Run-DMC was such a massive and undeniable force during this period that it feels immoral to separate any single part of them. Here's their résumé just during that stretch:

In March of 1984, they released *Run-D.M.C.*, a wildly influential album that pushed rap in a more assertive, more aggressive, more combative direction. (In 1989, *Spin* listed it as the eleventh greatest album of all time. In 1998, the *Source* not only selected it as one of the hundred best rap albums ever but also retroactively gave it a five-mic rating, which was the magazine's highest rating possible. In 2006, the *Observer* picked it as one of the fifty albums that changed music. In 2014, *NME* picked it for its 101 Albums to Hear Before You Die list.) In February of 1985, Run-DMC released *King of Rock*, which was their first platinum album. And then in October of 1985, they starred in the movie *Krush Groove* as themselves.[6] They were fucking running shit then.

As I mentioned in that Melle Mel blurb at the start of this: these first few years of rap, the picks were pretty easy to make. There were only a handful of viable people to choose from, really. (As a matter of setting the context, let me tell you that there were less than ten official rap albums released between 1980 and 1982.) From here going forward, though, things get a lot less easy.

Time Period: August of 1985 to sometime in 1986
Who Gets the Call? Slick Rick
Who Do You Call If Slick Rick Doesn't Answer? LL COOL J[7]

Here's where we get the first Really for Real Actually Difficult decision that has to be made. It's a proper toss-up. Because over here on one side, you have LL COOL J. He puts out his debut album,[8] absolutely sizzles during a seventy-second cameo appearance in *Krush Groove*, and becomes the flagship artist for Def Jam, which would go on to become an iconic record label. He's a behemoth.

HOWEVER, on the other side, you have Slick Rick. He puts out less material that year (his biggest contribution was being on "The Show" and "La Di Da Di" with Doug E. Fresh as part of the Get Fresh Crew), but he does something else that (I'd argue) is bigger and more undeniable and more fun to be a part of: he rolls up all of his wit and all of his charisma and all of his molten confidence and all of his crushed-velvet smoothness and, really all by himself, invents a whole new kind of cool in rap.[9]

Prior to Slick Rick's arrival, people were cool the way that LL COOL J was cool, which is to say they were cool in ways that felt intentional and loud and overt.[10] Slick Rick was the opposite of that. Slick Rick was cool in a way that was impossible to explain, because Slick Rick was cool in a way that nobody had seen yet in rap. You couldn't just describe him to someone like, "Oh, um, well, he wears an eye patch and he likes bracelets and also he kind of has an accent." That doesn't sound cool. That sounds like a pirate. But then you saw Slick Rick and you heard Slick Rick, and it was like, "Oh shit. Hold on a second. Should I start wearing an eye patch, too????"[11]

6. *Krush Groove* was, in effect, a retelling of the origin story of Def Jam Recordings, the iconic record label founded by Rick Rubin and Russell Simmons, who is Run from Run-DMC's older brother.

7. LL COOL J and Slick Rick have the same birthday. That was something I found out while I was researching for this book, and I wanted to mention it to you.

8. *Radio*, which included "I Can't Live Without My Radio" and "Rock the Bells," two extremely excellent songs.

9. And this is to say nothing of how he pretty much invented telling stories in rap songs.

10. LL COOL J's name literally has an all-caps "COOL" in it.

11. In 2012, Questlove wrote one of my very favorite things about Slick Rick. It was part of a list that he put together for *Rolling Stone* of what he felt were the fifty greatest hip-hop songs of all time. (He had "The Show" / "La Di Da Di" in the number nine spot.) He wrote that "Slick Rick's voice was the most beautiful thing to happen in hip-hop culture" and that Rick was "the blueprint" and that "no one bragged like him, no one name-dropped like him, no one sang like him, no one was funny like him."

Time Period: Sometime in 1986 to July 19, 1987
Who Gets the Call? Ice-T
Who Do You Call If Ice-T Doesn't Answer? KRS-One, Rakim, Run-DMC, anyone from 2 Live Crew

Three things here:

1. Schoolly D hinted at what would eventually become gangsta rap on 1985's "P.S.K. What Does It Mean?," but it was Ice-T who created it in 1986 with "6 in the Mornin'," a seven-minute-long song that hits all the cornerstone pieces of the subgenre.
2. I tipped my hand a little bit here with the Grandmaster Caz entry, which mentioned the documentary that Ice-T made. Ice-T is one of my longtime favorite people in pop culture. Separate even from music, he's also been in several movies that I care a great deal about, including but not limited to *Breakin'*, *Breakin' 2: Electric Boogaloo*, *New Jack City* (where he gives the unforgettable "I wanna shoot you so bad my dick's hard" line to the villain at the end), *Surviving the Game* (which taught me two important life lessons, the first of which being that if you find a gun, you should always check the barrel to make sure it's clean before trying to shoot it, and the second of which being that if a bunch of white guys invite you to a remote hangout in the wilderness, it means they probably want to hunt you), and *Mean Guns* (which has an all-time great Okay I'm Definitely Gonna Watch This Movie plot).[12]
3. I'm not certain I all the way believe this idea just yet, but since we were just talking about it: it feels like maybe there's a connection to be made here about how Ice-T was cool in a way that combined the way LL COOL J was cool and the way that Slick Rick was cool.

12. One hundred criminals who are associated with a crime syndicate are gathered in an empty prison. Ice-T, speaking from the second floor down to everyone on the first floor, tells them that they've all betrayed the syndicate in one way or another. Then he tells them that they were going to be killed and buried like normal but that he talked the bosses into something way more fun. He says that everyone is going to fight to the death over a six-hour period until there are only three people left and that those three people are going to split a prize of $10 million. Then his goons dump a bunch of containers of guns and bullets and metal bats down into the crowd.

WHO GETS THE PHONE CALL?

(1987–1996)

. . . cont'd

> **Time Period:** July 20, 1987, to June 27, 1988
> **Who Gets the Call?** Too Short
> **Who Do You Call If Too Short Doesn't Answer?** Rakim, Salt-n-Pepa, KRS-One, Flavor Flav

In 1987, Rakim rapped the following: "I take seven MCs, put 'em in a line / And add seven more brothers who think they can rhyme / Well, it'll take seven more before I go for mine / Now that's twenty-one MCs ate up at the same time." He said it on a song called "My Melody," which was on an album called *Paid in Full*. That same year, way on the other side of the country, Too Short rapped this: "So motherfuck you, bitch, goddamn ass ho." He said it on a song called "Dope Fiend Beat," which was on an album called *Born to Mack*. Both of those albums, in their own very specific ways, changed rap forever.

(A quick sidebar: The standout song from *Born to Mack* is "Freaky Tales." In it, Too Short quickly details forty or so different women that he slept with.[1] He explained in an interview in 2012 with *Complex* that the song originally started out as a jokey kind of thing from high school where he rapped "I got sixteen hoes sucking ten toes." And I'm very curious about the toe distribution in an arrangement like that. Like, does each person suck 62.5 percent of a toe? Or is it that some of the people get full toes and other people have to share toes? And if that's the case, then is it that the people with full toes to suck look down on the people with just pieces of toes to suck? And is it a one-person-at-a-time thing or are they all gathered around at once like when puppies get milk from their mom? There are a lot of questions here that I'd like answered.)

> **Time Period:** June 28, 1988, to November 6, 1989
> **Who Gets the Call?** Chuck D
> **Who Do You Call If Chuck D Doesn't Answer?** Anyone from N.W.A. (but especially Eazy-E), Sir Mix-A-Lot, Scarface, Kool G Rap

I can't remember exactly who it was who said it (it might've been Bomani Jones, or possibly Sean Fennessey), but one time on the internet someone said that Chuck D had the single most impossible-to-replicate voice in all of rap. I think about that a lot, particularly whenever I'm revisiting 1988's brilliant *It Takes a Nation of Millions to Hold Us Back*, wherein Chuck D raps with an unstoppable, seemingly uncontainable energy. You know how in the *Avengers* movies only the most powerful entities could directly hold the Infinity Stones without being incinerated?[2] Chuck D's rap voice is like that. It's too powerful for anyone else. He's the only one who could've ever had it, which is why he's the only one who's ever had it.

> **Time Period:** November 7, 1989, to September 3, 1990
> **Who Gets the Call?** Queen Latifah
> **Who Do You Call If Queen Latifah Doesn't Answer?** The D.O.C., Ice Cube

1. One of the people he mentions is someone named Betty-Jo, whom he describes as "a dick sucker." Six years later, he put out a song called "Blowjob Betty," which I think implies that there's an entire Freaky Tales Extended Universe.
2. Or something.

A thing I find very compelling about Queen Latifah is that, despite arriving to rap as a fully formed emcee, she displayed an interest in career diversification almost immediately. To wit: Her debut album, *All Hail the Queen*, came out in November of 1989. And it was very good. It was one of those albums where you turned it on and two songs in you said something like, "Okay, this person is already playing at the top level." But rapping wasn't enough for her. She was so full of energy and so full of talent and so full of ambition that she needed more places to put it. A permanent place in Hollywood was inevitable.

Less than seventeen months later, she'd appeared in her first TV show (she guest starred as a successful and confident movie star on a season-one episode of *The Fresh Prince of Bel-Air*)[3] and also her first movie (she had a bit role as a waitress in *Jungle Fever*). And what's more, she was fucking great in them. She had an obvious aura about her. By 1993, she was one of the leads on a highly rated and influential sitcom that ran for five seasons (*Living Single*). By 1996, she'd earned a starring role in a major motion picture (*Set It Off*) and turned in an all-time great performance. By 1999, she was hosting her own talk show. And by 2002, she'd been nominated for an Academy Award for Best Supporting Actress.[4]

A handful of years ago, *Billboard* put together a list of thirty-one women who changed rap. MC Lyte did the section about Queen Latifah. In it, she wrote the following: "My sister, the Queen, has single-handedly changed the way every female MC looks at their business and, perhaps more importantly, has no doubt changed the way the world views female MCs and their business potential." It's a very true sentiment. And that all started here. In November of 1989.

Time Period: September 4, 1990, to October 7, 1991
Who Gets the Call? Vanilla Ice
Who Do You Call If Vanilla Ice Doesn't Answer? Either Salt or Pepa from Salt-n-Pepa, MC Hammer, Chuck D, Ice Cube, Kid Frost

The *New York Times* ran an article about Vanilla Ice in February of 1991 that began with this sentence: "Everyone seems to hate Vanilla Ice—except the seven million or so fans who ignited his rocket ride to the top of the pop charts." It's a perfect summation of Vanilla Ice's pop-culture existence in the early '90s. He was a person whom a lot of people disliked a great deal[5] and was also wildly successful during a brief but frenzied stretch.

Here's what Vanilla Ice did from September of 1990 to October of 1991: First, he released his debut album, *To the Extreme*. It became the fastest-selling rap album[6] that had ever been made,[7] and the lead single from it, "Ice

3. In hindsight, this seems less like a coincidence and more like a sign. (Also: she returned in season two playing a completely different person, that time a love interest of Will.)

4. *Chicago*, which won the Best Picture award that year.

5. He was often referred to as the "Elvis of rap," a nickname that touched on how he showed up doing something that Black people had been doing for years, and because he was white, it was instantly seen as more accessible and consumer friendly.

6. It eventually sold more than 7 million copies in America and more than 15 million copies worldwide. For context, Jay-Z's best-selling album, *Vol. 2 . . . Hard Knock Life*, sold 5.4 million copies in America.

7. Regarding actual quality, *To the Extreme* wasn't even one of the twenty-five best rap albums of the year.

Ice Baby," became the first rap song to reach number one on the pop singles chart.[8] Then he entered into an eight-month-long relationship with Madonna, who was then one of the biggest stars on the planet. Then he cameoed as himself in 1991's *Teenage Mutant Ninja Turtles II: The Secret of the Ooze*, a movie that still fucking rules. Then he starred in *Cool as Ice*, a movie that was exactly as good as the title implies. All of that in eleven months. And then nothing ever again ever.

Time Period: October 8, 1991, to December 14, 1992
Who Gets the Call? Scarface
Who Do You Call If Scarface Doesn't Answer? Nas, Treach, Q-Tip, anyone from De La Soul, Redman

Two things here:

1. I almost went with Nas for this pick because of his verse on Main Source's "Live at the Barbeque," which was like the audio version of seeing a shark's dorsal fin before you feel the actual teeth of the shark. But Scarface, who'd already begun stepping toward excellence as the foundational member of the Geto Boys in the '80s, put out *Mr. Scarface Is Back* just a couple months later, and so in this particular case it's Really Great Album > Really Great Verse. Scarface wins.
2. Going from Queen Latifah to Vanilla Ice to Scarface is a real bit of whiplash. It's like going from *Mission: Impossible* (thumbs way up) to *Mission: Impossible 2* (oh no) to *Mission: Impossible 3* (thumbs way up again).

Time Period: December 15, 1992, to November 8, 1993
Who Gets the Call? Dr. Dre
Who Do You Call If Dr. Dre Doesn't Answer? Either of the Chrises from Kris Kross, any of the Beastie Boys, Pimp C or Bun B from UGK

There are six things that I immediately think about anytime I hear "Nuthin' but a 'G' Thang."

The first thing: This is a perfect song. It's all of the things that g-funk was hoping to be. The technical definition of g-funk is probably something like "a subgenre of rap that combined the melodic elements of previous iterations of music with gangsta rap." The regular definition, though, is something close to "It feels like a warm afternoon spent hanging out with your closest friends."

The second thing: "Nuthin' but a 'G' Thang" is the marquee song from *The Chronic*. *The Chronic* is not the best ever g-funk album (that'd be Snoop's *Doggystyle*, which, incidentally, was also produced in full by Dr. Dre), but it's the most important ever g-funk album.

The third thing: Snoop, who is a guest on the song, was only twenty years old when he recorded his parts for it. He was still just a baby. The older I get, the more I realize how incredible it is that so many very young people do so many very unbelievable things.

8. Vanilla Ice and MC Hammer were the first truly gigantic pop rappers.

The fourth thing: There's a documentary that came out a few years ago that's all about g-funk.[9] The very first real quote you hear in it is from Snoop. He says, "One thing about magic: When you're making magic, the ingredients sometimes don't come with instructions. You just gotta know how to put that shit together." I love that.

The fifth thing: It doesn't matter how many times I hear "Nuthin' but a 'G' Thang"—every single time somehow feels like the first time. It's mesmerizing.

The sixth thing: My dad deejayed a church function in 1993. He played this song as part of his set. I don't remember a lot of things from that year, but I definitely remember that. I thought it was hilarious then and think it's hilarious now. The people in charge, however, felt differently about things.

Time Period: November 9, 1993, to December 31, 1993
Who Gets the Call? Everyone from the Wu-Tang Clan
Who Do You Call If the Wu-Tang Clan Doesn't Answer? Q-Tip, Queen Latifah, E-40, anybody from Cypress Hill, nobody from Insane Clown Posse, 2Pac

How about this: over a two-week period in November of 1993, we got Wu-Tang Clan's *Enter the Wu-Tang (36 Chambers)*, A Tribe Called Quest's *Midnight Marauders*, E-40's *Federal*, Queen Latifah's *Black Reign*, and Snoop's *Doggystyle*. That's fucking crazy. I don't know that there's ever been a stronger, more interesting two-week stretch for albums released in the history of rap.

Time Period: January 1, 1994, to April 18, 1994
Who Gets the Call? Snoop
Who Do You Call If Snoop Doesn't Answer? Eightball & MJG, Da Brat, Scarface, Pimp C

Snoop has been an omnipresent figure in our lives for three-plus decades now. As such, he's reached a very rare level of fame. He's become so famous that he feels inevitable. There's no situation you can put him in anymore that would make everyone go, "Wait, what? Snoop's gonna do what now?"

For example, if I turned on the TV at this very moment and saw that, say, Kendrick Lamar or Cardi B was about to try and jump across the Grand Canyon on a skateboard, I would be very surprised to see that with my eyeballs. But if I turned on the TV at this very moment and saw Snoop doing that exact same thing, I would not be surprised at all. Not even a little. Because he's Snoop. And Snoop is everywhere at all times doing all things. Nothing he can do is surprising anymore. And that's a really weird thing to think about today, because when Snoop first showed up in the '90s, every single thing about him felt unpredictable: the way he rapped, the way he glided places instead of walking like a normal person, the way his voice felt like bathwater at the perfect temperature. All of it. And all of him.

1994 is (I would argue) the most purely great year in the history of rap. That's when Nas put out *Illmatic*

9. It's called *G Funk*.

and when Biggie put out *Ready to Die* and when Outkast put out *Southernplayalisticadillacmuzik* and when Scarface put out *The Diary* and when UGK put out *Super Tight* and when Da Brat put out *Funkdafied* and on and on and on. It was a monster year full of monster talents. And still, Snoop, whose debut album came out in November 1993, was the biggest thing in rap during that time. He pulled everything toward himself. He was just so undeniably smooth and inventive and invigorating and intoxicating. It was a perfect combination of powers.

Time Period: April 19, 1994, to December 31, 1994
Who Gets the Call? Nas
Who Do You Call If Nas Doesn't Answer? Either André 3000 or Big Boi from Outkast, Bun B, Jeru the Damaja, Warren G

Nas, potentially the word-for-word, line-for-line greatest pure rapper that has ever rapped, released *Illmatic*, potentially the word-for-word, line-for-line greatest pure rap album that has ever rap albumed.

Time Period: January 1, 1995, to July 24, 1995
Who Gets the Call? The Notorious B.I.G.
Who Do You Call If Biggie Doesn't Answer? DJ Quik, 2Pac, either Havoc or Prodigy from Mobb Deep, Skee-Lo[10]

First, some housekeeping: Biggie's debut, *Ready to Die*, came out in 1994. However, because we have that stupid You Can't Call More Than Two Rappers During Any Given Year rule in place, I couldn't pick him during 1994, because Nas and Snoop had already grabbed the two spots that were available there.

Second, a clarification: Biggie's *Ready to Die* is my favorite album of 1994. I find it to be a slightly more enjoyable experience than *Illmatic*, and I find Biggie to be a more accessible figure than Nas. And listen: I completely understand that Nas is a genius and that *Illmatic* is a masterwork. I don't want it to seem like I don't understand that. Because I do. I get that. There are actually two whole chapters dedicated to Nas and *Illmatic* earlier in this book. It's just I've always found myself more drawn to Biggie's brand of brilliance, which is rooted in a kind of rap populism, than to Nas's brand of brilliance, which, when he presses that gas pedal down all the way, feels more like we're watching a god create the cosmos.

Time Period: July 25, 1995, to December 31, 1995
Who Gets the Call? All of the members of Bone Thugs-n-Harmony
Who Do You Call If Bone Thugs Don't Answer? Not one single other person

I have no way to prove this, and I don't even really have a logic-based argument for why this is the case, but this is a theory that I firmly believe and will heartily argue: Mexicans fucking love Bone Thugs-n-Harmony. A lot. Like, *a lot*.

10. I fucking loved "I Wish" when I was a kid.

Now, I don't know why that's the case. Maybe it's a combination of (a) the way that they sing (which is genuinely beautiful and affecting) and (b) the things that they talk about in their songs ("Tha Crossroads" is very popular among the Catholics, lol)[11] and (c) the way they dress (if you squint, there are some hints of cholo in there)? Or maybe it's something else entirely that I've never even considered? I don't know. I just know that, again, Mexicans love Bone Thugs-n-Harmony. And Tasha, too.

Time Period: January 1, 1996, to July 29, 1996
Who Gets the Call? 2Pac
Who Do You Call If 2Pac Doesn't Answer? Jay-Z, Silkk the Shocker,[12] André 3000 and Big Boi, Lil' Kim, Master P, anyone from the Fugees, anyone from A Tribe Called Quest

2Pac's 1996 was, and remains, one of the most surreal, unbelievable, dominant stretches in rap history. It was an incredible confluence of events. He (a) had recently gotten out of prison; (b) joined Death Row Records, which was then the preeminent record label in rap; (c) had already given three brilliant performances in three brilliant movies[13] and had completed filming on three other movies that would all be released before 1997 was over;[14] and (d) put out *All Eyez on Me*, which was instantly successful and would eventually go on to become not only his most popular album ever but also one of rap's most popular albums ever. 2Pac was so big and so overwhelming and so blindingly charismatic that he took an entire subgenre of music (gangsta rap) and re-formed it entirely in his image. It was wild. It was a wild, Wild, WILD run that positioned him to be a high-profile public figure in our lives forever. And then he was shot and killed. And it fucking sucked.

---

11. Way more so than "Nuthin' but a 'G' Thang."
12. Shut up.
13. 1992's *Juice*, 1993's *Poetic Justice*, and 1994's *Above the Rim*.
14. 1996's *Bullet*, 1997's *Gridlock'd*, and 1997's *Gang Related*.

WHO GETS THE PHONE CALL?

(1996–2007)

. . . cont'd

Time Period: July 30, 1996, to July 14, 1997
Who Gets the Call? Bun B
Who Do You Call If Bun B Doesn't Answer?
Lil' Kim, anyone from A Tribe Called Quest, either guy from Outkast, Jeru the Damaja

Three things here:

1. *Ridin' Dirty*, the third proper album from UGK, is a goddamn masterpiece. It's smart and lush and brutal and beautiful. It's the best rap album that Texas has ever produced,[1] and also it's the best rap album ever in general that music has produced where someone makes reference to a mandolin. The opening five-song stretch—"One Day" into "Murder" into "Pinky Ring" into "Diamonds & Wood" into "3 in the Mornin'"—is like a twenty-minute-long version of that picture where Dwyane Wade has his arms out in boastful elegance while LeBron James tomahawk dunks it behind him.
2. A thing that I think about every time I see the *Ridin' Dirty* album cover: On UGK's first album, *Too Hard to Swallow*, Bun B and Pimp C are positioned on the cover in a manner that, if you're very nerdy and look for symbolism in places where maybe there's none, makes it seem a lot like Pimp C is the dominant figure. (Bun and Pimp C are both posing in front of a fence, with Pimp standing as Bun squats.) And that makes sense because Pimp C was the better rapper on *THTS*. On their second album, *Super Tight*, the two are positioned on the cover at the same eye level. (They're both squatting in front of a car.) And that makes sense because Bun had caught up to Pimp in terms of overall rapping skill by then. On the *Ridin' Dirty* cover, it's Bun who's in the more prominent position (he's in the driver's-side seat of a car, while Pimp rides shotgun). And that makes sense because by then he had become a truly top-level rapper, and really all you need to hear is his verse on "Murder" as proof of that. It's a fucking avalanche of Uzis and machetes.
3. There's not a PERFECT SONGS museum yet, but when someone finally gets around to building one, I'm going to be very excited to visit the wing of the museum they dedicate to "One Day."

Time Period: July 15, 1997, to October 27, 1997
Who Gets the Call? Missy Elliott
Who Do You Call If Missy Elliott Doesn't Answer? Jay-Z, J Dilla, Puff Daddy, Busta Rhymes

(There's an entire chapter on Missy Elliott during this exact time period. Go read that.)

Time Period: October 28, 1997, to August 24, 1998
Who Gets the Call? Ma$e
Who Do You Call If Ma$e Doesn't Answer?
DMX, Big Pun, Mystikal, either Eightball or MJG

Two things here:

1. DMX is the correct choice here. But there's a bunch of DMX stuff in this book, so I wanted to use this space to talk about another rapper I care about a lot.

1. The other two on that particular top-three list: Scarface's *The Diary* and the Geto Boys' *We Can't Be Stopped.*

2. The thing you have to know about Ma$e in 1997 is I just loved him. He was an excellent character in my life and an excellent character in rap. (*Harlem World*, his debut album, would go on to sell over 4.8 million copies.) I loved that soft lisp that he had, and I loved the way the front of his forehead stuck out just a little. I loved how his smile always felt like it was its own double meaning, and I loved how he always kind of danced in his videos but not really. I loved the way his voice seemed to brush just the edges of your ears, and I loved the way that even though he was marketed as Bad Boy's replacement for the Notorious B.I.G., he always made sure to say that he never saw himself that way. He was excellent.

Time Period: August 25, 1998, to September 28, 1998
Who Gets the Call? Lauryn Hill
Who Do You Call If Lauryn Hill Doesn't Answer? Either guy from Black Star

Here are seven stats for you: (1) Lauryn Hill put out *The Miseducation of Lauryn Hill* in 1998. It sold over 422,000 copies the first week, which was the biggest first week any woman ever had put up on the board in any music genre ever. (2) Her lead single, "Doo Wop (That Thing)," debuted at number one on the *Billboard* Hot 100, an impressive feat made all the more remarkable when you realize that only nine other songs in the chart's history had ever debuted in the lead spot.[2] (3) *TMOLH* received ten Grammy nominations (she was the first ever woman to be nominated that many times at once), five of which she won. (4) One of those wins was for Album of the Year, the most prestigious Grammy.[3] It marked the first time ever that a hip-hop album had taken home the award. (5) In 2020, *Rolling Stone* picked *TMOLH* as the tenth-greatest album in the history of recorded music. (6) The album was so good and so beloved and so successful that Hill is often credited with being one of the primary figures to help hip-hop cross over fully into the mainstream. (7) There's a hospital in New Jersey, which is where Lauryn Hill is from, where, rather than performing surgery on people, they just play the video for "Ex-Factor" two or three times in a row and it fixes whatever's wrong with the person.

Time Period: September 9, 1998, to February 22, 1999
Who Gets the Call? Juvenile
Who Do You Call If Juvenile Doesn't Answer? There was nobody else. I fucking loved Juvenile during this stretch.

I know that I'm probably supposed to pick Jay-Z right here, ha? Because this was the year that he put out *Vol. 2 . . . Hard Knock Life*, ha? It was the moment that he stepped into the space that had been left vacant by the Notorious B.I.G.'s murder the year before, ha? But I just don't want to, ha? Because Juvenile's "Ha" is one of music's most brilliant songs, ha? And Juvenile is one of my all-time favorite rappers ever, ha? Writing a song the way he wrote "Ha" is the kind of everlasting thing that only the most ambitious kind of person would do, ha? And I was hoping that the structure would

---

2. Michael Jackson's "You Are Not Alone," Mariah Carey's "Fantasy," Whitney Houston's "Exhale (Shoop Shoop)," Mariah Carey and Boyz II Men's "One Sweet Day," Puff Daddy's "I'll Be Missing You" tribute song that he did with Faith Evans and 112, Mariah Carey's "Honey," Elton John's "Candle in the Wind 1997" / "Something About the Way You Look Tonight," Celine Dion's "My Heart Will Go On," and Aerosmith's "I Don't Want to Miss a Thing."
3. The other four she won: Best R&B Song, Best Female R&B Vocal Performance, Best R&B Album, and Best New Artist.

translate well to this blurb that I'm writing for it right now, ha? But I don't think it is, ha? So I'm going to stop now, ha?

Time Period: February 23, 1999, to November 29, 1999
Who Gets the Call? Eminem
Who Do You Call If Eminem Doesn't Answer? Nas, Missy Elliott, Black Thought

There's a group of rappers who exist in this separate class from everyone else—rappers who, the first time you hear them, make you say something like, "Oh fuck. Wait. Who is this? What is this?" Rappers who you know instantly are going to be a force. Eminem is in that class. He showed up and nobody knew what the fuck to do. Nobody except Dr. Dre, who, after a handful of fruitless at bats in the mid to late '90s with Aftermath, bet his whole reputation on Eminem after their first recording session ended with them making "My Name Is."[4]

Time Period: November 30, 1999, to March 20, 2000
Who Gets the Call? Q-Tip
Who Do You Call If Q-Tip Doesn't Answer? Common, DMX, Jay-Z, Trick Daddy[5]

Q-Tip, from his very first days as a rapper in the late 1980s, was always cool. He showed up with a cool face and a cool style and a cool voice. He moved in a cool way and talked in a cool way and just, as a default setting, radiated coolness out into the universe in an impossible-to-grab-ahold-of kind of way. He was like that from the drop.

That being said, he was on a fucking whole different planet of coolness during the rollout for *Amplified*, his first album separate from his A Tribe Called Quest bandmates. It might've been because he was a little older (he was twenty-nine at the time) or because he was finally stepping out as a solo artist or because he was paired up for "Vivrant Thing" and "Breathe and Stop"[6] with people like Hype Williams and J Dilla, both of whom always served as cool multipliers. I can't say for certain. All that I know is that when he was on your TV, you had to negotiate with your own eyes to get them to blink, because your brain didn't want to miss even one one-hundredth of a second of what you were watching.

Time Period: March 21, 2000, to September 10, 2001
Who Gets the Call? Trina
Who Do You Call If Trina Doesn't Answer? Nelly, Jadakiss, either guy from Big Tymers, MC Eiht

This is only an unorthodox pick if you're someone who lived outside of Trina's bubble of influence in the early 2000s. Because if you lived in it—like, if you were from Miami, especially, but also if you were anywhere that could accurately be described as the South—you remember

4. Eminem has since sold more records than every rapper ever.
5. I would assume this is the first time that Trick Daddy has appeared in a list with Common, DMX, and Jay-Z.
6. "Vivrant Thing" and "Breathe and Stop" were released as singles three months apart. They were so earwormy and aesthetically similar, though, that it felt like they'd been built to snap together into one big piece, something like how *Kill Bill: Volume 1* and *Kill Bill: Volume 2* feel like one megamovie broken up into two parts.

NFL
Steelers
84
NFL

exactly how fucking bonkers everyone went when she took a chainsaw to Trick Daddy's chest on "Nann" in 1998, and you remember how she carried the momentum from that all the way through the run-up to her debut album *Da Baddest Bitch.*

Time Period: September 11, 2001, to August 19, 2002
Who Gets the Call? Jay-Z
Who Do You Call If Jay-Z Doesn't Answer? CeeLo, Cam'ron, Jean Grae, Project Pat

Two things here:

1. Jay-Z calling himself to get a guest verse makes me happy.
2. This is (I would argue) the moment when Jay-Z really started becoming someone who you couldn't leave out of the Greatest Rapper Alive conversation. (More on this later.)

Time Period: August 20, 2002, to February 5, 2003
Who Gets the Call? Both guys from Clipse (but especially Pusha T)
Who Do You Call If Pusha T Doesn't Answer? Devin the Dude, Lil Flip, Lil Jon or any of the East Side Boyz

Pusha T one time called himself "the L. Ron Hubbard of the cupboard." Pusha T one time called himself "the Black Martha Stewart." Pusha T one time called himself "Brick James." Pusha T one time called himself "the *Robb Report* of the snort." Pusha T one time called himself the "Jack Frost of sellin' that blast off." Pusha T one time called himself the "Hines Ward of the crime lords." Pusha T one time called himself "the hood's Obama, shovelin' McCain." Pusha T one time called himself "the grand wizard of that almighty blizzard." Pusha T one time called himself the "Kim Jong of the crack song." Pusha T is fucking excellent.

Time Period: February 6, 2003, to September 22, 2003
Who Gets the Call? 50 Cent
Who Do You Call If 50 Cent Doesn't Answer? T.I., Bone Crusher, Joe Budden

(There's an entire chapter on 50 Cent during this exact time period. Go read that.)

Time Period: September 23, 2003, to February 9, 2004
Who Gets the Call? André 3000 and Big Boi from Outkast
Who Do You Call If Outkast Doesn't Answer? Wyclef Jean, Z-Ro

The truth is I couldn't get over not being able to slide Big Boi or André 3000 somewhere into one of the selection spots during the years when they put out *Southernplayalisticadillacmuzik* (1994) or *ATLiens* (1996) or *Aquemini* (1998). That's how they ended up right here. It's like in basketball games when a ref messes something up and they know they've messed up, so they blow a bad whistle on the other side of the court just to balance things out. This pick here is a makeup call for Outkast. And even then,

I still feel kind of bad about it. Because despite the fact that this was when Outkast put out one of the best-selling albums of all time (*Speakerboxxx / The Love Below*), this would never be the album that I'd play first for someone who had never heard Outkast before and wanted to know what made them so special.

Time Period: February 10, 2004, to July 25, 2005
Who Gets the Call? Kanye West
Who Do You Call If Kanye West Doesn't Answer? Sean Price, the Game, Slim Thug, Lil' Kim, Ghostface Killah

The year that Kanye began his college-based albums trilogy. It goes *The College Dropout* in 2004, *Late Registration* in 2005, and *Graduation* in 2007. It's as loud and declarative of an opening three-album run to a career as we've ever gotten.

Time Period: July 26, 2005, to August 7, 2006
Who Gets the Call? Young Jeezy
Who Do You Call If Young Jeezy Doesn't Answer? Common, Beanie Sigel, Jim Jones

There's a full chapter on Young Jeezy and his album *Let's Get It: Thug Motivation 101* earlier in this book, but let me just say this here because it doesn't get said there: Young Jeezy says words in a way that makes them feel more alive than normal and more energetic than normal. Take "yeah," for example, his most famous ad-lib. When you or I say "yeah," it doesn't sound like anything except for the word "yeah." It sounds lame and boring and uninspired; in certain instances, it can even begin to sound like what you really mean to say is "no, not really." When Young Jeezy says "yeah," though – when he stretches it and bends it and shapes it and pumps it full of enthusiasm – it sounds massive. It sounds like it's stuffed fat with life and with love and with sunlight. It's no longer just a word; it's an affirmation of purpose in the universe.

Time Period: August 8, 2006, to September 15, 2006
Who Gets the Call? Rick Ross
Who Do You Call If Rick Ross Doesn't Answer? Jay-Z

Rick Ross is an interesting case study in rap. Prior to him, credibility was a wildly important part of someone's rap existence. It's what each person would build everything around. (50 Cent famously got shot nine times. Eazy-E famously used money he'd earned from the drug game to start Ruthless Records. Drake famously was a cast member on a Canadian teen drama.) After Ross, though – after he (a) spent a bunch of time telling everyone he was a drug kingpin who bathed in a Jacuzzi of diamonds and caviar but then (b) was outed as a former correctional officer at Miami-Dade County's South Florida Reception Center who made about $23,000 a year and then (c) just sort of shrugged it off and kept it moving – it didn't seem to matter anymore. Nobody really cared about that part of it. The only thing that mattered was that he was willing to play the role and that he could make a song like "Hustlin'" or a song like "B.M.F." or a song like "Santorini Greece" or a song like "Aston Martin Music."

Time Period: September 16, 2006, to September 10, 2007
Who Gets the Call? Lupe Fiasco
Who Do You Call If Lupe Fiasco Doesn't Answer? Ludacris, Lil Wayne

Three things here:

1. Lupe Fiasco is an incredible name.
2. A thing I have occasionally asked myself is, "Do you think Lupe Fiasco would've been able to become Lupe Fiasco if Kanye West hadn't become Kanye West? Do you think we would've gotten *Lupe Fiasco's Food & Liquor* in 2006 if we hadn't gotten *The College Dropout* in 2004?" (For the record, I think the answer is "Yes. Lupe Fiasco was inevitable, as was *Lupe Fiasco's Food & Liquor*." But it's a fun thing to think about and to argue about.)
3. Here's what Lupe Fiasco said about *LFFAL* while talking about it at the Red Bull Music Festival in 2019: "This album is merely motivation; it's not the blueprint. It ain't got the answers. It's flawed. It's imperfect. But it's a fucking try—hopefully a try that pushed some of you all in the right direction." I love that as the general ethos not only for the album but also for Lupe Fiasco.

Time Period: September 11, 2007, to October 1, 2007
Who Gets the Call? Kanye West
Who Do You Call If Kanye West Doesn't Answer? Gucci Mane, Devin the Dude, Lil Wayne

A thing that I think about a lot whenever I find myself feeling nostalgic is that 2007 was one of the best years of my life. I got married that year. I became a dad that year. I started my career as a teacher that year and also began freelance writing that year. The Spurs won the championship that year. A bunch of really great movies came out that year.[7] And, to add to all of that, Kanye West released *Graduation*, which, even all this time later, remains my personal favorite Kanye West album, in no small part because every time I listen to it, I'm reminded of all of the things that I mentioned before this sentence. Music is good.

7. *300* (shut up), *Shooter* (I liked it; I don't care), *Stomp the Yard* (one of my favorite stories is one of my most curmudgeonly uncles going to see this at a theater and then swearing to everyone who would listen that it was one of the best movies he'd ever seen), *Alpha Dog* (exceptionally underrated), *Ocean's Thirteen*, *Superbad*, *3:10 to Yuma* (my all-time favorite western), *No Country for Old Men* (I know that it's purposely left unsaid, but I am certain that Anton Chigurh is Mexican), *I Am Legend* (Will Smith rules), and *There Will Be Blood* (fuck yes).

WHO GETS THE PHONE CALL?

(2007–2020)

. . . cont'd

Time Period: October 2, 2007, to June 9, 2008
Who Gets the Call? Soulja Boy
Who Do You Call If Soulja Boy Doesn't Answer? Lupe Fiasco, Jay-Z

It's commonplace now for rappers to fully integrate parts of the internet into their albums and into their music. But the reason that it's commonplace is because of Soulja Boy, who, over the course of just a few weeks in 2007, changed rap forever when he weaponized the internet for "Crank That" and catapulted himself up into the cosmos.[1] That sort of innovation—figuring some shit out to help you get to a spot that you want to get to—is always interesting to me. That's why Soulja Boy gets the nod here.

Time Period: June 10, 2008, to September 14, 2009
Who Gets the Call? Lil Wayne
Who Do You Call If Lil Wayne Doesn't Answer? Jay-Z, Jeezy, Q-Tip

I'm aware of the hypocrisy of starting this block of chapters off by talking about Lil Wayne during his brilliant mixtape stretch but then waiting until the release of *Tha Carter III*, which was a proper album, to finally choose him for a section. HOWEVER, there's a reason I did it that way, and that reason is this: Waiting until after *Tha Carter III* is released to dial up Lil Wayne means you're not only getting him when he was the best rapper on the planet but also getting him when he was the most popular rapper on the planet. And it's not too often that those two things align. So, I mean, I figured that was worth waiting for.

Time Period: September 15, 2009, to December 7, 2009
Who Gets the Call? Kid Cudi
Who Do You Call If Kid Cudi Doesn't Answer? There was nobody else here. Only Cudi.

My grandma passed away in 2008. And when she did, it fucked me up a lot. It was the first time that someone I really loved and cared about had died. Everything in my universe was good and fine and normal, and then one day she went to the doctor and they told her she had cancer, and then six months later she was dead. Just that fast. It was awful. I hated all of the parts of the situation. I hated how the cancer robbed her of all of the years she should've had left as a mother and grandmother, and I hated how the cancer robbed her of her zest and of her spirit, and I hated how the cancer robbed her of the tiny bit of peace that she'd built up for herself in the world. Again: It fucked me up real bad. It felt like a part of me had been ruined, like a part of me had rotted out, like a part of me had been soaked in infested water for six hundred years. Honestly, I imagine parts of that damage are still in me, though I'll never know for certain, because I don't figure I'll ever work up the courage to peek inside that particular memory chest.

Anyway: There's a part on Kid Cudi's "Soundtrack 2 My Life" where he mentions his father, who passed away when Cudi was eleven. (Also from cancer, by the way.)[2] Here's the

---

1. The song was nominated for a Grammy, spent seven nonconsecutive weeks atop *Billboard*'s Hot 100 chart, and eventually sold over five million downloads.
2. Fuck cancer, by the way.

line: "I'm super paranoid, like a sixth sense / Since my father died, I ain't been right since." It'll always be the first line I arrive at whenever someone mentions Kid Cudi. Because I remember hearing it for the first time less than a year after my grandma had died, and I remember hearing Kid Cudi say the "I ain't been right since" part, and I remember thinking to myself something like "That's it. That's what's going on inside of me. My grandma died, and I ain't been right since." It felt a little bit like relief, really, just hearing him say that. I'll always carry a very acute appreciation for Kid Cudi in my chest because of that. Again: music is good.

Time Period: December 8, 2009, to October 22, 2010
Who Gets the Call? Gucci Mane
Who Do You Call If Gucci Mane Doesn't Answer? Rick Ross, Drake

There's probably some very clever observation to be made here about how the song "Lemonade," which is the standout track from Gucci Mane's *The State vs. Radric Davis* album and also a standout track from Gucci Mane's career, is some sort of extended metaphor. You can probably draw some line to the way that Gucci Mane was able to turn an early life of hardships into a bracelet with lemonade-colored diamonds and earrings with lemonade-colored diamonds and a lemonade-colored Corvette and so on and so forth–something about when life gives you lemons and such. But I don't want to do that here. I don't want to chase that. I just want to say "Lemonade" fucking ruled then and still rules today.

Time Period: October 23, 2010, to August 7, 2011
Who Gets the Call? Nicki Minaj
Who Do You Call If Nicki Minaj Doesn't Answer? Tyler, the Creator; Kendrick Lamar

Nicki Minaj, who had done well to build a proper amount of buzz for herself via mixtapes and guest appearances in the two or so years prior, was about a month away from the release of her debut studio album[3] when it happened. That's when "Monster" came out–the third single from Kanye West's upcoming *My Beautiful Dark Twisted Fantasy*–and that's when she became a top-level star. Her verse there, set up in the closing position behind Rick Ross, Kanye, and Jay-Z, was an instant all-timer. It was gigantic and ferocious and confident and unbelievable. Listening to her perform it was like watching someone windmill dunking it from two feet behind the free-throw line; it somehow felt both unbelievable and also inevitable. It was one of those very rare moments when everyone listening seemed to agree on at least one point: that Nicki Minaj had shown up to collect a handful of skulls and that she had done exactly that.

Time Period: August 8, 2011, to August 13, 2012
Who Gets the Call? Jay-Z
Who Do You Call If Jay-Z Doesn't Answer? Mac Miller, Drake, Black Thought

Two things here:

1. You know what I always think of anytime I revisit *Watch the Throne*, the joint album that Jay-Z and Kanye West

3. *Pink Friday*, which would go on to sell over 375,000 copies the first week and eventually hit the top of the *Billboard* 200 chart.

did together in 2011? The part in 2016's "Feedback" where Kanye said that if Jay-Z, often cited as the greatest rapper to have ever existed, is Michael Jordan, then that makes Kanye West the Dennis Rodman of their relationship. It's a pretty good comparison, I think.

2. Jay-Z and Kanye West were so good together that part of their live show when they toured for *Watch the Throne* included performing the same song ("Niggas in Paris") multiple times in a row, *AND PEOPLE FUCKING LOVED IT.* They did it three times in a row in New York. They did it five times in a row in Houston. They did it ten times in a row in Los Angeles. They did it TWELVE TIMES in a row in Paris.

Time Period: August 14, 2012, to October 21, 2012
Who Gets the Call? 2 Chainz
Who Do You Call If 2 Chainz Doesn't Answer? Killer Mike, Nicki Minaj

Here are the eleven funniest things 2 Chainz has ever said in a song, because 2 Chainz is excellent and 2 Chainz is funny:

1. "My wrist deserve a shout-out, I'm like, 'What up, wrist?' My stove deserve a shout-out, I'm like, 'What up, stove?'" (from "Fork")
2. "She got a big booty, so I call her Big Booty" (from "Birthday Song")
3. "If I die, bury me inside the Louis store" (from "Birthday Song")
4. "I look you right in your face / Sing to your bitch like I'm Drake" (from "Good Drank")
5. "I don't know nothin' 'bout iChat / I'm working this iPhone, they need an app called iTrap" (from "Where U Been?")
6. "I hope you get testicular cancer in the brain, dickhead" (from "Beautiful Pain")
7. "My girl got a big purse with a purse in it / And her pussy so clean I can go to church in it" (from "Like Me")
8. "Drinkin' breast milk out a lean cup" (from "3500")
9. "My favorite dish is turkey lasagna / Even my pajamas designer" (from "G.O.O.D. Morning")
10. "Wood grain, chestnut / Titty fuck, chest nut" (from "Like Me")
11. "Turn the camel toe into a casserole" (from "Yuck!")

Time Period: October 22, 2012, to March 17, 2014
Who Gets the Call? Kendrick Lamar
Who Do You Call If Kendrick Lamar Doesn't Answer? There was nobody else here. Only Kendrick.

You know the scene in *Predator* after Jesse Ventura dies, when Bill Duke briefly sees the Predator and so he just starts shooting into the jungle, hoping to kill whatever it is he's just seen? He eventually runs out of bullets for his first gun, so he picks up the big Gatling gun and starts firing that one into the jungle, too. He shoots something like a thousand bullets into the trees and leaves and bushes and vines over the course of a few seconds. Then Arnold Schwarzenegger and Carl Weathers and Sonny Landham and Shane Black run over, and they all start shooting into the jungle, too. And they shoot a thousand rounds each as well. It's just an onslaught of wayward bullets and indiscriminate mayhem. That's how Kendrick Lamar raps on *Good Kid, M.A.A.D City*, except instead of the bullets going everywhere all at once like that, they only go directly at your forehead like a fucking laser beam.

Time Period: March 18, 2014, to March 14, 2015
Who Gets the Call? Freddie Gibbs
Who Do You Call If Freddie Gibbs Doesn't Answer? There was nobody else here. Only Freddie.

This is only going to make sense to a small number of people, but to that small number of people, it is possibly going to make more sense than anything has ever made sense: Freddie Gibbs raps the way Isiah Thomas used to dribble a basketball. There's a probing nature to it and an economy of motion tucked within it that turn everything just a little more sinister and a little more assertive and a little more I'm Gonna Go Where the Fuck I Want and There's Nothing You or Anyone Else Can Do About It. It's really beautiful.

Time Period: March 15, 2015, to July 7, 2016
Who Gets the Call? Kendrick Lamar
Who Do You Call If Kendrick Lamar Doesn't Answer? There was nobody else here. Only Kendrick.

Please reread the Kendrick Lamar entry from two time periods ago. It's all true again here.

Time Period: July 8, 2016, to February 16, 2017
Who Gets the Call? ScHoolboy Q
Who Do You Call If ScHoolboy Q Doesn't Answer? Any of the guys from Migos, either guy from Run the Jewels, Travis Scott, Young Thug

ScHoolboy Q's *Blank Face* LP is one of the sharpest rap albums of the past ten or so years. It's mean ("Groovy Tony / Eddie Kane," featuring Jadakiss, who yanks the fucking doors off a tank with his verse), and it's aggressive ("Ride Out," featuring Vince Staples, whose pinpoint inflections are the perfect counterbalance to ScHoolboy Q's rake-across-gravel voice), and it's ambitious ("Kno Ya Wrong," where ScHoolboy Q turns everything warm and rubbery), and it's textured ("John Muir," which feels in your ears the way that tweed feels at your fingertips), and it's sewn together in a way that feels unexpected yet purposeful (the transition from the end of "Lord Have Mercy" into the beginning of "That Part" is its own little masterpiece).

Time Period: February 17, 2017, to June 22, 2017
Who Gets the Call? Future
Who Do You Call If Future Doesn't Answer? There was nobody else here. Only Future.

Future released two separate albums over the course of a week in 2017. They were both surprise projects. The first one was called *Future* (named after himself), and it debuted at number one on the *Billboard* 200. The second one was called *Hndrxx* (named after his alter ego), and it also debuted at number one on the *Billboard* 200, knocking *Future* out of that spot. It was the first time ever that an artist pulled that feat off. And that's not even the wildest part of all of this. The wildest part of all of this is that Future was possessed of such otherworldly confidence during this stretch that, on a song called "Comin Out Strong," he claimed that he invented doors. Doors. DOORS. *DOORS*. He said, "I opened up Bentley doors, I invented doors." Doors. DOORS. *DOORS*. HE SAID THAT HE INVENTED DOORS. And he said it with so much faith and so much conviction that I heard it and couldn't help but be like, "Wait . . . Did Future really invent doors?"

Time Period: June 23, 2017, to April 5, 2018
Who Gets the Call? Vince Staples
Who Do You Call If Vince Staples Doesn't Answer? Any of the guys from Migos, Maxo Kream, Lil Uzi Vert

Vince Staples has a song called "Big Fish," which is from an album called *Big Fish Theory*. In the video for it, he sits alone on a very nice sailboat as it slowly sinks into the ocean. Eventually, he peeks over the side and notices that there are a few very large sharks circling. It's a disastrous situation, clearly. He is, quite literally, looking at his own eventual death, either by drowning or by shark or by some horrible combination of the two. And yet despite the dire circumstances, he seems totally unfazed. He reacts less like he's just looked at the possibility of being eaten alive and more like he's just looked at an alert on his cell phone letting him know that his Uber driver has canceled his ride. And it's not that he doesn't understand the circumstances or that he doesn't want to be alive – clearly he does, which is made obvious by the rescue flares that he fires into the air in search of help that he knows is never going to arrive. It's just that he doesn't care. Because . . . I mean . . . fuck it, you know? Why bother caring, you know? Even when you do care, you know?

Or something like that.

I don't know.

Vince Staples is smarter than everyone else, is what I'm saying.

Time Period: April 6, 2018, to June 28, 2018
Who Gets the Call? Cardi B
Who Do You Call If Cardi B Doesn't Answer? There was nobody else here. This whole year really was a victory lap for Cardi.

Can I just give you a list of all of the places that put Cardi B's *Invasion of Privacy* in their top-ten albums of the year in 2018? Because I feel like that's a pretty compelling argument here. Because *Rolling Stone* had it there. So did the *Ringer*. So did *Time*. So did *Billboard*. So did *Entertainment Weekly*. So did *Esquire*. So did the *Guardian*. So did *Stereogum*. So did *Vibe*. So did NPR Music. So did the *New York Times*. So did *Spin*. So did *Complex*.

Or maybe you want a list of the awards that Cardi won, like when she won the Grammy for Best Rap Album or when she won Album of the Year at the BET Awards?

Or how about some fun numbers? Numbers like this: *Invasion of Privacy* debuted at number one on the *Billboard* 200 chart (and it stayed on the chart for more than 150 straight weeks, which is the longest ever run by a female artist); it eventually sold over three million copies; all thirteen of the songs on the album were eventually certified as gold or higher by the RIAA; the album helped Cardi place thirteen separate songs on the *Billboard* Hot 100 chart AT THE SAME TIME, which gave her the record at the time for singles charted simultaneously by a female artist; and it eventually became the most streamed album by a female artist in Spotify's history.

Time Period: June 29, 2018, to May 16, 2019
Who Gets the Call? Drake
Who Do You Call If Drake Doesn't Answer? DaBaby, Mac Miller, Noname, Young Thug

The truth is you can grab Drake from any year after 2010 and slot him in wherever you'd like in this chapter. He's been that good and that dominant for that long. He's his own planet, and if not his own planet, then at least his own moon, and if not his own moon, then at least his own comet or asteroid. Or whatever. He's all-caps BIG, is the point. I'm going with this version of him because I just really like the stretch of singles he had in 2018. He touched on all the different versions of Drake that I enjoy. He was Benevolent Drake on "God's Plan." And he was Above-the-Law Drake on "Diplomatic Immunity." And he was Empowering Drake on "Nice for What." And he was Gatekeeper Drake on "Yes Indeed." And he was Dancing Drake on "In My Feelings." And he was Fuck-Your-Feelings Drake on "Nonstop." It was fun. It was a real fun time with Drake.

Time Period: May 17, 2019, to February 28, 2020
Who Gets the Call? Megan Thee Stallion
Who Do You Call If Megan Thee Stallion Doesn't Answer? Tyler, the Creator; Lil Nas X

There are two versions of Megan Thee Stallion that you have to choose from for this particular exercise that we're participating in right now. The first version of Megan Thee Stallion is the 2019 version. That's when she officially moved from standing on the precipice of stardom to getting a proper seat at the stardom table. (2019 is when she did "Big Ole Freak,"[4] as well as "Cash Shit," "Sex Talk," and "Hot Girl Summer," the first two of which stemmed from her very excellent mixtape *Fever*.) The 2020 version of Megan Thee Stallion is when she took everything that she'd done in 2019 and turned the volume up as far as the little knob would let her (that was when her debut album, *Good News*, came out; and also when she did the "Savage" remix with Beyonce, which tilted the internet at a thirty-degree angle; and also when she "WAP" with Cardi B, and if the "Savage" remix tilted the internet at a thirty-degree angle then "WAP" flipped that whole shit upside down). I think I'm gonna go with the 2019 version, mostly because I like the way that *Fever* jumps out of your speakers when you play it in your car.

Time Period: February 29, 2020, to November 19, 2020
Who Gets the Call? Bad Bunny
Who Do You Call If Bad Bunny Doesn't Answer? Either guy from Run the Jewels, Freddie Gibbs, Action Bronson

I only ever understand, like, 15 percent of what Bad Bunny is saying, but I know that he's going hard 100 percent of the time.

Time Period: November 20, 2020, to December 31, 2020
Who Gets the Call? Megan Thee Stallion
Who Do You Call If Megan Thee Stallion Doesn't Answer? Benny the Butcher, 21 Savage, Pop Smoke

I changed my mind. Let's get 2020 Megan in here, too.

4. "Big Ole Freak" appeared originally on 2018's *Tina Snow* but wasn't released as a single until 2019.

WHAT JOKE WAS IT THAT DMX TOLD THAT ONE TIME?

A note: This was the second chapter that I did when I started working on this book. I wrote it somewhere around March of 2020. Just thirteen months later, DMX passed away. I was very sad when it happened. DMX is one of my favorite rappers ever and one of the most impactful rappers in my life ever. He was such a force. He still is, honestly. I went back and revisited this chapter in the days after his passing. It made me feel a tiny bit better. I hope it does the same for you. I didn't change any of the "DMX is ..." kinds of lines to "DMX was ..." kinds of lines. I couldn't bring myself to do it. I hope that's okay.

–SHEA

IN JULY OF 2000, DMX released a song called "What These Bitches Want." It was a rap and R&B mashup between him and Sisqó, a platinum-haired dragonfly,[1] where they shared wayward relationship advice[2] and recounted past lovers.

On paper, the pairing should've never worked. DMX and Sisqó seemed diametrically opposed, and we needn't look any further than the beginning of their solo careers for evidence of that.

On "Get at Me Dog," for example, which was DMX's first single, he spends pretty much all of his time either (a) daring people to confront him or (b) talking about the results that have come from people daring to confront him.[3] Also: the entire video was shot in black and white. Also: the video was filmed inside of a dungeon-y New York City nightclub, with DMX in an understated pair of overalls, performing for a packed-in crowd of people in what felt like a suffocatingly small space.

On "Got to Get It," Sisqó's first single, he spends pretty much all of his time either (a) talking about how he wants to have sex with a woman or (b) talking about how he's extremely willing to perform oral sex on the woman.[4] Also: the entire video was shot in vibrant, undeniable color. Also: the video was largely filmed on the roof of a building, with the free and open night sky above Sisqó, in a matching white fur hat and white fur vest, dancing for himself and no one else.

They were opposites, both in style and presentation. And yet "What These Bitches Want" worked. And more than that: It was perfect. There was an instant chemistry. It took all of ten seconds to tell that they were going to be great together. They seemed to balance each other out, is what it felt like. DMX's titanium-heavy presence gave new gravity to Sisqó's impassioned singing, and Sisqó's preternatural zeal somehow turned all of DMX's growls and barks into momentary bursts of joy. It was great back then and remains great now, more than two decades later.[5]

---

1. This song caught Sisqó at the perfect moment in his career. Five months earlier, he had released "Thong Song," an earworm novelty song about underwear that earned him four Grammy nominations. The same month "What These Bitches Want" was released, so too was Sisqó's "Incomplete," his first (and only) song to reach number one on *Billboard*'s Hot 100.
2. There are lots of bits of bad relationship advice, the most egregious being when DMX explains that if a woman starts to care about him, then that's when he steals a bunch of shit from her and disappears into the night.
3. Mostly they died, though there was at least one person who ended up "only" being paralyzed from the waist down.
4. The opposite of being paralyzed from the waist down, as it were.
5. The obvious misogyny notwithstanding.

And on that song – right around the start of the third verse – DMX references a time that he told a joke. That's what this chapter is about.

•••••

Parts of DMX's life, starting from the time he was a child, could be described as "inordinately painful" or "Sisyphean" or "Shakespearean in their tragedy" or, perhaps most succinctly, "super fucking shitty."

If you want to get a glimpse of the way that his demons have wobbled his existence, you can dig his autobiography up online. It's called *E.A.R.L.: The Autobiography of DMX*, and it details, among other things, a childhood filled with abuse and abandonment. It does a really good job of allowing you to wander around in the haunted hallways of his brain for a bit. The whole thing is really pulverizing, and it probably says a lot that he released that autobiography so shortly after ascending into legitimate stardom and acclaim.

Whenever I try to whittle down all of everything around DMX and about DMX to find a thesis statement for his career, I find myself always arriving at the same spot: the "Prayer (Skit)" part on his debut album, *It's Dark and Hell Is Hot,* where he yells, "So if it takes for me to suffer for my brother to see the light / Give me pain till I die / But please, Lord, treat him right." I think it speaks to how special he is, how even under the worst kind of stress and the worst kind of pain, his first instinct is to somehow use it as a way to make things better for the rest of us.

•••••

The thing about the joke in "What These Bitches Want" happens at the start of the third verse. In the video, we see DMX standing alone on an empty city block, rapping downward at the camera. And as he does, he explains that he told a joke one time back before he was rich and famous, and nobody laughed at it. And listen, there are things that DMX has said in songs that have made me feel worse than the time he told a joke and nobody laughed at it. There was the time on "Slippin'" when he asked, "Was it my fault? / Something I did? / To make a father leave his first kid." That one made me feel real bad. And there was the time on "Let Me Fly" when he said, "You can't blame me for not wanting to be held / Locked down in a cell where a soul can't dwell." That one made me feel real bad, too. And there was the time on "Damien" when he wished for a guardian angel and got one, but then his guardian angel ended up being evil and forced DMX to either kill his friend or cut off his own right hand. That one also made me feel bad.

But the line about him telling a joke and nobody laughing at it is the one I've thought about the most in an anthropological sense. There are just so many parts of it that I have follow-up questions for.

- **I mean, the first thought here is obvious:** What joke was it that DMX told? What funny thing was it in DMX's head that made him – the same person who one time started a song by saying, "I got blood on my hands and there's no remorse / And I got blood on my dick 'cause I fucked a corpse" – decide he wanted to tell a joke? (More on this in a bit.)

- **The second thought:** What do you think his delivery was like when he told the joke? Part of me thinks that it was really, really bad, but the other part of me thinks that maybe actually it was really, really good. I don't know.

- **The third thought:** In the clean version of the song, the line is "Ay, yo / I think about when a dog didn't have / And a dog told a joke / And the chickens didn't laugh." That imagery always makes me smile. It makes me think about a literal dog telling a joke to a literal flock of very unimpressed chickens. (The idea that chickens are judgmental is one of those things you never really spend any time thinking about, but then as soon as you hear it, you go, "Oh, well, yeah. That makes sense.")

•••••

"Sometimes people wanna feel worse, you know what I mean? They don't always wanna feel better. However the fuck you wanna feel, there should be a song that helps you feel that way, you know what I'm saying? That you can just ride to and then, you know, just feel like you wanna feel."

–DMX, to *GQ* in 2019

In 2019, I was at a Barnes & Noble in Detroit for a book signing as part of a promo tour that my publisher had arranged for *Movies (And Other Things)*. The way that book signings usually work is everyone gets in a line, and you sit at a table, and a person walks up and hands you a book, and you sign it and then make some small talk and maybe take a picture and then keep it moving. And that's exactly how this particular Detroit signing was going, all the way up until it super wasn't.

What happened was that my grandma (who had passed away a little over a decade earlier) was from Detroit. And she had a relative who was still alive who lived there and whom I'd not seen since I was in middle school. And I'd heard a few times from my mom and my uncles about how much they looked alike and how much they sounded alike, but I always assumed that it was just one of those things you say, you know?

Anyway, the book-signing line is moving, and I get ready to call the next person up, and so I look up and there she is. She's standing right there. And, man, all of the parts were the same—she was the same size as my grandma and the same shape that my grandma was, and they had the same face and the same posture. I honestly couldn't fucking believe it. I very loudly said, "Oh my God."

She walked up, held me by the shoulders, and said hello. And I was doing semi-okay when I was just looking at her. But to hear her voice—which sounded EXACTLY like my grandma's voice—I couldn't handle it. I gave her a hug and just held her real tight and did my best not to cry. It was wild. My brain and my eyes and my heart and my legs didn't know how to react. I'd spent so much of the most important parts of my early life with my grandma; she'd taken care of my sisters and me as children, and then we'd all lived together for pretty much all of my middle school and certainly all of my high school. As such, when she passed away, it put a whole bunch of anger in my chest that took a long time to go away. And so to see a version of her again and to hear a version of her again, it was . . . I don't know. It was fucking wild. I remember spending that night in my hotel room alone, eating way too much food and thinking about her.

DMX has a song called "I Miss You." On it, he helplessly asks for just one more hug from his deceased grandma. That's how those two things are related here, more or less.

•••••

SO, WHAT JOKE WAS IT THAT DMX TOLD?

It seems unlikely that it was a knock-knock joke. The only way I can see it being one is if DMX told that same knock-knock joke that Tom Hanks's character tells in 2002's *Catch Me If You Can*. The way that joke works is that Carl Hanratty, a stodgy FBI agent who works in the bank-fraud department, is riding around in a car with a couple of other FBI agents, who are giving him a hard time about being so serious all the time. Hanratty, fed up with their criticism and also fed up with the unprofessional way he thinks they approach the job, asks them if it'd make them feel better if he told them a joke. They both agree that it would. "Knock, knock," says Hanratty. The agent sitting in the passenger seat asks who's there, and so Hanratty, proud to have snared them in his trap, lets a tiny piece of a smile sneak out of the side of his mouth. Then he straightens himself out, says, "Go fuck yourselves," and turns the radio up. If DMX told a knock-knock joke that did not elicit laughs, then it was probably that one.

It also seems unlikely that DMX would go with anything especially madcap or zany for his joke. The closest to "zany" DMX has ever gotten was when he rapped an impromptu version of "Rudolph, the Red-Nosed Reindeer" during an interview in 2012. Even that felt a little bit ominous, though. I greatly enjoy thinking about the night that Donner and Dasher and Blitzen and the rest of Santa's reindeer heard that DMX had officially endorsed Rudolph as the alpha reindeer. A lot of DMX's music has a through line in it about how important it is that your friends will be there for you whether you're famous or not. And because there's that line in "Rudolph, the Red-Nosed Reindeer" where we find out that the other reindeer hated Rudolph and made fun of Rudolph all the way up until Santa declared that Rudolph was special, I have to assume that DMX does not think favorably of those reindeer.

The obvious choice is that it was something vulgar or offensive, but I feel like that's too easy. I feel like if DMX was going to tell a joke, he'd know that people would be expecting him to show up with something vulgar or offensive. And because he'd know that they were expecting that of him, he'd probably go in a totally different direction. (If he did end up going with something from this category, it'd probably be something really out there, like the one about the child murderer and the nine-year-old that popped up on the internet several years ago. I'm gonna slide that one down into the footnotes; that way it seems like I'm whispering it to you in private, which is the only way I have ever told this particular joke.) (Also: I don't know who it was that came up with that joke, by the way. And I refuse to search "child murderer nine-year-old joke" on Google because, I mean, what good can come from that? Sorry in advance if I messed up any of the parts of it. And sorry in advance for not crediting the person who thought of it. Anyway, here's the joke.)[6]

I think DMX would end up going with a word-play kind of joke. That feels the most right to me. He'd surprise them, because he knows what we all know, and that's that the best kinds of jokes are the ones that catch you off guard. That's why I think he'd show up with something that was pun based—a dad joke, if you will. Probably something like "Why are dogs like iPhones? Because they have . . . *collar ID*."

---

6. A child murderer and a nine-year-old are walking deep in a spooky forest as the sun sets. "Man, it sure is scary out here," says the nine-year-old. "You're telling me," says the child murderer. "And I'm gonna have to walk back to the car alone after this, too."

HOW MUCH IS THE [RAPPER] ROOKIE CARD WORTH?

SOMEWHERE NEAR THE END OF 2019, I bought a Luka Dončić rookie card. I didn't just buy a regular one, though. I bought one that had been professionally graded by Professional Sports Authenticator (PSA), an authentication company that scores the condition of trading cards (and comics and whatnot) on a scale of 1 to 10.

Now, there are a lot of alleyways and backtrails you can travel down once you get to talking about trading cards, but the main three details for the conversation you and I are about to have are (1) trading cards have exploded in value over these past couple years, (2) graded cards are always going to be worth more than nongraded cards, and (3) the most valuable cards are the ones from good sets that feature players whose legacies either are already secure[1] or have the potential to be something really gigantic.

That's why I bought the type of Luka card that I bought when I bought it. A friend of mine whom I knew to be an expert in the space[2] told me that Luka cards were likely going to jump up in value very soon, and so I picked up a PSA 10 rookie card of his from the 2018 Panini Prizm set. It cost me about $600, which I considered to be wholly unreasonable at the time. About a week or so after I got it, Luka recorded his first triple-double of the 2020 season. Shortly after that, he put up two triple-doubles back-to-back. Five days later, he set a new career high in points (thirty-eight), and then ten days after that, he set a new career high in points again (forty-two this time, including eleven rebounds and twelve assists just for fun). And things just kept going on and on like that for him.

By the end of the regular season, Luka had been named to the All-Star team and named to the All-NBA First Team, the second distinction unofficially dubbing him one of the five best basketball players on the planet. In his first playoff game, he scored forty-two points, the most ever in a debut. Later in the series, he became the youngest player ever to hang a forty-point triple-double on an opponent, a feat made all the more overwhelming by the fact that he scored the final seven points of the game for his team during the last minute of overtime, including a crossover step-back 3 at the buzzer to win the game.

And somewhere around that time, the rookie card that I'd bought for $600 had begun selling for upward of $9,000.[3]

All of that is to say, this chapter is about rapper rookie cards. The idea is to lay out what the rookie cards for various rappers would be worth right now if they existed, and also to lay out what they'd be worth a decade from now.[4]

•••••

THREE THINGS BEFORE WE MOVE ON

Firstly: Mos Def actually had a song where he talked about this exact thing. It was called "Oh No" and it came out in 2000. In it, he warned during the first verse, "The kids better buy my rookie card now / 'Cause after this

---

1. Two Michael Jordan rookie cards from the 1986 Fleer set that had been graded as 10s by PSA sold for $738,000 each in 2021.
2. Josh Luber.
3. This is why I now have a rule in place that if a rich white person gives me any sort of financial advice, I make sure and take it seriously.
4. As a general rule here, let's say that a rapper's rookie card would come from whatever year it was that the rapper released their debut album. So for example, Nas released his debut album in 1994. That's when his rookie card would have been released. Rapsody's debut album came out in 2012. That's when her rookie card would have been released. On and on like that.

BECKETT
RAPPER
MAGAZINE

Issue #3 Oct/Nov 2021 $2.95

year, the price ain't comin' down." So because of that, his will be the first card that we appraise.

Secondly: There was a trading-card company in the late '80s and early '90s called Pro Set. It was mostly known for football cards but also made cards for other things, including a one-off series of *Yo! MTV Raps* trading cards. I collected those when I was a kid. It was never a prestigious set, which is why they're all pretty much worthless now. But they're still fun to open and look at. You can buy entire boxes of unopened packs online for less than twenty dollars. I bought one while I was working on this book. I opened one of the packs and found three identical Beastie Boys cards in there. I thought this to be a very fortuitous turn of events and have since refused to open any other packs. There's nowhere to go but down after that. There's no beating a Beastie Boys three of a kind in a single pack.

Thirdly: For the purposes of this chapter, let's pretend we're talking about rapper rookie cards that (a) have been graded a 10 by PSA and (b) are from a make-believe set that is universally regarded as being of high quality and covetable scarcity. And, as is the case in most rap-based hypotheticals, let's use Jay-Z to set the market here. In March of 2021, an autographed Jay-Z card that was part of the 2005–2006 Topps Chrome Autographs series and had been graded a 9 by an authentication company sold at auction for over $105,000. Let's make a rule that no card can be appraised higher than that.

•••••

Mos Def's Rookie Card: This will be either very controversial or not controversial at all, and the thing that's maybe going to decide where you land on that debate is your opinion of stylish hats. If we were to gather together and give scores to (1) An Ear for Beats, (2) Lyrical Dexterity, (3) General Coolness, (4) Specific Likability, and (5) Overall Output, then Mos Def would be one of the fifteen greatest rappers who has ever lived. He can do pretty much anything you need a top-level rapper to do on a song. And that means his rookie card should be worth tens of thousands of dollars. However, given that the Mos Def Is One of the Fifteen Greatest Rappers Who Has Ever Lived story line isn't one that is widely accepted, it knocks the value of his card down some. Mos Def's rookie card is currently worth $3,600. In ten years, it'll be worth $4,300.

MC Lyte's Rookie Card: Did you know that MC Lyte was the first woman ever to release a full rap album as a solo artist? That's a true thing. It happened in 1998 when she put out *Lyte as a Rock*, which went on to become one of the most influential rap albums ever. (The *Source* picked it as one of the hundred best hip-hop albums of all time. *Pitchfork* picked it as one of the two hundred overall best albums of the decade. *NME* declared that it was one of the twenty-five most impactful hip-hop albums ever.) MC Lyte's rookie card is currently worth $18,000. In ten years, it'll be worth $23,500.

Dr. Dre's Rookie Card: I would argue that Dr. Dre is the most important producer in the history of rap and also the most talented producer in the history of rap. (That's why his rookie card is going to come in at such a high price. More on this in a second.) His production has never felt overwhelming or intrusive on songs, but it's always felt unforgettable and essential on songs, which is the hardest place to land in production. He could go from a song for himself in his twenties ("Nuthin' but a 'G' Thang," for example), to a song for himself in his thirties ("Still D.R.E.," for example), to a song for Eminem ("My Name Is," for example), to a song for 50 Cent ("In da Club," for example), to a song for Mary J. Blige ("Family Affair," for example), to a song for 2Pac ("California Love"), to a song for N.W.A. ("Fuck tha Police," for example), to a song for Bilal ("Fast Lane," for example). He has, for the entirety of his career, been able to hit any pitch that someone could throw at him. Dr. Dre's rookie card is currently worth $53,000. In ten years, it'll be worth $62,000.

Megan Thee Stallion's Rookie Card: A thing that happens in card collecting is a new person will pop up that everyone will get excited about because they have a clear amount of big potential, and so the rich collectors will buy up as many of that person's cards as possible. (They might buy one hundred to two hundred of the player's cards when they're relatively cheap in hopes of that player taking off into the stratosphere and pulling the price of said cards along with them.) That's the move with a Megan Thee Stallion rookie card. You grab as many of them as you can find and then sit on them until it's time to buy some beachfront property somewhere in twenty-five years. Megan's rookie card is currently worth $1,600. I have no idea how much it'll be worth in a decade; I just know it'll be a lot.

Mac Miller's Rookie Card: Tracing the arc of Mac Miller's musical career from his earliest stuff (2007's *But My Mackin' Ain't Easy*, which he released when he was just fifteen) to his final tapes (*Swimming*, which was released in August of 2018, about a month before he passed away, and *Circles*, which was released in January of 2020 with the blessing of his family) is a very beautiful and emotional look at the way an artist homes in on what it is exactly that makes them special, aims all of their creative energy toward it, and then creates something undeniable.[5] You can feel it playing out over the course of the albums, and you can feel it when he fully arrives there on *Swimming* and *Circles*. It's really stunning to hear that change, especially in revisiting the entirety of his work after his passing. And I know I'm supposed to be doing the rookie-card thing here for a bunch of rappers, but I don't want to do that with Mac Miller. I just want to go watch the video for his NPR Tiny Desk Concert on YouTube again. It came out during his promo run for *Swimming*. It's one of the very last videos of him performing. He does "Small Worlds," "What's the Use?" (featuring Thundercat), and "2009." It's really something special. He's in complete control of his musicianship. So that's what I'm gonna do. And I think you should do the same.

Actually, you know what? I'm going to abandon the rapper-rookie-card thing entirely. I was gonna do, like, twenty of them. But I'm not gonna do any more of those. The rest of this chapter is just going to be some stuff about Mac Miller.

•••••

My favorite non-music Mac Miller memory is when he responded to being name-dropped alongside several other rappers by Kendrick Lamar. What happened was

5. He had a great quote about this in a 2018 profile of him at *Vulture* written by Craig Jenkins, saying of the HBO documentary *The Zen Diaries of Garry Shandling*, "He was always writing the words, 'Just be Garry.' 'Just be Garry.' And that shit struck a chord with me because that's the goal, to get better and to try to make this shit the most of a reflection of who I am."

Kendrick had gotten tapped by Big Sean to deliver a guest verse for a song called "Control." And so Kendrick, maybe because he just felt like warring or maybe because he'd been surfing a massive months-long tidal wave of praise following the release of his brilliant debut album *Good Kid, M.A.A.D City* or maybe because of some combination of the two or maybe because of something else entirely, showed up with a flamethrower and a machete and just started destroying things.

The verse started off, and Kendrick was more growly than normal and angrier than normal and meaner than normal. It was excellent, and he was excellent. And then came his big surprise. First, he aligned himself with who he (presumably) considered to be the greatest rappers ever (Jay-Z, Nas, Eminem, and André 3000). Second, he demanded that all the new rappers move along because they weren't allowed to be in the conversation. And then third, he listed off a bunch of names of people he considered to be his contemporaries ("Jermaine Cole, Big K.R.I.T., Wale, Pusha T, Meek Mill, A$AP Rocky, Drake, Big Sean, Jay [Electronica], Tyler, Mac Miller") and said he had love for them but that he was going to try to rap murder them. And that's where my favorite Mac Miller moment happened.

One of the lines that Kendrick said was about how he wanted to make it so that fans wouldn't "wanna hear not one more noun or verb" from any of the rappers he listed ever again. And so Mac Miller heard that, then went on Twitter and playfully tweeted, "If I can't do no more nouns or verbs ima start comin with the wildest adjective bars that anyone has ever heard." You were reading the words on a screen, but you could somehow hear him laughing. It was a perfect response.

•••••

My second-favorite non-music Mac Miller memory happened in 2012. I'd been working on a coloring book with the rapper Bun B (it was called *Bun B's Rap Coloring and Activity Book,* and it was, quite simply, a coloring and activity book filled with illustrations of rappers for people to color). And Mac Miller was one of the artists that Bun had arranged to be in there. And as part of a TV appearance that Mac was doing, the people who were interviewing him had handed out copies of his page to the audience and told them to color them so Mac could see them when he arrived. Mac got there, and the interviewer mentioned what they'd done, and so Mac looked out into the audience to see a bunch of copies of his page from the coloring book being held up at him. He laughed about it, then made a quick joke about how some of the people didn't even bother to color his face, because he was white and the drawing was on a white page, and then he laughed again. He was three or four levels past charming. It was a perfect response.

•••••

Somewhere around July of 2020, my wife and kids and I had started to go a little stir-crazy because we hadn't really left our house for a couple months, because we'd been doing the social-distancing thing because of the pandemic. We decided to try and figure out a way to get away for a weekend. And so we got on Airbnb and searched for a spot that we could rent that (a) was within reasonable driving distance of our house, (b) was secluded enough that we wouldn't have to worry about running into people, and (c) was not too expensive. After

a not-small amount of time of location hunting, we found one. It was only about forty minutes away, and also it had private access to a small piece of a river that ran through the house's backyard, and also it was available for a reasonable rate. So we rented it and then drove there, and it was a very pleasant couple of days.

On our second morning there, I sat outside on the back porch alone and stared at the trees and the water. After maybe ten seconds of doing that, I reached for my phone. I opened up iTunes, tapped the little Browse icon, then started scrolling. I wanted to listen to something besides the birds and the bugs because in my estimation, birds and bugs are wildly overrated musical artists.

Eventually I came across Mac Miller's *Circles*, an album I'd avoided listening to prior to that moment because everything I'd read about it talked about how emotional it was to hear Mac on it even almost two years after his passing. I put my headphones on, then connected them to my phone, then tapped the *Circles* album cover, then tapped on the first song ("Circles"). And, I mean, *goddamn.*

It starts off in the most pulverizing way possible. You hear this very warm, very mellow, very welcoming arrangement of cymbals and a bass guitar and a xylophone and (maybe) some slightly distorted keys; it feels exactly like the morning on a day that you know ahead of time has the potential to carry a significant emotional toll, like if a close friend of yours was moving to a new town to start a dream job they were very excited about, or like if you were going to see your family for the first time in months.

And then you hear Mac. And his voice feels like soft sand under your fingertips. And he says, "Well / This is what it looks like / Right before you fall." And, I mean, *goddamn.*

I listened to that whole album on that back porch by myself before anyone else in the house was awake. And I didn't do anything else. I just sat there. Listening. And I don't know why I didn't move. And I don't know why I didn't pick up my phone to scroll the internet or Twitter or whatever like I normally do when I listen to music in a recreational capacity. But I didn't. All I did was listen. And feel. And it was sad in the beginning, but only in the beginning. Because after that sadness began to disintegrate away, it started to feel . . . *comforting*, I think. It made me feel safe and like things were going to be okay. And, to be sure, I didn't sit down out there feeling particularly stressed out about anything; I didn't have a problem that needed to be solved – at least, not one that I directly understood. But I still felt that relief. And it was wonderful. It was a feeling that I knew I was going to carry in my chest for a long time. And as the album drifted its way through the last song, I kept thinking about how I was feeling a way that I couldn't all the way explain, or even understand.

And then Mac finished the album. And as he closed out that last song, he sang, "And everybody means something / When they're stuck on your mind / But every now and again, why can't we just be fine?"

It was a perfect response.

WHICH VERSION OF DRAKE DO WE NEED FOR THESE HYPOTHETICALS?

BY 2011, DRAKE WAS ALREADY A STAR. He'd put out a few different mixtapes;[1] he'd gotten a career-generating co-sign by Lil Wayne (this happened in 2008, when Wayne was the biggest rapper in the world); he'd released his big-label debut, *Thank Me Later*, which was very successful;[2] and he'd put eight different songs in a row up on the Platinum- or Multiplatinum-Selling Singles scoreboard.[3] But we'd not yet witnessed the kind of personality whiplash that he was gonna hit us all with that summer. And what I mean is this:

Drake does this thing where he recalibrates his Rapper Persona so that it best fits whatever it is he's trying to accomplish during a particular song. It's something we all know now. If, for example, he wants a song to feel especially aggressive, like what he did with "Energy" on 2015's *If You're Reading This It's Too Late*, he becomes Vengeful Drake. If he wants a song to feel like you're supposed to listen to it while sipping a colorful drink on a beach, like what he did with "Controlla" or "One Dance" on 2016's *Views*, he becomes Caribbean Drake. If he wants a song to feel very thoughtful, like what he did with "Look What You've Done" on 2011's *Take Care*, he becomes Contemplative Drake. He has a ton of different versions of himself that he can tap into and make use of. It's maybe his single greatest strength as a rapper.

Anyway, up through 2011, we'd seen several different versions of Drake. However, it felt like it was one of those things that maybe was happening but also maybe wasn't happening – you know what I'm saying? But then that summer rolled around. And it wasn't a question anymore. And what I mean is this:

At the time, Drake was prepping for the release of his sophomore album, *Take Care*. And, as most every musician does during an album-rollout period, he began releasing singles for it. The first one he put out was called "Marvins Room," and it was a doozy of a song. It was groggy and foggy and transitory. The whole thing was just Drake, completely bare, drunk, on the phone, singing to an ex-girlfriend late at night, telling her that he missed her and that she should leave her current boyfriend and that he was having a hard time dealing with being famous, and asking her to please talk to him. He was emoting insecurity and vulnerability and just trying to find a way to keep from falling over.

The single he put out after that was called "Headlines," and it drove a hundred miles per hour in the opposite direction. It was big and fast moving and vibrant and assertive.[4] It literally started with him talking about how he might overdose on confidence, and then it just carried forward that energy from there. He spent the whole song talking shit. There was even a part in it where he proclaimed that other rappers were too emotional and were wasting too much time talking about their feelings. It was nuts. Everyone heard that line and was like, "Wait,

---

1. *Room for Improvement*, *Comeback Season*, and *So Far Gone*.
2. Over two million copies sold.
3. "Best I Ever Had" (4× platinum), "Successful" (platinum), "I'm Goin' In" (platinum), "Forever" (6× platinum), "Over" (3× platinum), "Find Your Love" (3× platinum), "Miss Me" (platinum), and "Fancy" (platinum).
4. Even the videos were diametrically opposed. In the "Marvins Room" video, Drake was alone in a nightclub, drinking and staring at himself in a bathroom mirror. In the video for "Headlines," he was surrounded by people, and he wore batting gloves just because he thought they looked cool, and he sat at the head of a large table for a meal with a bunch of his underlings, and he held an unlit cigar while riding an elevator. (The cigar is how you know he was really feeling himself. Tony Soprano is the only guy in history who has smoked a cigar because he enjoyed it. Every other guy who's held a cigar only did so because they couldn't find a big enough megaphone to shout into about how interesting they thought themselves to be.)

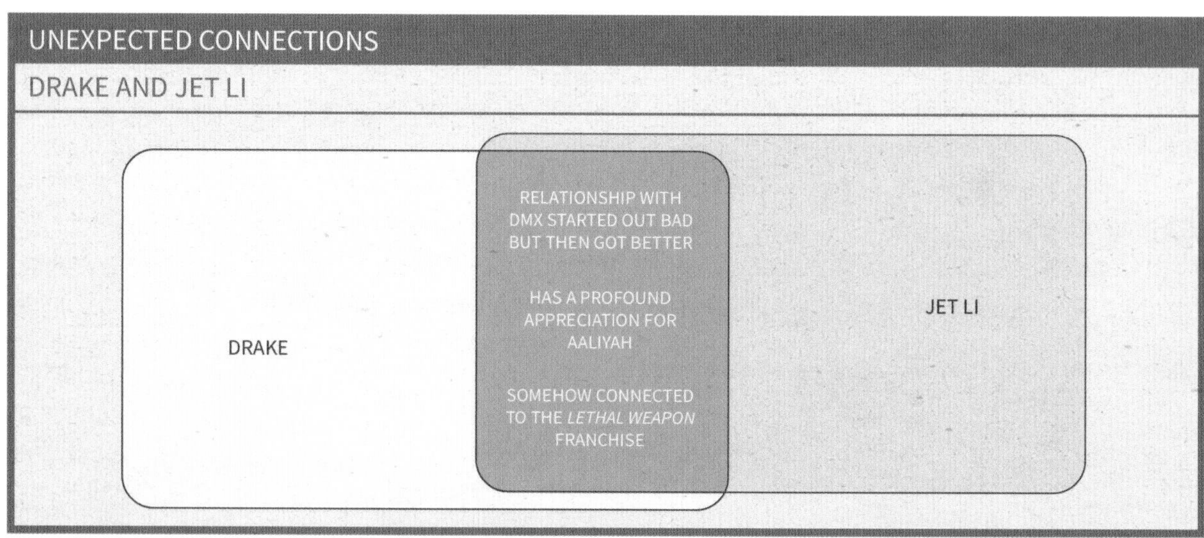

wait, wait. You *just* put out a song doing exactly that! What's happening right now?!" But it didn't matter. He just kept cruising along. And what's more: he was so confident with the contradiction that, ultimately, it felt like we must've been overreacting.

And that was that. He knew going forward he could do whatever he wanted; he could be whoever he wanted to be, whenever he wanted to be him.

And now, a decade later, Drake has seven hundred different versions of Drake that he can call upon whenever he needs to.

•••••

There's this movie I like called *The One*. It came out back in 2001, but I still watch it every so often. It stars Jet Li and Jason Statham and Delroy Lindo and Carla Gugino, and Jet Li and Statham and Lindo and Gugino are all great, and so that's part of why I like it, but mostly I like it because I'm fascinated with the core idea of the plot.

In *The One*, it gets explained that the universe isn't actually a universe; it's a multiverse (a whole bunch of universes that are interconnected), and so rather than there just being one of you, there are a bunch of you, each one existing "in present time in parallel universes." (Picture there are fifty different versions of Earth, and each Earth has a different you on it. That's what's going on.) There's some other stuff that happens in the movie,[5] but that's the main part of it, or at least the part that seemed "main" to me. It's also the foundation for this particular chapter.

Let's you and I pretend three things:

First, let's you and I pretend that the hypotheticals presented in the following section are of extreme and utmost importance.

5. That "other stuff" includes, but is not limited to, a bomb hidden inside of a rat, Jet Li running literally fifty miles per hour on foot as cops chase him in cars, Jet Li in dreadlocks (which is somehow more surprising than him running faster than a Ford Focus), and a fight scene set to "Bodies" by Drowning Pool.

Second, let's you and I pretend that all of the different versions of Drake that he's played in his songs exist in present time and in parallel universes. There's an Earth where Benevolent Drake from "God's Plan" lives, and there's a different Earth where Arrogant Drake from "All Me" lives, and there's yet still a different Earth where War Drake from "Back to Back" lives. On and on and on like that, every different Earth containing a different version of Drake.

And third, let's you and I also pretend that, through some unexplainable and likely very improbable manner, we can transport whatever version of Drake we want to wherever we might need him.

That all being the case, the question here becomes obvious: What version of Drake would be the most helpful in each of the following hypotheticals?

•••••

The Hypothetical: You're at the grocery store. And you see the parent of a child in your kid's class. And you don't like this person. But because your children are in the same class, you've been forced into enough situations with him that you definitely know his name. (His name is probably something like Steve, although you only ever refer to him in your head as Fucking Steve.) And as you stare at him and happily imagine one of the aisle signs that hang from the ceiling breaking off and bonking him on the head, he looks up. And the two of you make eye contact, which he considers to be a great turn of events because he likes you a lot and has no idea that you pray every day that he closes his fingers in a door. He smiles a big smile and he heads your way. It's clear he's going to try and talk to you for a few seconds that, inevitably, will feel like a few hours.

So, which version of Drake do you need for this hypothetical?

Drake has a song called "No Lie." And there's a part in it where he mentions seeing someone he used to talk to, and then, because he's petty, he pretends not to know her name. ("Aw, that looks like what's her name / Chances are it's what's her name.") That's the version of Drake you need here. You need Pretends to Be Bad with Names Drake. Because a good way to run someone off is to let them know that you don't care about them or even like them all that much, and a surefire way to do that is to pretend not to know their name once or twice. It's a sneaky way to be disrespectful. It lets you exert your superiority over the person while sidestepping any of the culpability otherwise attached to those sorts of actions. Pretends to Be Bad with Names Drake is the move here.

The Hypothetical: It's September. And you've just opened your mailbox. And you see you've received a letter from the IRS. You open it. And you read it. And then all of your insides fall out of your butt, because the letter says that you owe the government a not insubstantial amount of money because you misfiled your taxes earlier that year. Which version of Drake do you need for this hypothetical?

You need Experience with the IRS Drake. He did that version of himself on 2013's "Jodeci Freestyle," saying that he had the Feds rooting around in his finances, trying to catch him on tax evasion. He'd have some good advice for you here. And if you feel like you're past the point of needing advice and want to go straight to preparing to fight the charges, then you could probably call Legal Defense Drake. He's had a few different

songs where he's mentioned how talented his lawyers are, including but not limited to "Going in for Life" and "The Winner," both of which were released early in his career.[6] And if you're like, "Fuck it. I'm just gonna not pay this and hope it goes away," then go ahead and dial up Fuck Paying Taxes Drake, who appeared on 2020's "Life Is Good."[7]

The Hypothetical: You chose to get re-bar-mitzvahed as a recommitment to the Jewish religion. Which version of Drake do you need for this hypothetical?

You need I Chose to Get Re-Bar-Mitzvahed as a Recommitment to the Jewish Religion Drake. He was that version of himself for the video for "HYFR" in 2011. (I was very excited when I watched this video the first time, because I turned thirty in 2011, and in the weeks leading up to that birthday, I was going around telling everyone that I was gonna have a double quinceañera to celebrate, and everyone kept saying I was stupid for wanting to do that. Then, eight or nine months later, Drake showed up basically doing exactly that same thing.)

The Hypothetical: You're scrolling through your various social-media feeds. And you see a person has posted a picture celebrating something they like. There are twenty-seven comments on there from people also celebrating the thing and being happy. You, however, want to comment on the picture to let everyone know that you don't like the thing that they all like. Which version of Drake do you need for this hypothetical?

You need the Drake from "Hotline Bling," which is a song where he complains about how a woman he used to talk to did not seal herself off in a tomb and wait for him after he left the city. You need Overstepping Your Bounds Drake.

The Hypothetical: You play basketball professionally for whatever professional basketball team happens to be your favorite. During the second quarter of an inconsequential game three months before the playoffs start, you sprain your ankle while attempting to secure a rebound. You fall to the ground in a heap. It hurts a lot, but you're certain that it's not broken. And because you are a professional athlete with a fiercely competitive spirit, your brain tells you that it's fine, that you can play through it, that you owe it to your team to try and play through the pain. Which version of Drake do you need for this hypothetical?

You need Orthopedic Doctor Drake. He did that version of himself on 2009's "Forever" when he reminded everyone that ankle sprains should be taken seriously. (The full line is "Like a sprained ankle, boy, I ain't nothing to play with.")

The Hypothetical: It's time for you to ask for a raise at work, but your insecurity is getting the best of you. You feel like you definitely deserve a raise, but your boss is annoying and difficult with these types of conversations. Which version of Drake do you need for this hypothetical?

---

6. By the way: In 2013, I made a rap coloring book with Bun B. He wanted Drake to be in it, which meant I had to reach out to Drake's lawyer to get a form signed saying that it was okay for us to use Drake's likeness in the book. I found his lawyer (or whoever it was on the other end of those emails) to be perfectly pleasant and prompt.

7. "Haven't done my taxes / I'm too turnt up."

You need I'm the Motherfucking Man Drake. You need the Drake from "All Me," who shouts, "Should I listen to everybody or myself? / 'Cause myself just told myself, 'You're the motherfucking man, you don't need no help!'" That's who you want in your ear, powering you up.

The Hypothetical: You didn't get the raise. Your boss told you that he came by your office to talk to you, and he saw you in there on your computer pulling up Drake song after Drake song after Drake song on YouTube. "It looked like you were trying to pump yourself up for something," he said, and he smiled just enough to let you know that he thought it was a ridiculous thing. So now you're sitting in your car at home. And you're in the garage. And you're frustrated. And mad. And you can tell that you're about to walk into your house and pick a fight with your significant other because you're an asshole. So you walk in and you see your significant other. And they say hello and you grunt back, and they can tell that you're upset. They ask what's wrong. You say, "Nothing. I don't wanna talk about it." And they say, "Okay. Well, my day off today was good. I got some yard work done. And I dropped off some stuff at the Goodwill. And I talked to my mom for a bit." And you can't help yourself. You wanna make a biting comment. Which version of Drake do you need for this hypothetical?

Drake has a song called "Trophies." And the chorus includes a part where he says, "Shit don't come with trophies / Ain't no envelopes to open." That's the Drake you need right here. You need They Don't Have No Award for That Drake.[8]

The Hypothetical: You invent a small item that changes everything forever. And because of it, you grow to be wildly rich. Year after year, money piles its way into your bank account. At twenty-five, you're a millionaire. At thirty-five, you're a multimillionaire. At forty-five, you're worth upward of 100 million dollars. Here's the thing, though: You grew up poor. And that's why you feel like you're grateful for everything you have. But your children were born when you were thirty-two, which means they have only ever known a life of means. And you slightly resent them for it. So you decide that when you die, you're not going to leave them anything. You want them to build their own fortunes. Which Drake do you need for this hypothetical?

There are two Drakes that need to be called on here. The first Drake you need is Very Bad with Money Drake. He did that version of himself on 2019's "Money in the Grave," during which he tells everyone that when he dies, he would like to be buried with all of his money. So there you go. If you don't want to give your money to your children, then just get buried with it. It's a really bad idea, but also it's kind of an incredible idea, if for no other reason than because it guarantees that someone will eventually dig you up from your grave. And the second Drake you need is Very Good with Money Drake. He's there to talk to your kids and to help them figure out how to generate income. (He has a song called "No Tellin'" where he explains that the goal is to try and build multiple income streams.)

The Hypothetical: You're a Jewish American woman in your twenties. You live in New York. You're an aspiring artist, and you spend a lot of time with your best friend, whom

8. I know that he's using the "They don't have no award for that" phrase with a different intent on "Trophies," but the words themselves still work in this context.

you love dearly. Through a certain turn of events, a piece of art you drew was purchased by a nude-dating website. You were paid $8,000 for your work. Now you and your best friend are walking into the bank to deposit the check. Which version of Drake do you need for this hypothetical?

This was actually an episode of *Broad City*, which was a TV show that aired on Comedy Central for five years. I liked it a lot. In the episode here, the two stars, Abbi and Ilana, strut into the bank in celebratory fashion with Abbi's check while Drake's 2013 hit "Started from the Bottom" plays. On that song he's My Friends and I Used to Be Poor but Now We're Rich Drake. That's the version of Drake you need here.

The Hypothetical: You were at the grocery store earlier, and you saw the parent of a kid who's in your kid's class at school. You walked over and said hello and were expecting a warm conversation. However, that was not what happened. What happened was they called you by the wrong name twice in a row. And you're certain that they know what your real name is, because y'all have interacted a number of times outside of the school while y'all waited to pick up your children, which means you're certain that they called you the wrong name on purpose, which means you're certain this person you'd assumed liked you actually does not. Which version of Drake do you need for this hypothetical?

You need Fake Love Drake from 2017's "Fake Love." He's the one who said, "I got fake people showing fake love to me."

YES OR NO IS A MANAGEMENT STRATEGY that I would occasionally employ while I was teaching. It's a very simple, very effective (and, if we're being very honest, very manipulative) tactic that you utilize when you want to try and pin down one piece of a knotty, complicated situation. Here's the way it works:

Let's say that you're in your class and you're walking around the room, checking in on the students as they work independently on whatever assignment it is that you've given them. And a kid raises her hand because she has a question about something. So you listen as she begins to tell you why she doesn't quite understand how the tilt of the Earth on its axis is partly responsible for the seasons that we experience. And right as she's talking her way through her question, you hear a noise behind you. And you turn around just in time to see a kid angrily throw a textbook at someone two seats over. It's clear they're about to fight, so you hustle over there and get in between them.

Now, the student who threw the book (let's call him John) is one of your favorite students. He's a good, smart, sweet kid who has zero history of throwing books (or any other classroom materials) at anyone in class. And the student who got the book thrown at him (let's call him Mario) is one of your least favorite students. He's a rude, unruly, unpleasant kid who leads the league in getting shit thrown at him, because he is constantly bullying other students. And frankly, your initial reaction inside your brain when you see who the participants are in the exchange is something close to "Fuck yes. Way to go, John. I wish more people would throw books at Mario. It should be part of the gym-class curriculum, if you ask me." But you don't say that. Instead, what you say is "You two come with me," and then you escort both of the students to your desk and talk to them about what's just happened.

John explains that the reason he threw the book at Mario was that Mario, who'd been talking shit to him about various things for the past three days, called him a very nasty combination of words when you weren't looking.

"I just couldn't take it anymore," John says.

Mario doesn't deny it. In fact, he says that everything John has said is true.

"I just think he's a bitch," says Mario.

And here's where the YES OR NO thing becomes useful.

Because if you say something to John like "John, do you think it's okay to throw a book at someone," he's likely going to respond with something like "Not usually, no. But in this case, yes. Because Mario has been bullying me. It's been happening all week." And John would be 100 percent right in that assessment of things.

But if you preface it by saying, "John, listen to me. You can only answer this question I'm going to ask you right now with either a YES or a NO. You can't say anything else. Don't say any other words. Only YES or NO: Do you think it's okay to throw a book at someone? Yes or no?" Then (typically) what happens is that question sits differently in John's head. He (typically) won't think of the situation directly as it relates to Mario. He'll (typically) think of it as it relates to all of humanity. Which is why he'll respond then with "No."

And listen: Robbing a situation of the entirety of its context is not the way to go when you want to arrive at equitable justice. That's not the point of YES OR NO as a management strategy. The point of it is to pin down one tricky piece of a complicated situation. Because if you do that, then maybe you can get your arms around all of the other pieces.

At any rate, this chapter is a version of the YES OR NO thing. Each of the other chapters in *Hip-Hop (And Other Things)* has presented one question in pursuit of one well-reasoned, well-researched, well-argued answer. This time, though, things are headed in the opposite direction. Rather than the chapter asking one question with one big answer, it's asking ninety-nine questions, each with a direct answer and only a direct answer. They're not YES OR NO answers exactly, but they're YES OR NO answers in spirit. Nothing is explained. No reasoning is outlined. No context is set. No anything is anythinged.

- **Do you prefer LL COOL J when he needed a beat on "I Need a Beat" or LL COOL J when he needed love on "I Need Love"?** LL COOL J when he needed love.
- **Which rapper looked the coolest getting a haircut?** Big Daddy Kane.
- **Kool Moe Dee when he was by himself or Kool Moe Dee when he was with Treacherous Three?** Kool Moe Dee when he was by himself.
- **MC Lyte on "Paper Thin" or MC Lyte on "Lyte as a Rock"?** MC Lyte on "Paper Thin."
- **What's the order of the songs Grandmaster Flash used in "The Adventures of Grandmaster Flash on the Wheels of Steel" if you arrange them from Most Exciting to Least Exciting?** It's "Another One Bites the Dust" by Queen in first place. Then it's "Good Times" by Chic. Then it's "Apache" by the Incredible Bongo Band. Then it's "Freedom" by Grandmaster Flash and the Furious Five. Then it's "Monster Jam" by Spoonie Gee and the Sequence. Then it's "Rapture" by Blondie. Then it's "The Decoys of Ming the Merciless" by Jackson Beck. Then it's "8th Wonder" by the Sugarhill Gang. Then it's "The Birthday Party" by Grandmaster Flash and the Furious Five. Then it's "Life Story" by the Hellers.
- **What's a song that made you say "You probably should not have combined those two things" when you heard it?** It was when T Ski Valley tried to turn Marvin Gaye's "Sexual Healing" into a rap song.
- **Cooler name: Boogie Down Productions or Public Enemy?** Boogie Down Productions.
- **Whose stock rose the most during the Roxanne Wars?** Roxanne Shanté's.
- **Would you rather be able to rap like Slick Rick or beatbox like Doug E. Fresh?** Rap like Slick Rick.
- **Better sound: the first big electronic drop on Afrika Bambaataa & Soulsonic Force's "Planet Rock" or the recurring teakettle whistle on Public Enemy's "Rebel Without a Pause"?** The recurring teakettle whistle on "Rebel Without a Pause."[1]
- **Does the dictionary know the definition of "friend"?** No.
- **When do the freaks come out?** At night.
- **What's the best part of Kurtis Blow's face?** His eyebrows.
- **Which benefited more from a Run-DMC co-sign: the shoe brand Adidas or the rock band Aerosmith?** Aerosmith.
- **Better video: Salt-n-Pepa's "Shake Your Thang" or Salt-n-Pepa's "Push It"?** "Push It."
- **Whose stock rose the most during the Bridge Wars?** KRS-One's.

1. Technically, it's the pitched-up sax from "The Grunt" by the J.B.'s.

- **Worse outcome: when the Fresh Prince missed the Run-DMC concert on "Girls Ain't Nothing but Trouble" or when Freddy Krueger haunted the Fresh Prince's dreams on "A Nightmare on My Street"?** Freddy Krueger haunting the Fresh Prince on "A Nightmare on My Street."
- **Which of Queen Latifah's wraths was more wrathful: when she talked about feeling the wrath of the giver of all life in "Latifah's Law" or when she talked about feeling the wrath of her madness on "Wrath of My Madness"?** The wrath of the giver of all life.
- **Who do you think would be more fun to hang out with: Kool G Rap & DJ Polo or De La Soul?** De La Soul.
- **Why did Rakim feel like he needed to let everyone know that fish was his favorite dish on "Paid in Full"?** I don't know, but I love it.
- **Ice-T in *Breakin'* or Ice-T in *Breakin' 2: Electric Boogaloo*?** Ice-T in *Breakin' 2: Electric Boogaloo.*
- **What's the best verse on N.W.A.'s "Straight Outta Compton"?** That first verse from Ice Cube.
- **Better comeback album: Queen Latifah's *Black Reign* or Big Daddy Kane's *Looks Like a Job For . . .* ?** Queen Latifah's *Black Reign.*
- **Chuck D or Flavor Flav?** Chuck D.
- **A Tribe Called Quest's "Bonita Applebum" or A Tribe Called Quest's "Can I Kick It?"** "Can I Kick It?"
- **Do you think the twelve-year-old girl that the Fresh Prince talks about in "Parents Just Don't Understand" is the same twelve-year-old girl that 2Pac talks about in "Brenda's Got a Baby"?** No.
- **Naughty by Nature's "Hip Hop Hooray" or Naughty by Nature's "O.P.P."?** "Hip Hop Hooray."
- **Which barbecue would you rather go to: the one that happens in the video for Dr. Dre's "Nuthin' but a 'G' Thang" or the one that happens in the video for Snoop's "Who Am I (What's My Name)?"?** The barbecue in the video for "Nuthin' but a 'G' Thang."
- **What order would you put the songs that appear on the soundtrack for the movie *Juice* in if you were arranging them based on how good they are?** It's "Juice (Know the Ledge)" by Eric B. & Rakim in first place. Then it's "Is It Good to You" by Teddy Riley and Tammy Lucas. Then it's "Uptown Anthem" by Naughty by Nature. Then it's "He's Gamin' on Ya" by Salt-n-Pepa. Then it's "Sex, Money & Murder" by MC Pooh. Then it's "Nuff Respect" by Big Daddy Kane. Then it's "Shoot 'Em Up" by Cypress Hill. Then it's "People Get Ready" by the Brand New Heavies and N'Dea Davenport. Then it's "It's Going Down" by EPMD. Then it's "So You Want to Be a Gangster" by Too Short. Then it's "Don't Be Afraid" by Aaron Hall. Then it's "Flipside" by Juvenile Committee. Then it's "Does Your Man Know About Me" by Rahiem. Then it's "What Could Be Better Bitch" by Son of Bazerk.[2]

---

2. Typically, Dart Adams, who fact-checked this book, stayed invisible during the process. But he made sure to ping me on this to tell me how wrong I was here. His note: "WHOA. The order is definitely 'Juice,' 'Uptown Anthem,' 'It's Going Down,' 'Shoot 'Em Up,' 'Nuff Respect,' 'Don't Be Afraid,' and 'What Could Be Better Bitch.' Then you either fast-forward past the remaining songs or rewind if you overshoot any of these songs listed to get to these songs and these songs only. Please print this as a footnote."

- **Ice-T in *New Jack City* or Ice-T in *Surviving the Game*?** Ice-T in *New Jack City.*
- **What's the most impressive thing that Ice Cube mentions in "It Was a Good Day"?** That he somehow got a triple-double during a game of pickup basketball.
- **Who had the best performance on Wu-Tang Clan's "C.R.E.A.M."?** Raekwon.
- **Who had the second-best performance on Wu-Tang Clan's "C.R.E.A.M."?** Method Man.
- **Better Nate Dogg moment: his work on Warren G's "Regulate" or his work on Snoop's "Ain't No Fun"?** "Regulate."
- **What do you think is Too Short's SECOND-favorite word?** Probably just "bitch" in a different voice.
- **Is there a line on Biggie's "Juicy" that does a better job of simultaneously looking backward and forward in rap than when he says, "You never thought that hip-hop would take it this far"?** No.
- **Would you rather spend a night in the Thunderdome from *Mad Max Beyond Thunderdome* or the Terrordome from Public Enemy's "Welcome to the Terrordome"?** The Terrordome.
- **EPMD's "Gold Digger" or Kanye's "Gold Digger"?** Kanye's.
- **When EPMD said they made a million bucks every six months or when Kanye said that he and Kim made a million a minute?** EPMD.
- **EPMD's series of album titles connected by a theme (*Strictly Business*, *Unfinished Business*, *Business as Usual* . . .) or Kanye's series of albums connected by a theme (*The College Dropout*, *Late Registration*, *Graduation*)?** Kanye.
- **What's a thing a rapper did in a movie that you'll never forget in your whole life?** When Busta Rhymes electrocuted Michael Myers in the dick in *Halloween: Resurrection.*
- **If you were at a rapper dinner party with assigned seating, which two rappers would you hope to get seated next to, because you suspect they'd make for very good dinner conversation?** 1997 Foxy Brown and 2020 Drake.
- **If you take every rapper who's ever appeared in a movie and add up their rapping ability with their acting ability, who gets the highest score?** 2Pac.[1]
- **2Pac or Dr. Dre: who's more memorable on "California Love"?** 2Pac.
- **Mia X on Master P's "Bout It, Bout It" or Mia X on "Make 'Em Say Uhh!"?** Mia X on "Make 'Em Say Uhh!"
- **Rank these Bone Thugs-N-Harmony songs: "Thuggish Ruggish Bone," "Foe tha Love of $," "1st of tha Month," "Tha Crossroads."** It's "Thuggish Ruggish Bone" in first place. Then it's "Tha Crossroads." Then it's "1st of tha Month." Then it's "Foe tha Love of $."
- **What's the first line you think of when someone says the name "Missy Elliott"?** "Beep beep / Who got the keys to the Jeep?"

---

1. Mahershala Ali, who used to rap under the name Prince Ali, is second place.

- **What's the first line you think of when someone says the name "Mos Def"?** "I'm Mos Definite, not Think So"
- **What's the first line you think of when someone says the name "Ma$e"?** "Can't a young man get money anymore?"
- **What's the first line you think of when someone says the name "Mobb Deep"?** "Ain't no such thing as halfway crooks"
- **What's the first line you think of when someone says the name "Lil' Kim"?** "Wanna bumble with the bee, huh?"
- **What's the first line you think of when someone says the name "Eazy-E"?** "Cruisin' down the street in my 6-4"
- **What's the most Jay-Z beat that Jay-Z has ever rapped on?** The one from "Dead Presidents."
- **What overlooked album by one producer do you prefer: Akinyele's *Vagina Diner* or Prince Paul's *A Prince Among Thieves*?** *A Prince Among Thieves.*
- **Which solo Wu-Tang album had the most interesting name?** GZA's *Liquid Swords.*
- **1988 or 1994?** 1994.
- **1996 or 1998?** 1998.
- **2015 or 2017?** 2017.
- **What's the best time someone who wasn't Latino spoke Spanish in a rap song?** When Puff spoke Spanish on "Señorita."
- **Dr. Dre and Snoop on "Deep Cover" or Big Pun and Fat Joe on "Twinz (Deep Cover '98)"?** Big Pun and Fat Joe.
- **DMX on top of the bus in the video for "Ruff Ryders' Anthem" or DMX on top of the building in the video for "Party Up (Up in Here)"?** DMX on top of the building in the video for "Party Up (Up in Here)."
- **Beats by the Pound or Mannie Fresh?** Mannie Fresh.
- **Juvenile or Master P?** Juvenile.
- **Better hype man: Diddy for Biggie or Jermaine Dupri for Da Brat?** Diddy.
- **Method Man or Redman in the video for "Da Rockwilder"?** Redman.
- **Rank the animals in Outkast's "Ms. Jackson" video.** It's the owl in first place. Then it's the snapping turtle. Then it's the dogs. Then it's the cats.
- **Lil' Bow Wow or Lil' Romeo?** Bow Wow.
- **50's *Get Rich or Die Tryin'* or the Game's *The Documentary*?** *Get Rich or Die Tryin'.*
- **Which James Brown sample source is most crucial to rap production?** "Funky Drummer."
- **Nelly's Band-Aid on his face or Murphy Lee's mask on his face?** Nelly's Band-Aid.
- **Does Jay-Z saying that he has ninety-nine problems "but a bitch ain't one" mean that he doesn't care what someone he's deemed a bitch has to say or that the people he's deemed a bitch never present their concerns or worries or frustrations to Jay-Z?** Probably that first one.
- **Lloyd Banks or Meek Mill?** Lloyd Banks.
- **"This Is Why I'm Hot" by MIMS or "Chain Hang Low" by Jibbs?** "This Is Why I'm Hot" by MIMS.
- **Rick Ross rhyming "Atlantic" with "Atlantic" on "Hustlin'" or Chance the Rapper rhyming "Friday" with "Friday" on "Baby Blue"?** Rick Ross.
- **The tuba on Young Buck's "Get Buck" or the tubas in Trick Daddy's "Shut Up"?** Trick Daddy's tubas.

- **50 Cent using candy as a metaphor for his penis on "Candy Shop" or Lil Wayne using candy as a metaphor for his penis on "Lollipop"?** 50 Cent.
- **What grandparent-related line made you say "Now wait just a second" louder: when Lil Wayne said "Your flow never wet like grandma pussy" or when Lil Wayne said "The only time I will depend is when I'm seventy years old / That's when I can't hold my shit within, so I shit on myself"?** The grandma one.
- **Young Jeezy's verse on Kanye's "Amazing" or Kanye's verse on Young Jeezy's "Put On"?** Jeezy's.
- **Kid Cudi's *A Kid Named Cudi* or Wale's *The Mixtape About Nothing*?** Wale's *The Mixtape About Nothing*.
- **In the entire history of rap, who claimed the most amount of ground for themselves with a guest verse?** Nicki Minaj on "Monster."
- **Big Sean playing football in the "I Don't Fuck with You" video or Drake playing football in the "Laugh Now Cry Later" video?** Big Sean playing football.
- **The song "I Like That" by Houston or the song "I Don't Like" by Chief Keef?** "I Don't Like" by Chief Keef.
- **Would you rather have a full version of that song from the beginning of the "Alright" video that Kendrick Lamar did or a full version of that song from the Beats by Dre commercial that Kendrick Lamar did?** The full version of that song from the beginning of the "Alright" video.
- **Nicki Minaj's performance as a rapper in the song "Anaconda" or Jennifer Lopez's performance as an actor in the movie *Anaconda*?** Nicki.
- **D.R.A.M. or Lil Yachty in "Broccoli"?** D.R.A.M.
- **Lil Baby or DaBaby?** Lil Baby.
- **Is Fetty Wap's 2015 album *Fetty Wap* good?** Duh.
- **What rap song made you cry actual tears?** This is dumb, but it's "See You Again" by Wiz Khalifa.
- **Remixes with whole new beats and new verses or remixes with the same beat but new verses and new guest verses?** Same beat, new verses.
- **Cardi B's "Bodak Yellow" or Cardi B's "WAP"?** "WAP."
- **Tyler, the Creator's *Flower Boy* or *Goblin*?** *Flower Boy.*
- **Would you rather an album was way too short or way too long?** Way too short. Word to Tierra Whack's *Whack World*, which is excellent. I wish it was four hours long.
- **Who has the best guest verse on ScHoolboy Q's *Blank Face* LP?** Jadakiss on "Groovy Tony / Eddie Kane."
- **What's the first song you think of when you hear someone say "Mac Miller"?** "Come Back to Earth."
- **What's the first song you think of when you hear someone say "Pusha T"?** I just think of a big pile of cocaine like what Scarface had on his desk at the end of *Scarface*.
- **What's the first song you think of when you hear someone say "Chance the Rapper"?** "Angels."
- **What's the first song you think of when you hear someone say "Young Thug"?** "Harambe."
- **What's the first song you think of when you hear someone say "Megan Thee Stallion"?** "Cash Shit."
- **Mario or John?** John.

GOOD COP / BAD COP: DID ANYONE HAVE A BETTER 2018 THAN CARDI B?

THIS IS A GOOD COP / BAD COP argument about whether or not anyone had a better 2018 than Cardi B. Good Cop is arguing that Cardi had the best 2018. Bad Cop is arguing she didn't.

Good Cop: Here's how massive and influential Cardi B was during her 2018 campaign: In January of that year, the band Maroon 5 put out a single called "Wait." And it w–

Bad Cop, interrupting: Awesome. Great start. You're supposed to be talking about Cardi B, and here you are talking about the guy who used to be on *The Voice*. Not even somebody who's currently on *The Voice*. You picked someone *who used* to be on there.

Good Cop: Relax. I'm gonna get there.

Bad Cop: Was there a video for the song you're talking about?

Good Cop: For Maroon 5's "Wait"? Yes.

Bad Cop: Did Adam Levine take his shirt off in it?

Good Cop: You know that he did. That's actually how the video opens. He's at a funeral, standing in front of a casket. And he's shirtless for some reason. And he places a scorpion on the stomach of the woman who's in the casket (Alexandra Daddario, whom you maybe remember from *San Andreas* or *Baywatch*). And the scorpion stings her. And then she comes back to life.

Bad Cop: That's terrible funeral etiquette. Or . . . wait. Maybe it's *really good* funeral etiquette, what with him bringing her back to life and all? I'm not sure. I don't know the rules there. Scorpions are a no-go at funerals, right?

Good Cop: Here's the point I was making: Maroon 5 put out that song "Wait." And it's pretty clear it was designed to be one of those earworm songs built to dominate the radio. Except it didn't. It never really grabbed on like they were hoping it would. The highest it charted was the twenty-fourth spot. And their single before that ("What Lovers Do") never got past the ninth spot on the chart. And the one before that ("Cold") only got up to sixteenth. At that particular moment, it had been six years since Maroon 5 had a number one hit. And then they tagged Cardi B in for a song. And that was the end of that.

Bad Cop: What do you mean?

Good Cop: What I mean is Maroon 5, one of the biggest and most successful bands of the modern era, went well over half a decade without scoring a number one hit. That's how hard it is to score one of those. And then Cardi B gave them a verse for a song in 2018 ("Girls Like You"). And then, just like that, they finally got another number one hit. Because of Cardi B. And what's more: their single with Cardi B sold more copies by itself than their previous seven songs combined. And what's double more: Cardi B has not given them any more verses for songs since then, and Maroon 5 has not had any more number one hits since then. That was the 2018 Cardi B effect.

Bad Cop: If this is the best argument you could think of for why Cardi B had the best 2018 of anyone, then I have some bad news for you, buddy: this isn't gonna turn out that great for you.

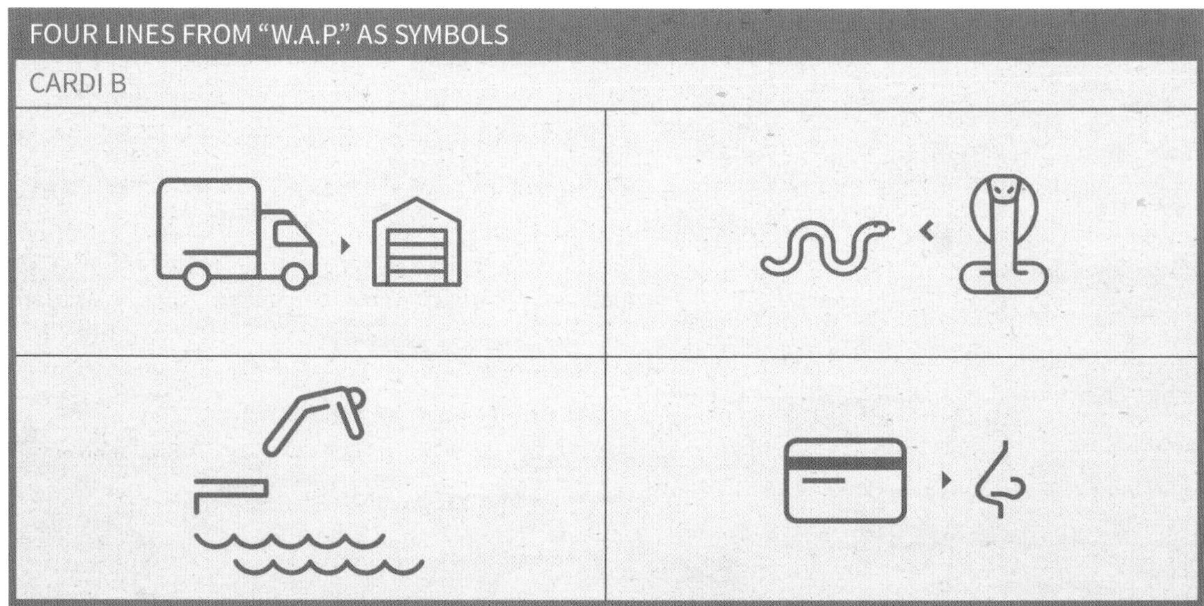

Good Cop: I'm just getting started. There's honestly so much ammo here for this argument that I don't even really know what gun to shoot at you with first. Let's do this. Let's start with 2017. Let's start with "Bodak Yellow."

Bad Cop: Cool. You started your Nobody Had a Better 2018 than Cardi B argument by talking about a musical act that wasn't Cardi B, and now you're gonna talk about a year that wasn't 2018. Awesome. You're doing a wonderful job right now.

Good Cop: Just listen, dummy. Because you need the pre-2018 context to fully understand why (or how) her 2018 was so impactful. Here's the shortest possible version of Cardi B's backstory: around 2013, she started making a tiny name for herself on the internet through videos that she was posting on social media.

Bad Cop: *2013?!*

Good Cop: And she was so charming and so funny and so sharp in those that she flipped those videos into a two-season run as a cast member on *Love & Hip Hop: New York*. And she was so charming and so funny and so sharp on there that she flipped that into a career in rap.

And of course in the beginning there was a crowd of people who were like, "Take it easy, Cardi. Sure, you were great on the show, but that doesn't mean you can rap." But then she started rapping. And pretty much instantly, those same people were like, "Oh, fuck. She's good at this, too."

Bad Cop, sarcastically: What year are you up to? Did you jump back again? I feel like I'm in a fucking Christopher Nolan movie.

Good Cop, ignoring Bad Cop's comment: And all of the stuff that made her feel so special in her social-media videos and on *Love & Hip Hop*—how open she was, how insightful she was, how bombastic she was, how she managed to make you feel like some of her confidence might somehow work its way into your spirit—translated perfectly over to rap. It was immediately clear that she was a star. She was just someone you wanted to see on your TV or phone screen as much as possible.

So Cardi worked through the early parts of her rap career, and she just kept getting better and better. And her voice—this big, imposing, undeniable weapon—just kept getting more and more deadly, and more and more accurate.

So in January of 2017 she puts out a mixtape.[1] And then in February of 2017 she signs her first major deal.[2] And when the BET Awards announced their nominations that May, Cardi, despite the fact that she'd not even put out a proper album yet, got nine (!!!) of them. And then that's when Atlantic Records officially released "Bodak Yellow." And it was fucking over after that.

It was the exact right song at the exact right moment. The *New York Times* called it "the rap anthem of the summer." *Pitchfork* and the *Washington Post* both picked it as the best song of the year. The Grammys nominated it for two different awards. By September, "Bodak Yellow" had climbed its way to the top of the *Billboard* Hot 100 chart, making Cardi the first woman who was a rapper to put a song up there by herself since Lauryn Hill did it in 1998.

Bad Cop: Okay. So clearly, 2017 was a great year for Cardi. But, again, WE'RE SUPPOSED TO BE TALKING ABOUT 2018. You're supposed to be arguing that she had the best 2018 of anyone, not the best 2017. So I'm still winning this argument right now just by default.

Good Cop: I know what I'm supposed to be arguing. But you need all of that information to get to the next section of information.

Bad Cop: Which is what? Are you gonna tell me about something that happened in 2007 now? And then maybe tell me something about a movie from 2014 that doesn't have anything to do with anything? You're the worst Good Cop I've ever seen. You're in the interrogation room, talking about everything *except* what you're supposed to be talking about.

Good Cop: I hate you so much.

Bad Cop: Before you blather on, can I say some stuff for a second now? Can I say some names to you of other people who were big in 2018? Because I would like to do that.

Good Cop: Sure.

Bad Cop: How about this, then? You want a big impact? How about Pusha T puts out his album *Daytona*, which eventually leads to his big rap battle with Drake? That was a huge moment. That was a Stop the Internet for a Few Minutes moment. That was a great year for Pusha.

---

1. *Gangsta Bitch Music, Vol. 2.*
2. With Atlantic Records.

26 WA
3M
wonder
wonder
wonder

Or how about just Drake in general? He put out an album that was 5× platinum and had seven singles that all placed in the top twenty on *Billboard*'s Hot 100. That's not light work.

Good Cop: I mean, it feels like you gotta pick one person or the other there, man.

Bad Cop: Jay-Z and Beyoncé put out a tape in 2018, too. Are we just discarding them? And there was an Eminem album, too. It wasn't that great, but I feel like I should say his name here since he's Eminem. And Travis Scott had a nice little stretch in there. Vince Staples was really exciting on his *FM!* album. Don't forget Tierra Whack. Mac Miller had *Swimming.* There's a bunch.

Good Cop: Without looking it up, can you name two songs off the Jay-Z and Beyoncé tape?

Bad Cop: I don't suppose I can.

Good Cop: Listen: I don't want to make it seem like I'm saying that everyone else had a bad year and that only Cardi B had a good year. That's not the case at all. In fact, it's the opposite. There was a lot of cool stuff that happened in 2018, and certainly some people had great years. It's just that Cardi's was bigger. Because let me run you through some of the stuff that she did now that you know how she teed herself up for 2018.

Bad Cop: Cool. Can't wait to hear more about Maroon 5.

Good Cop: So, like I was saying, Cardi has this breakout year in 2017. She announces herself as a star in rap. But 2018 is when she became a full-on galactic superstar.

First, right there in January, she shows up on the remix of Bruno Mars's "Finesse." And that's where her crossover into that top, Top, TOP level officially starts. So she does that. And then, because of some other guest features she's done, she becomes only the third person ever in the then-sixty-year history of the Hot R&B/Hip-Hop Songs chart to have five songs on there at the same time (and the first woman to do it). And that's before January is even over.

Bad Cop: That's a solid start to the year.

Good Cop: I know.

Bad Cop: Keep going.

Good Cop: By the time April rolled around, which is when *Invasion of Privacy* came out, everyone was so crazy for Cardi that it was an immediate success. It debuted in the top spot on both *Billboard*'s Top 200 chart and *Billboard*'s Top R&B/Hip-Hop Albums chart. And everything just kept getting bigger and wilder. The album eventually went triple platinum. EVERY SINGLE SONG on there eventually charted on the *Billboard* Hot 100 chart (she was the first woman ever to do that). It became the most streamed album by a woman in the history of Apple Music. It was the best-performing rap album of the decade by a woman per *Billboard*'s decade-end chart. It seemed like every day there was some new record or accomplishment she'd pulled off. And that's nothing to say of the actual quality of the actual album.

Bad Cop: Was it good?

Good Cop: Was it good?! It fucking ruled. It was consistently listed among the best albums of the year by every major publication. *Rolling Stone* picked it as the best of the year. So did the *Ringer*. So did *Time*. So did *Entertainment Tonight*. *Billboard*, *Esquire*, and *Entertainment Weekly* had it second. And this is across all genres, not just rap. It was on all of the lists.

And Cardi was incredible on it. The opening track, "Get Up 10," was her just Godzilla-ing her way through one four-minute-long verse. It was masterful. And she leaned into that momentum all the way through the rest of the album. She was affecting ("Be Careful"), and she was funny (the second verse on "Bickenhead" is great), and she proved to have an ear for hits ("I Like It" is an obvious winner here), and she proved to have the kind of talent required to skate across even the most complicated beats ("Money Bag").

Bad Cop: Okay. Well, if I can interje–

Good Cop: Oh, no, no, no. I'm not done yet. We're still in April. There's a bunch more stuff to hit. She also announced that she was pregnant during a performance on *Saturday Night Live*. And it was really wonderful. She performed "Be Careful," perhaps the most tender track on *Invasion of Privacy*. And the camera was in on her real tight. And she was wearing a white dress and holding a mic and rapping into it in a way that felt different than what we'd seen from her before. And then, near the end of the song, the camera pulled back to reveal her belly, and everyone went wild.

She also performed at Coachella and it was a mega-party. Then she went on *Ellen* and talked about both performances. She also co-hosted an episode of *The Tonight Show Starring Jimmy Fallon*. She also popped up at the Met Gala. She was everywhere, at all times, for the entirety of the year. Every month. In July, she had her baby. In August, she pulled up to the MTV Video Music Awards to see how many of the twelve nominations she'd received were going to end in victory. In September, there were rumors that she'd thrown a shoe at Nicki Minaj during an altercation.[3] On and on and on.

Meanwhile, during all of that, she was still putting out singles and still breaking records. She put out that "I Like It" song with Bad Bunny and J Balvin, and there she was again up on top of the Hot 100 chart.[4] "I Like It" eventually became the first song led by a woman to get a billion streams on Spotify. And then there was that song she did with DJ Snake ("Taki Taki") that put her at the top of the Spotify Global Top 50 chart. More and more and more shit just kept happening.

And then in December, *Invasion of Privacy* got nominated for five (!!!) Grammys, including Album of the Year. I can keep going, but I don't think I should have to. I don't know how anyone could argue that someone had a better 2018 than Cardi. It was a twelve-month-long victory lap.

Bad Cop: I didn't know most of that stuff.

---

3. There was a nice bit of circularity here. Because she also threw a shoe at someone during a reunion show after a season of *Love & Hip Hop: New York*. And then she moved on from that show and became super-duper famous because of rap. And people wondered if the level of fame she'd achieved would cause her to corral her rowdiness. And then she reportedly threw a shoe at Nicki Minaj.

4. *Rolling Stone* called it "the best summer song of all time."

Good Cop: That seems to be usually what it is. I've had versions of this same conversation with other Bad Cops, and each time I find out the only reason they were arguing against the idea that Cardi B owned 2018 is because they just didn't know what type of year she'd put together.

Bad Cop: Yeah.

Good Cop: Really, the question here shouldn't be "Did anyone have a better 2018 than Cardi B?" but rather "Where does Cardi B's 2018 rank in the Best Single Year for a Rapper conversation?" That's the level at which she was operating. Her 2018, if we're measuring impact and success, is up there in that top ten or fifteen ever. You can mention her 2018 alongside, say, Snoop's 1994 or, say, Kendrick's 2012.

Bad Cop: Yeah. You're probably right. But I'm supposed to be the Bad Cop. So I'm just gonna argue with you, because that's what I'm supposed to do, like in that old fable where the frog agrees to carry the scorpion across the river, and halfway there the scorpion stings the frog because that's what scorpions do.

Good Cop: I think you might've missed the whole point of that story.

A beat.

Bad Cop: I wonder if that scorpion was related to the one from the Maroon 5 video you mentioned earlier?

Good Cop: Gah, you're the worst.

IGOR

THERE'S A LOT TO GET THROUGH over these next two chapters, so rather than a long introduction that meanders its way toward a point, I'm just going to lay out the vital information here:

- In August of 1995, the *Source* magazine, which by then was the biggest media voice in rap, put on an awards show.
- It was called the *Source* Hip-Hop Music Awards, although everyone just called it the Source Awards.
- It was the second time the *Source* had done a full awards show, but it was the first time it'd been televised.
- More than twenty-six years later, it remains the biggest, most historic, most impactful awards-show night in rap history. (I'll get into all the reasons why later.)
- I didn't watch the show when it happened, because we didn't have cable at my house during that time. I'd seen the big clips from it on the internet, but up until recently, it was impossible to watch the whole thing in its entirety.
- But it's since been loaded to YouTube for everyone to see.
- This chapter and the following chapter are a tick-tock recounting of the 1995 Source Awards.
- There are little time stamps at the beginning of each entry so that you know where we are in the show.
- The first four time stamps are all marked "0:00" because Dr. Dre's section of the Death Row medley performance that started the show is curiously cut off from the only full-length video of the show. That being the case, I just watched a different version to see his parts, then jumped over to the full version when the parts synced up.

0:00: "Ladies and gentlemen, the Source Hip-Hop Music Awards proudly presents the inmates of death row." The show opens with a Death Row medley performance. The stage is set up to look like a stretch of eight prison cells, each of which has an artist inside. One cell doesn't have an actual person in it, though. Instead, what's in there is a cardboard cutout. It's of 2Pac. (He was, at this moment in time, in real-life jail.) Remember when Dr. Dre had that special-effects company resurrect 2Pac via hologram[1] so he could perform at Coachella in 2012? This is like the 1995 version of that.

0:00: The first person out is Dr. Dre, although he doesn't come out of one of the cells; he enters via a door that separates four cells on the left from four cells on the right. If you feel like being especially clever, you can maybe argue that this foreshadows how a bunch of other artists were trapped on Death Row Records, but Dre, who famously walked away from Suge Knight and created Aftermath Entertainment, wasn't.

0:00: Dre does "Keep Their Heads Ringin'." A small fact about "Keep Their Heads Ringin'": it's the only single that was released from the *Friday* soundtrack. (The soundtrack went double platinum, by the way.)[2]

0:00: Another small fact about "Keep Their Heads Ringin'": It's the only rap song ever to use the phrase

---

1. Technically speaking, it wasn't actually a hologram. It was an updated version of an old theater trick called Pepper's Ghost, wherein a projection is reflected up onto something (typically glass, but in the case of Hologram 2Pac, the design studio used Mylar foil). It's all very complicated. Really, all you need to know is that the same people who did special effects for *Avengers: Endgame* are the ones who built Hologram 2Pac.

2. Ice Cube's song "Friday" was released as a promo, but it wasn't eligible to chart.

"ring-a-ding-ding-ding-dong" and make it to the top of the *Billboard* Hot Rap Songs chart.

1:05: The Lady of Rage is here. Awesome. She's performing "Afro Puffs." This is an excellent song. So much so, in fact, that it leads us to one of rap's great WHAT-IFs: The Lady of Rage was a member of Death Row Records when it was as powerful a record label as rap had ever seen. And, per what Rage said in an interview she did with Clover Hope for the book *The Motherlode: 100+ Women Who Made Hip-Hop*, the original plan was for Death Row to release Dr. Dre's *The Chronic* (they did, and it was gigantic), then release Snoop's *Doggystyle* (they did, and it was gigantic), then release her debut album.

They never got around to her part, though, because Death Row had already begun to crumble under the cumulative weight of various tragedies and controversies (as Hope outlines in her book, "Dr. Dre left Death Row, 2Pac was murdered, Suge Knight got locked up, and Snoop Dogg left the label"). What would've happened if the Lady of Rage would've gotten that Dr. Dre–produced album she was supposed to have? What would've happened if it would've come out with the full momentum of Death Row behind it? How much differently would we remember the Lady of Rage today?

2:15: NATE DOGGGGGGGGGGGG! Nate gets a huge ovation from the crowd. And don't forget, this is not only happening as the East Coast vs. West Coast feud begins to brew but also happening in New York. And they're *still* cheering for Nate. This is like LeBron walking into the Boston Garden in 2012 and the crowd cheering for him. Nate Dogg is endlessly unhateable.

3:37: As the members of Death Row make their way out of each cell, I'm reminded of an interview that former co-owners of the *Source* (Dave Mays and Ray Benzino) did with Paul Cantor for *Complex* in 2015 where they mentioned that Suge Knight spent over $100,000 to build the set for their show.

5:07: Here comes DJ Quik. Mostly everyone remembers the combustible moments that Suge and Puff Daddy and Snoop and Outkast had, but DJ Quik was actually the first one at the show to unsheathe his sword and point it at someone's throat. He'd been engaged in a longtime beef with MC Eiht, who he knew was going to be in attendance at the show. As such, he decided to perform "Dollaz + Sense," a diss track he'd written in response to a bunch of stuff that MC Eiht had said about him. And just because he thought it'd be fun to pour a little gasoline on the fire, he began his performance by saying, "I'd like to dedicate this song to my fiancé: MC Eiht."

5:08: Just for the record, if MC Eiht said something about me, then all that means is MC Eiht said something about me. There's no way I'm about to pick a fight with A-Wax from Menace II Society.[3]

5:43: An outstanding line from "Dollaz + Sense": "E-I-H-T / Now shall I continue / Yeah, he left out the *G* / 'Cause a G ain't in you." That's great writing. DJ Quik was so good here. Imagine you're sitting in a theater full of the biggest rappers on the planet, and a guy with a perm is up onstage using your name for a Scripps National Spelling Bee bit.

5:44: Regarding the 5:43 time stamp: The cool news is that DJ Quik and MC Eiht eventually ended their beef in 2002. The other cool news is I just paused this show for a minute to listen to MC Eiht's verse on Kendrick Lamar's "M.A.A.D City" again, and I'm happy to report that verse is still fucking great and MC Eiht is still fucking great.

3. MC Eiht played A-Wax in 1993's *Menace II Society*. He actually won the Acting Performance, Movie or TV award for it at the 1994 Source Awards.

6:47: Oh fuck. They're playing police sirens and a heartbeat sound real loud as DJ Quik makes his way back to his cell. And it looks like they're rolling someone out onto the stage on a gurney via that same door that Dr. Dre came through earlier. Is that …

I think it's . . .

It's gotta be . . .

6:49: SNOOOOOOOOOOOOOP! He sits up on the gurney right as the tombstone bell hits for "Murder Was the Case."[4] The crowd goes bonkers. What an entrance. It's my favorite ever pop-culture use of a gurney. The second-place finisher is when Ginuwine used one when he performed "Pony" on BET's *106 & Park*.[5] The third-place finisher is when they wheeled Hannibal Lecter into that meeting with Senator Ruth Martin in *The Silence of the Lambs*.

6:50: "Murder Was the Case" is a really beautiful song, and it's clear that Snoop wants to perform it well for New York.

7:16: Man, there really isn't anything like mid-'90s Snoop. All of his parts—his voice, his face, his talent, the length of his arms and legs, the control he has over his body—are perfectly perfect.

7:50: Snoop's real name is Calvin Broadus. Calvin Broadus is an exceptionally cool name, which makes it all the more wild that Snoop doesn't even have the coolest name in his own family. His mom beats him (Beverly Broadus Green), and his birth father beats him, too (Vernell Varnado).

8:10: Wait, hold on. All of the people from the Death Row performance just climbed up onto a small platform and hung a white sheet in front of themselves so we couldn't see them, then a couple seconds later someone walked over and yanked the white sheet away to reveal that they'd all disappeared. THEY DID A FUCKING MAGIC TRICK?!?! The most intimidating record label in rap planned out their performance (which was excellent), and someone was like, "That all sounds great. But you know what would be a great closing? Let me ask y'all a question: Have any of y'all ever heard of David Copperfield?" I love this.

8:12: Immediately after the magic trick, the camera cut to a bomb that one of the Death Row inmates left onstage. It detonated, a bunch of pretend explosions went off, and now the show has officially started. And just knowing what we know now about how things in this show eventually are gonna go, the whole Death Row Setting Off Some Explosions as the Opening Act thing is an incredible bit of foreshadowing.

10:10: The official hosts are Doctor Dré and Ed Lover. That's a neat little hat tip, given that (a) Doctor Dré and Ed Lover were the hosts of *Yo! MTV Raps* and (b) the Source Awards originally started out as a special episode of *Yo! MTV Raps* in 1991.

11:58: Heading into the first commercial break for the show, a narrator says that the Source Hip-Hop Music Awards are brought to us by the *Source* magazine, which makes sense, and also, curiously, by "Crooked I: all natural, real fruit juices. They're untouchable!" Crooked I was a part of St. Ides, but it's hard to tell here if this one was alcoholic or nonalcoholic. Either way, it's at least 30 percent funny to go from a performance by Death Row into an advertisement for fruit juice just a couple minutes later.

4. Snoop was charged with murder in 1993. He was eventually acquitted in 1996.
5. This is on YouTube. Go watch it. It's completely ridiculous.

13:25: Time for the first award of the night. It's a big one, too: New Artist of the Year – Solo. The nominees are Biggie, Warren G, Method Man, and Da Brat. That's a solid lineup. Da Brat had just come off being the first woman ever to have a platinum-selling solo album (*Funkdafied*), Biggie had just come off the gargantuan success of *Ready to Die*, Method Man had just come off not only his participation in Wu-Tang Clan's *36 Chambers* but also his own solo album (*Tical*, which had been certified platinum the month before), and Warren G had given us "Regulate," a song so obviously perfect that, as soon as you heard it, you said, "Well, okay, so that's gonna be in all of our lives forever."

One question, though: HOW DOES NAS NOT GET A NOMINATION HERE??????????? He delivered *Illmatic*, which is regularly mentioned as the greatest rap album ever, less than sixteen months before. The only thing I can think of is that maybe he was nominated for the award in 1994? I don't know. I know that Snoop won it that year, but I don't know who was nominated. That information isn't available anywhere on the internet. It seems unlikely that Nas was nominated that year, though, given that the show was held on April 25, 1994, and *Illmatic* had come out just six days earlier.

15:26: And the winner is . . .

15:27: BIGGIE! Bang. Good pick. It had to be him. He was so very clearly the biggest name in rap at that moment. Even if Nas had been nominated, you probably still would've had to go Biggie there.

15:56: "Yo, I got much love for everybody up in here." That's a thing Biggie just said. And I know that he was saying it because that's what people say in those situations, but also . . . I mean . . . you know who wasn't up in there? 2Pac. And I would feel very comfortable betting that if someone had told 2Pac that was what Biggie said there, 2Pac would've taken it to be a sneaky diss of sorts. And to be clear, I don't think that that was what Biggie was actually doing . . . but maybe?

16:28: Next award. It's the New Artist of the Year – Group category. The nominees: Bone Thugs-n-Harmony, Outkast, Ill Al Skratch, and Smif-n-Wessun. This is a two-horse race here. It's gotta be either Bone or Outkast. What a fun battle between those two. They're completely different groups, with completely different energies, headed in two completely different directions.

16:31: Okay, this is the last time I'm going to bring this up, but Outkast being in this category can be taken as further proof that Nas was supposed to have been nominated for New Artist of the Year – Solo this year but wasn't. Because Outkast's *Southernplayalisticadillacmuzik* was released the week after *Illmatic*. If they were eligible for the 1995 iteration of the show, then Nas would've been, too.

18:11: And the winner is . . .

18:18: OUTKAST! Bang. Good pick again. The *Source* is 2 for 2 on winners so far.

18:20: Aaaaaaaand the crowd is booing Outkast. Booing Outkast, who would eventually go on to be perhaps the most impactful duo in rap ever, for winning Best New Artist – Group is way, way, way up on the Things That Have Aged Poorly list. Remember when Indiana fans booed the Pacers for picking Reggie Miller over Steve Alford (???) at the 1987 NBA draft? That's this but multiplied by fifty or sixty.

19:01: André 3000 is absorbing the boos from the crowd. He looks so fucking mad or disappointed or sad or some combination of all three of those things. You can see him silently calculating how best to respond to the situation. Jermaine Dupri, who was raised in Atlanta and who was also at the show, recounted the night to a documentary crew some years later.[6] He said, "It was pretty brutal to just be in a room full of people that don't even really, really care about what you do."

André, who, I'll remind you right here, had just turned twenty years old, takes a breath, steps to the microphone, centers himself, then breathes fire from his nose: "But it's like this, though. I'm tired of folks, you know what I'm saying . . . Close-minded folks, you know what I'm saying . . . It's like we got a demo tape and don't nobody wanna hear it, but it's like this: the South got something to say. That's all I got to say."

That's fucking beautiful. This moment right here is the Declaration of Independence for southern rap. You have one of southern rap's most talented and most brilliant acts up onstage, in a hostile environment—*in the birthplace of rap*—in front of what is essentially every important figure in the business, being booed on a vast scale. And rather than bow to the pressure of the situation, he pretty much says, "You know what? Fuck y'all. We're coming for the throne. Get ready." I love it. I love it so much. I love André 3000 deciding to show up with the same kind of energy that Thor had when he showed up to that fight in Wakanda at the end of *Avengers: Infinity War.*

20:23: A new commercial. It's for an upcoming album from Death Row called *Dogg Food* (from Kurupt and Daz Dillinger). The commercial includes a couple of liquid-metal dogs that can shape-shift like the T-1000, a prison escape, and a bomb. Man, Death Row fucking loved bombs in the mid-'90s.

20:50: The 69 Boyz are performing. They're doing the remix version of "Tootsee Roll." It's just the two members of the group (Thrill da Playa and Fast Cash) and two backup dancers. That's it. There's nobody else onstage, and there aren't any props or anything. Just the four guys. And they're all dressed like members of the Harlem Globetrotters. It's incredible. And everyone in the crowd hates it—everyone, that is, except for one person: Biggie Smalls. He looks like he's having a great time. And I'm real happy about that. Every candid video clip I've ever seen of Biggie makes it seem like he was just the nicest guy having the greatest time.

23:13: Three of the four guys onstage have taken their shirts off and are now air humping. This is my favorite performance so far. Suge Knight wasted $100,000.

23:33: Okay, listen. I know I said earlier that I wasn't going to bring this up anymore, but I have to come back to it one more time: I couldn't stop thinking about the possible Nas non-nomination thing from the start of the show. I mean, the *Source* gave *Illmatic* one of their very rare, very coveted five-mic ratings when they reviewed it. It had been three years since the last time they'd handed one out,[7] and it'd be another three years after that before they handed out another.[8] So I messaged the rap historian Dart Adams and asked him if he knew who'd gotten nominated for the New Artist of the Year—Solo award in 1994. He dug through his archives and found an issue of the *Source* that confirmed it: no Nas on the list. The nominees in 1994 were Snoop (the winner), Fat Joe, Apache, Kam, Diamond D, and Erick Sermon.

---

6. The documentary is called *ATL: The Untold Story of Atlanta's Rise in the Rap Game.*

7. A Tribe Called Quest's *The Low End Theory.*

8. Biggie's *Life After Death.*

23:34: Hey, another commercial for that Crooked I fruit juice. This one's an animated spot with Snoop (as a cartoon dog) re-creating the baseball-bat scene from *The Untouchables*. Still no word if it's an alcoholic beverage or not. I have to assume yes at this point, though. I just can't see someone in, say, a Minute Maid commercial cracking someone in the side of the head with a baseball bat as a way to sell more tropical punch or whatever, you know?

24:33: IT'S DA BRAT! She's performing "Give It 2 You" with Jermaine Dupri. A true thing: just based off the strength of the g-funkiness of her music, I went, like, a solid fifteen years of my life before I realized that she wasn't from California.[9]

29:05: Another award. This time it's the R&B Artist of the Year. And it's being presented by the Wu-Tang Clan. The nominees: Mary J. Blige, who rules; TLC, who rule; Brandy, who rules; and R. Kelly, who has been charged twenty-two times with various sex-related crimes, including but not limited to child pornography and human trafficking.

30:50: And the winner is...

30:56: MARYYYYYYYYYYY! A perfect pick. She won the same award in 1994, making her the first ever champion to successfully defend a title at the Source Awards. She's been the top level for literal decades now.

32:11: Fab 5 Freddy is presenting the Pioneer Award, which is the *Source*'s answer to the Lifetime Achievement Award that the Grammys hand out. It goes to Run-DMC. Here's a great section about them from Freddy's prerecorded segment that played before they came up onstage to accept the award: "They made compelling party rap, message rap, hardcore rap, and their example has gone on to influence damn near every rap group that's followed them, from LL COOL J and the Beastie Boys to Public Enemy to Ice Cube, even Biggie Smalls and Salt-n-Pepa. And that's to say nothing of the fact that their groundbreaking record 'Walk This Way' brought Aerosmith back to life. Run-DMC's impact cannot be measured by musical milestones alone. They've been responsible for the introduction of new dances, new fashions—that's right, my Adidas and them fat gold chains—new slang, and new flavor." Run-DMC is so excellent.

36:35: As Run-DMC gives their acceptance speech, I'm just now realizing that they're all still so young here. DMC is the oldest of the bunch, and HE'S BARELY THIRTY-ONE YEARS OLD. (Run and Jam Master Jay are both thirty.) For comparison, the five people who received the Lifetime Achievement Award from the Grammys this same year[10] were, on average, over sixty-three years old. You could take their average age, subtract thirty-one years from it, and still nobody in Run-DMC would even be alive yet. Watching them receive the Pioneer Award just a decade removed from their most seminal work (1984's *Run-D.M.C.*, 1985's *King of Rock*, and 1986's *Raising Hell*) shows how rap as a genre had begun moving at light speed by the mid-'90s.

9. She's from Chicago.

10. Patsy Cline, Peggy Lee, Henry Mancini, Curtis Mayfield, and Barbra Streisand.

DO YOU WANNA REWATCH THE 1995 SOURCE AWARDS?

PART 2

. . . cont'd

38:45: Another award. This time it's Lyricist of the Year. And it's being presented by Patra and Charles Oakley, an all-time great basketball bruiser.

38:47: There are an advertised five NBA players at the show. Oakley is there. Penny Hardaway is there. Chris Webber is there. Dennis Scott is there. And Sam Cassell is there. Of those five, Oak is the last one I'd associate with lyricism. The word "lyricism," to me, feels sleek and slick and dexterous and like a scalpel being used by a ninja. (Penny Hardaway is the obvious pick here.) Oak is not those things. Oak is broad and a bully and uncompromising and like a bulldozer being driven by Colossus. When you say "lyricism," the first thing I think of is that time Big Pun said, "Dead in the middle of Little Italy / Little did we know that we riddled two middlemen who didn't do diddly," or that time Nas said, "Deep like *The Shining* / Sparkle like a diamond / Sneak a Uzi on the island in my army-jacket lining." When you say "Charles Oakley," the first thing I think of is that time he tried to take Bo Outlaw's head off during a February basketball game in 1998, or how there's a twenty-two-minute-long compilation video on YouTube of all the times he got into a fight during his career.[1]

39:22: The nominees: Redman, Biggie, Nas, and Big Mike. This is an all-caps TOUGH list of nominees. You gotta go with Nas, though, right? He's the guy here who does the thing here. He's the one who said, "I never sleep, 'cause sleep is the cousin of death." He's the one who said, "True in the game, as long as blood is blue in my veins / I pour my Heineken brew to my deceased crew on memory lane." He's the one who said, "You couldn't catch me in the streets without a ton of reefer / That's like Malcolm X catching the Jungle Fever."

40:26: And the winner is …

40:35: BIGGIE! Wow. I'm not sure if this counts as an upset or not. Part of me feels like yes, but part of me also feels like no.

40:38: Here's a thing that Questlove wrote in his 2013 book, *Mo' Meta Blues*, about being at this show and watching Nas get ignored again and again for *Illmatic*. It's really smart and really insightful, because Questlove is really smart and really insightful: "And for every award Biggie got I watched Nas just wilt in defeat, and that killed me inside. There was a look of shame and defeat. I remember turning to Tariq and saying, 'He's never going to be the same. You just watch.' That was the night Nas's Clark Kent turned into Superman, the night this mild-mannered observer realized he had to put on a suit and try to fly. But maybe he didn't have flying power in that way. When he released his next record, *It Was Written*, there was debate over whether he was following his own course or trying to be Biggie."

40:39: Here's another thing Questlove wrote in *Mo' Meta Blues*. I especially liked this part, because he gives you a seating chart and a temperature check for that night: "The ceremony was held at the Paramount Theater at Madison Square Garden. As you came in, you could see that there was a kind of aesthetic apartheid at work. They sat the artistic rappers, the have-nots of hip-hop, on the far right side: Nas, Mobb Deep, Wu-Tang, Busta Rhymes, and us. In the center of the place you had the Death Row crew and all the non–New York acts. On the

1. Oakley had a guest appearance in the video for LL COOL J's "Back Seat," a song I only remember because LL rhymes the word "cornea" with "hornier."

far left of the place, you had the Bad Boy team. That room was like *Apocalypse Now: The Hip-Hop Version*. If you had sparked two rocks together the place would have exploded."

41:35: Next award. It's Video of the Year. The nominees: The video for Dr. Dre and Ice Cube's "Natural Born Killaz." The video for Craig Mack's "Flava in Ya Ear." The video for Snoop's "Murder Was the Case." And the video for Coolio's "Fantastic Voyage."

43:13: And the winner is . . .

43:16: DR. DRE AND ICE CUBE'S "NATURAL BORN KILLAZ"! That's a good pick. That's the right pick. The video is great. I was secretly hoping that it'd be Snoop's "Murder Was the Case," because I just really love Snoop, and also I was *super secretly* hoping it was Coolio's "Fantastic Voyage," because there's a part in that video where some mariachis climb out of a trunk, and I just really love mariachis, too. But "Natural Born Killaz" deserved to win. It was bigger and more indicative of what the peak era of rap videos was headed toward. (It was one of those the Police Are After Us mini-movie things that people were doing back then. It ends with a surprise appearance from 2Pac as a police sniper who has a clear headshot on Ice Cube.)

43:17: The main detective in pursuit of Dr. Dre and Ice Cube in the video is John Amos, a wonderful actor probably most famous for his role in the movie *Coming to America* and his role in the TV show *Good Times*.

43:18: I love the line from "Natural Born Killaz" when Ice Cube says, "Terror illustrates my era / Now I can't hang around my mama 'cause I scare her."

43:19: The video was directed by F. Gary Gray, a brilliant director whose filmography includes *Friday*, *Set It Off*, *Law Abiding Citizen*, *Straight Outta Compton*, and *The Fate of the Furious*. Big fan.

43:45: Dr. Dre, while accepting his award: "First of all, I gotta say, peace to everybody from the Death Row camp." I wonder if this is him trying to soften the evening, to preempt aggression, to quell things? I bet yes.

44:45: Ooooooooh. We're getting a Bad Boy performance now.

45:10: It starts with a thunderstorm and Puff Daddy resting his head on a podium as he delivers a prayer via voice-over. "Now I lay me down to sleep. I pray the Lord my soul to keep. And if I should die before I wake, I pray to God I die a Bad Boy." Do you think Jesus was a Bad Boy fan during their run? Do you think he was in heaven trying to convince God to let him change his default clothes from that white robe thing he was always wearing to one of the shiny suits that Puff and Ma$e wore in the "Mo Money Mo Problems" video? Church would've been way more fun as a kid if I knew that Jesus was part of the Bad Boy family.

45:54: The final line of the Puff prayer: "I live in the East. And I'm gonna die in the East." That seems like a not-so-subtle shot at Death Row.

46:00: Craig Mack is the first out to perform. He does "Flava in Ya Ear." (The horn in that song is perfect.) Faith Evans does "You Used to Love Me." (She always had such a great speed about her. She never felt hurried.) Biggie shows up and starts off Total's "Can't You See," and then they come in behind him and close it out. (Total and Biggie were a perfect combo on this song.) "Player's Anthem" is next. They didn't announce Lil' Kim as part of this showcase at the start of this performance, but she has a verse on this song...so...fingers crossed.

53:12: LIL' KIM IS HERE!!!!!!!!!! The place goes yo-yo when they see her. Imagine how electric of a performer you have to be to walk out on a stage with Biggie and Puff in the mid-'90s and have the crowd get even louder when you show up.

53:24: Lil' Kim raps words with the same kind of ferocity that assault rifles let bullets loose with in movies. It's really something special. It's part of the reason that she was so great whenever she popped up for a surprise appearance or verse somewhere. And this was still true more than two decades later: There was a Bad Boy reunion performance as part of the 2015 BET Awards, and she came rising up out of the floor to do her verse on the "It's All About the Benjamins" remix, and she was in that famous squat pose when everyone saw her and the whole place fucking went nuts. It was awesome.

54:10: "One More Chance." What a song.

56:17: Puff intentionally shouts out the West Coast. I wonder if he did it because he saw Dr. Dre trying to press some peace into the room immediately before Bad Boy's performance?

56:43: They just announced that Ice Cube won the Best Acting Performance in a TV or Movie Role award earlier in the evening during an unaired part of the show. He got it for his portrayal of Fudge in John Singleton's *Higher Learning.*

57:10: Another award. It's the Motion Picture Soundtrack of the Year. One of the presenters is Flavor Flav, who has shown up with what appears to be two broken arms. (The result of a motorcycle accident that took place a few weeks before the awards.) If you'd have said to me before the show, "Shea, listen, someone during this show is going to walk out onstage with two broken arms. Take a guess who," my first guess would have been Flavor Flav. He has a very strong Two Broken Arms kind of energy about him.

59:29: The soundtrack for *Above the Rim* wins. (The other nominees were the soundtracks for *Jason's Lyric*, *Poetic Justice*, and the short film *Murder Was the Case.*) Suge Knight is onstage to accept the award. Which means it's time for . . .

1:00:14: Suge thanks God, then he thanks the Death Row family, then he reminds 2Pac to "keep his guards up" in prison. Then he stands there for six seconds not saying anything at all, just gathering together all the villain momentum that he can. Then he speaks: "And one other thing I'd like to say: any artist out there that want to be an artist and wanna stay a star and don't wanna have to worry about the executive producer trying to be all in the videos...all on the record...dancing...come to Death Row!" It's met with immediate boos from the crowd, who know that he's just taken a gigantic bear swipe at Puff Daddy. Things are beginning to tumble forward very quickly.

1:01:06: Ed Lover and Doctor Dré try and steady the ship a little by saying some very general nice things about nobody and everybody, but it doesn't work. And they can tell it hasn't worked, so they just keep it moving and tee up the next presenters. It's acclaimed director John Singleton (*Boyz n the Hood*, *Poetic Justice*, *Higher Learning*, *Baby Boy*, *2 Fast 2 Furious*) and NBA player Sam Cassell. They're presenting the award for Producer of the Year. I hope someone from New York wins it, because otherwise it's gonna get real hot real fast.

1:01:28: As a way to help lighten the mood, Singleton asks Cassell if he wants to say something about the Knicks, whom Cassell's Rockets beat in the NBA Finals a year earlier. Poor Cassell. He looks like he's been covered

in chum and then shoved into a tank full of great white sharks. He laughs and then declines.

1:01:45: Singleton is trying to play peacemaker now: "Before we pass out this award, we gotta say something, all right? You know, we gotta kill all this East Coast, West Coast, South, Midwest dissension in rap. Because, you know, there's a lot of devils out there that would be damned if they could ban it, and we wouldn't be having no show, and a lot of y'all wouldn't be making no money. So, you know, with that, we're gonna pass out the award for Producer of the Year." The nominees: Dr. Dre, DJ Premier (the crowd cheers loudly), Easy Mo Bee, and Pete Rock.

1:03:25: The crowd is already yelling. They know what's coming...

1:03:45: Singleton gets the envelope open, sees who it is, looks up, then says, "Uh-oh. We're gonna have some trouble here." Then he announces that Dr. Dre is the winner. The California section of the audience erupts in a good way. The rest of the audience erupts in the opposite direction. Dr. Dre tried earlier to keep everything calm, so I'm curious to see how he responds here.

1:04:12: Snoop is up onstage with Dre. The crowd boos as Dre gets ready to speak. Snoop takes the mic from him. "Wait, wait, wait," he says, and his whole face is snarled up. "The East Coast don't love Dr. Dre and Snoop Dogg?!" He takes the mic off the stand and starts walking around with it. "The East Coast ain't got no love for Dr. Dre and Snoop Dogg?! And Death Row?! Y'all don't love us?! Y'all don't love us?! Well, let it be known, then! We don't give a fuck! We know y'all East Coast! We know where the fuck we at! East Coast in the motherfucking house!" You could tell that half of Snoop wanted to make it clear that he wasn't backing down and the other half of Snoop wanted to make it clear that he still respected New York and its position as Mecca in rap. It made the crowd feel a little off balance. They weren't sure how to react.

1:05:09: Ed Lover and Doctor Dré are completely caught up in the tumble of the waves that Snoop's just caused. Ed Lover claps softly and tries to just throw any good energy out into the room that he can. Doctor Dré keeps it moving, introducing David Mays and Mike Elliot, the executive producers of the show. They're giving the Lifetime Achievement Award posthumously to Eazy-E, who passed away five months earlier due to complications from AIDS.

1:08:50: Bone Thugs-n-Harmony perform in honor of Eazy-E. (He signed them to a deal at Ruthless Records, the label he founded.) I fucking love Bone Thugs. They do "Thuggish Ruggish Bone" (a perfect song), "Foe tha Love of $" (another perfect song), and "1st of tha Month" (yet another perfect song, and also the only song that ever made me feel good about buying stuff with food stamps when I was a kid).

1:14:27: Another award. It's for Artist of the Year – Solo. It's being presented by Puffy and Faith Evans and Chris Webber. Puff, getting his first chance at the microphone since Suge Knight threw a wrench at him, responds: "Check this out. I'm the executive producer that a comment was made about a little bit earlier.[2] Contrary to what other people may feel, I would like to say...that I'm very proud of Dr. Dre, of Death Row, and Suge Knight for their accomplishments, you know what I'm saying. I'm a positive Black man and I make music to bring us together, not to separate us. And all this East and West, that needs

2. In 2016, Puff Daddy walked this statement back and said that Suge Knight was actually talking about Jermaine Dupri, a claim that Jermaine Dupri denied.

to stop. So give it up for everybody from the East and West that won tonight. One love."

1:15:36: The nominees for Artist of the Year – Solo: Scarface, Queen Latifah, Snoop, and MC Eiht. I am so confused right now. Biggie's already won New Artist of the Year and Lyricist of the Year[3] (and he's nominated for Album of the Year as well), but he doesn't get a nomination here? And no Nas again????

1:16:43: And the winner is . . .

1:16:45: SNOOP! And nobody's booing! Excellent.

1:17:33: Snoop is in much better spirits. "Oh, we doing it like players now? That's right. Now that we done made the East Coast / West Coast thing officially one love, I wanna thank..." Snoop being happy makes me happy, too.

1:18:35: It's time for Artist of the Year – Group. Nas is one of the presenters. It's forever going to be crazy to me that we've gotten to the end of an awards show dedicated to rap released in 1994 and somehow this is the first time Nas has been onstage.

1:18:50: The nominees: Wu-Tang Clan, Salt-n-Pepa, Gang Starr, Heavy D & the Boyz. Again, I'm a little confused. Outkast won Best New Artist – Group, and also they're nominated for Album of the Year, but they don't get the nod here. I hope they explain at some point how all these nominations and winners were decided.

1:19:41: And the winner is...

1:19:42: WU-TANG! Fuck yes. They were such a force in the mid-'90s.

1:20:47: Oh shit. They just explained via voice-over the selection and voting process for the awards. They said that recorded material had to have been released between March 1, 1994, and February 28, 1995, to be eligible for an award. They also said that the nominees were determined democratically by the staff of the *Source* magazine and that the winners in each category were determined via tabulated ballots that were mailed to ten thousand subscribers of the *Source.*

1:21:30: Down to the final three awards of the night. Single of the Year is up next. Honestly, despite the obvious misses on a couple of nominations, they've mostly nailed the winners. Really the only one you could legitimately argue about is Biggie for Lyricist of the Year, and even then your argument isn't gonna be all that strong. Anyway, the nominees for Single of the Year: Craig Mack's "Flava in Ya Ear," Bone's "Thuggish Ruggish Bone," the Lady of Rage's "Afro Puffs," and Warren G's "Regulate." The winner: Craig Mack. I probably would've gone "Regulate" here, but it's fine.

1:25:13: Last performance of the night. It's Method Man. He's a great closer. One time – this was back when I was teaching middle school and coaching the football, basketball, track, and soccer teams – a former student who'd gone off to college to play basketball came back over the break and asked if he could come by the gym to get some practice in. The head coach and I both thought it'd be cool to see him, so we told him yes. And when he walked in, I couldn't believe it. He was a giant. He'd been maybe five foot nine when he was in the eighth grade, but apparently he spilled some plutonium on himself or something in high school, because he'd shot up to a solid six foot eight before the end of his junior year.

Anyway, he came by the gym after school one day and did a bunch of drills and dunked it a few times for

3. He also won Live Performer of the Year, but it wasn't televised. The other award that wasn't televised that I haven't mentioned yet was Reggae/Hip-Hop Artist of the Year, which went to Mad Lion.

some kids there, and it was great. After he was done with his workout, he asked if I wanted to play one-on-one. And, I mean, I definitely didn't want to do that, because there are few things that are worse for your ego than competing in something against a college-level-or-above athlete. But I couldn't say that to him, so I said, "Yes, definitely, I would love that." So we started playing, and he let me have the ball first (this is when I should've known that I was completely fucked), and I checked it to him and he checked it back. And then, right when I started dribbling, he got down into a defensive stance and stretched his arms out wide. I'll never forget what that looked like. It felt like his arms stretched from sideline to sideline. There was nowhere for me to go and nothing for me to do. I was toast; I was utter and total toast. That's what Method Man's voice sounds like in my head: like it stretches from sideline to sideline, like you're completely outmatched, like all you can do is hope that he decides to end things quickly. He's great.

1:29:30: Here it is. The last award. It's for Album of the Year. The nominees: Biggie's *Ready to Die* (obviously), Nas's *Illmatic* (obviously), Outkast's *Southernplayalisticadillacmuzik* (a surprising inclusion but certainly not an undeserving one), and Scarface's *The Diary* (man, it feels like Scarface is a world away from what's been happening here tonight). If things go the way they've gone so far, it's Biggie who's taking this.

1:30:52: And the winner is...

1:30:56: BIGGIE! Malibooyah! What a night. It's almost unbelievable going back and watching this show knowing all of the stuff that was going to happen in rap over the next five or so years.

WHICH WAS THE BEST MINUTE DURING BLACK THOUGHT'S FREESTYLE?

(AND SOME OTHER QUESTIONS ABOUT IT, TOO)

SEVERAL YEARS AGO, MY WIFE AND I went to Italy to celebrate our ten-year anniversary.[1] And there are a bunch of pieces of the trip that I like to think about—I bought a leather notebook in a little shop and briefly convinced myself that I was going to move to Venice and sketch doves and people and whatnot on the street for the rest of my life; we saw Nick Jonas while walking around one day, because it just so happened that he was on vacation in the same general area at the same exact time;[2] Larami accidentally got drunk on wine at dinner one night and then spent a sizable part of the evening leaning out of our hotel-room window catcalling Italian men as they rode past on those boat taxis.[3] It was a wonderful time. But the part of the trip that will stay with me forever is when we watched some dancers perform in a theater.

All of the stuff that I know about dance is only the stuff that I've seen in dance movies.[4] If you try and talk to me about dance and it doesn't have something to do with, say, DJ in *Stomp the Yard* or Nora in *Step Up*, I'm useless. You might as well be talking to a box of bricks. Which is why I wasn't that interested when Larami told me she'd gotten us two tickets to go watch some modern dance company.

But here's the thing: Turns out, modern dance is fucking awesome. Ten minutes into the show, I was in love. By twenty minutes in, all of everything else in the world had dissolved behind me. It was wild. The things that the dancers were doing onstage—the jumps and spins and twists and such—were mesmerizing. And then they got to the big finish, and that's when my whole goddamn head exploded. Because here's what they did:

There was one woman out on the stage. And she was all by herself. And she was dancing. And the whole rest of the theater was black. The woman was literally the only thing you could see. And she was gliding around the stage in this very flowy and fluid and incredible way. And as she danced, that last light on her went out. And it was all the way dark. You couldn't see two inches in front of you. It was like we were swimming underwater in a swimming pool filled with black paint.

And then this strobe light kicked on. And it started flashing. Over and over and over, flash, flash, flash. And each time it flashed, you got just a half-second glimpse of the woman again. And she'd timed things so that each time the strobe light flashed, she'd jumped up into the air and done a kick where one of her legs would go forward and the other would go backward.[5] You never got to see her land, and you never got to see her jump. All you saw was her up in the air each time the strobe light flashed. And after a couple of seconds, it began to look like she was flying. The whole theater, all at once, realized what was happening, which was why the whole theater, all at once, exploded in cheers. It was incredible. I'll have that moment in my brain for as long as I have a brain, and maybe even a few minutes after that.

---

1. Technically, it was a two-for-one deal. We couldn't afford to go on a honeymoon after we got married, so the Italy trip was a honeymoon plus an anniversary trip.
2. Nick Jonas is somehow more handsome in person than he is on-screen.
3. I assume that this was somehow related to having seen Nick Jonas earlier in the day, though I can't say for certain.
4. Or, in a pinch, that dance-contest show that Wade Robson had on MTV in the early 2000s.
5. If you're having a hard time picturing it, take your hand, hold up just your index finger and middle finger like you were signaling the number two to someone, then stretch your index finger as far forward as it'll go while stretching your middle finger back in the opposite direction. That's what she was doing with her legs each time she jumped.

I had no clue who any of the people were up onstage. And I had no clue who'd choreographed that dance or come up with that idea. And I had no clue about anything at all related to modern dance. But I knew that what I was looking at was of the highest caliber.

Black Thought's ten-minute-long freestyle that he did on Funkmaster Flex's show in December of 2017 was the same thing. You didn't have to know anything about Black Thought when it came out. And you didn't have to know anything about the Roots. And you didn't even have to know anything about rap. All you had to do was watch his performance to know that you were looking at something special, to know that what he was doing was something only the masters could.

ONE CLARIFICATION

Generally speaking, there are two different ways that people will use the term "freestyle" in rap. Neither is better than the other; they're just different.

The first version means something along the lines of "to make up a rhyme on the spot." There's no prewritten material included. You just insta-generate everything in the moment.[6] In fact, it's seen as a bad thing if a person makes use of preplanned material when the other people who are participating aren't using preplanned material.

The second version of "freestyle" means something close to "any kind of rap that's performed outside of the parameters of a traditional song." It's an evolution of that first kind. That's what Black Thought did. He made use of unheard material that he already had in his head. He talked about it with *Rolling Stone* afterward, saying, "As an actor, the theatrical side of me identifies with the concept of having a script, memorizing the lines, then being able to go off book, so to speak. If you know your lines, everybody else's lines, you have those beats in your muscle memory, then you can improvise and go off-script."

NINE QUESTIONS ABOUT BLACK THOUGHT'S FREESTYLE

Black Thought indirectly references two very different movies during his freestyle. The first one (*The Talented Mr. Ripley*) stars Matt Damon as a handsome serial killer with incredible luck. The second one (*Coming to America*) stars Eddie Murphy as a good-hearted prince of a foreign land who gets overcharged for a haircut. Can you make at least six connections between those two movies?

Sure. Here you go:

- **Both movies have leading men who travel to another country and fall in love with someone.** Eddie Murphy's Prince Akeem travels from Zamunda to America and falls in love with Shari Headley's Lisa McDowell, while Matt Damon's Tom Ripley travels from America to Italy and falls in love with Jude Law's Dickie Greenleaf.
- **Both movies have scenes where someone is standing up in a bathtub and we see their butts.** We see Jude Law's butt in *Ripley*, and we see one of Prince Akeem's royal bathers' butts in *America*.

6. Lil Flip, a regionally famous rapper in Houston who briefly stepped into the national spotlight in 2004 with his hit "Game Over," is a savant of this kind of freestyling.

- **Both movies have characters who purposely hide their true identities as a means to accomplish a mission.** Damon pretends to have attended school with Dickie at Princeton. Murphy pretends not to be of royal descent. And to that end …
- **Both movies have characters who are envious of the lifestyle lived by people on the opposite end of the social spectrum.** Damon covets the life that wealthy people live in *Ripley*; Murphy covets the life that normal people live in *America.*
- **Both movies have scenes where the leading man sings an emotional song after receiving some positive attention from the person they're in love with.** Damon sings "My Funny Valentine" in *Ripley*; Murphy sings "To Be Loved" in *America.*
- **And both movies have side characters that the main character needs to get rid of.** Damon has to get rid of Freddie, a friend of Dickie Greenleaf who immediately senses that Damon is not on the up and up, and Murphy has to get rid of Darryl, who is Lisa McDowell's current boyfriend. They do it in super-different ways (Murphy just turns on the super charm, which leads to Lisa falling in love with him, and Damon does it by smashing Freddie over the head with a marble sculpture, killing him), but they do it nonetheless.

Black Thought mentions several other rappers during his freestyle. If someone made a list of all the best rappers ever, in what order would the rappers Black Thought mentioned appear on that list?

There are eight different rappers that Black Thought mentions: 2Pac, Kendrick Lamar, Rakim, pre-Kardashian Kanye, pre-accident D.O.C., Pharoahe Monch, Kool G Rap, and the fictional rap group CB4. That's not the order they appear in during the freestyle, but that is the order they'd appear in on that list.

Is there a part of the song that makes you wish that Black Thought had been your dad when you were a kid?

Yes. It's when he says, "I'm sneaker shoppin' with my son / A size 8 / Prior to the release, 'cause why wait?" I imagine getting sneakers early when you're a kid is just about as good as it gets.

Is there a part of the song that makes you glad that Black Thought wasn't your dad when you were a kid?

Yes. It's when he says, "I put a couple bodies in a brown bag, then I'm en route." And let me be clear here: I don't think that Black Thought is a murderer. I suspect he has killed zero people in his lifetime. But the confident ease with which he says this line makes me feel like I don't want to do any more digging into the situation—you know what I'm saying?

What's the single best minute of Black Thought's ten-minute-long freestyle?

Here's how we answer this: Let's take the freestyle, break it up into ten different minute-long sections, then treat each of those as its own mini-song. We can chart (a) the best line from each section, (b) the most unexpected reference from each section, (c) the hardest Goddamn That's Hard as Fuck moment from each section, and (d)

G
XXV
FLORENTIA

the greatest That Sent Me Down a Real Deep Rabbit Hole bar from each section. Then we just tally up all the scores. And if we do all of that, it becomes clear that Minute 3, which stretches from the "Give me the proper respect, motherfucker, we back again" line to the "The microphone doctor / Black Deepak Chopra" line, is the single best minute of Black Thought's ten-minute-long freestyle.[7]

- **The Best Line in It:** "The anomaly sworn solemnly, high snobbidy"[8]
- **The Most Unexpected Reference in It:** The best-selling book *Freakonomics*, which came out in 2005. I've never read it, but *Wikipedia* tells me it's about applying "economic theory to diverse subjects not usually covered by traditional economists."
- **The Hardest GODDAMN THAT'S HARD AS FUCK Moment in It:** "Comin' from where only kings and crowns permitted the darkness / Where archaeologists found my image in parchment / Rolled into a scroll, holdin' a message for you / It said, 'The only thing for sure is taxes, death, and trouble."
- **The Greatest THAT SENT ME DOWN A REAL DEEP RABBIT HOLE Bar in It:** "That's heaven and Hades / Tigris and Euphrates / His highness, the apple of the Iris[9] to you ladies." I started out by searching to see who Iris was (she's "the personification of the rainbow"), and I just followed my feet forward from there, and twenty minutes later I was watching that clip of Whitney Houston performing the national anthem at the 1991 Super Bowl.[10]

Is there a part of the song that you're very confident your mother would enjoy?

Yes. It's when he says, "I ain't one of y'all peers / I'm the sum of all fears." That's pretty much his version of when I'd get too saucy with my mom and she would bark some version of "I'm not one of your little friends" at me.

Is there a part of the freestyle that really spoke to your science-teacher spirit?

Yes. It's when Black Thought says, "I'm made of elements you can't combine." It's a darling little line for science nerds. Two things happened when I heard it. The first thing was that it just really made me want to have a conversation with someone about valence electrons and atomic numbers. I miss talking about that stuff. The second thing was it reminded me of a story from when I was teaching.

Every so often, I would get assigned a student teacher who either (a) had just graduated college and

7. The full order goes Minute 3, Minute 7, Minute 1, Minute 4, Minute 10, Minute 6, Minute 9, Minute 5, Minute 8, Minute 2.

8. Black Thought explained via Twitter that the phrase "high snobbidy" is a play on Highsnobiety, which is a fashion website. He said that he "bent the words to make it rhyme."

9. There's a chance that Black Thought used "iris" to mean part of the eyeball, but, I mean, he's Black Thought, so there's really no telling.

10. The rabbit hole went like this: Iris is the personification of a rainbow. → Remember when Robin Williams played Rainbow Randolph in that movie *Death to Smoochy*? → Edward Norton was in that movie, right? → Edward Norton double-crossed Mark Wahlberg in *The Italian Job*, but Wahlberg outsmarted him in the end. There's no way Mark Wahlberg could've ever outsmarted Edward Norton in real life. → Marky Mark and the Funky Bunch was a terrible band. → New Kids on the Block were better. I should listen to "Hangin' Tough." No, I should listen to New Edition. → New Edition music. → Bobby Brown music. → Whitney Houston music. → I should watch some Whitney Houston live performances. → I should watch Whitney Houston's Super Bowl performance.

was trying to get some practice in before moving into their own classroom or (b) was about to graduate college and was trying to get some practice in before moving into their own classroom. And usually the way that relationship worked was they would show up, observe a few classes, ask some questions about being a teacher, and then try and teach their own lesson while I looked on and wrote down my notes on their performance.

One year, I had this guy who was young and eager and white. And because of that, I knew that my students – eighth graders at a school with a Latino population somewhere in the high 90s percentage-wise – were gonna fucking eat him alive. I told him as much, and he was like, "I'll be okay. I got this. Just watch me. You might learn some things." He was a fun guy, and I appreciated his confidence.

Anyway, he showed up to teach his lesson this one day, and we were supposed to be talking about the structure of atoms and the periodic table of elements and blah, blah, blah. So he was up at the front of the class. And he started his lesson. And I could tell he was nervous but he was working his way through it. A couple of kids tried to trip him up, but he just kept on moving. You could tell he had good teacher instincts. And in my head I was like, "Man. He's doing pretty good. This is neat." And that was when everything fell apart.

As he was talking about the periodic table of elements, he made a comment about how much of a mouthful that phrase was. And he said, from there going forward, he was going to shorten it. He said, "Instead of calling it the periodic table of elements, we're all gonna call it the *P-TOE* today." And as soon as he said that, all of the kids looked at me. And I looked at him. And my eyes were real big, and I was giving him that You Need to Stop Right Now headshake. He didn't catch the cue, though. He moved right on. "Go ahead and write that down on your worksheets, everyone. P-TOE. Say it out loud. P-TOE. It's fun." And the kids couldn't take it anymore. They burst into laughter. All of them. Crazy loud. Just laughing and laughing. And then one kid shouted "P-TOE!" And then another. And then another. Each one drawing more laughs. And that student teacher was so fucking confused. Because here's what he didn't know that everyone else in the room knew: he was pronouncing "P-TOE" the same as someone would pronounce "pito," and "pito" is a slang term in Spanish that basically means "dick." That's what he was accidentally telling the kids to say. That's what I had to explain to him after class was over.

I don't know what happened to that guy, because I never kept in touch with any of the student teachers I got assigned. But I have to assume that that afternoon he got into his car, threw his cell phone and wallet and all manner of identification out of the window, then drove to some small town several hundred miles away and restarted his life under a fake name.

What would you ask Black Thought about the freestyle if you got to talk to him for ten seconds about it?

That's easy: He starts off the freestyle by saying, "I'm sorry for your loss / It's a dead body in the car, and it's probably one of yours." That's the very first line. Then, ten minutes later, he ends the freestyle with "I tell a story like fingerprints and blood splatter." That's the very last line. I would ask him to please confirm or deny if he did that on purpose. Are the fingerprints and blood splatter related to that dead body in the car?

Why do you think so many people have such strong feelings about Black Thought's freestyle?

Here's my guess, and it goes back to the point I was making at the start of this chapter:

There was a period of time from the mid-'90s to the early 2000s in rap where, because everything was being filtered to us through the same five or six places, something would happen—be it a new big song or album or event of varying magnitude—and everybody would talk about it for the next few days or weeks or whatever. It was an easy process to understand. Someone would show up on MTV, and Sway Calloway would be like, "This is the person you need to know, and here's their backstory," and then we would all suddenly care about that person and their backstory.

But then the internet began to fuse itself into everybody's brain stems, and as people began to consume more and more content online, all of that changed. There was suddenly an overwhelming amount of information being beamed out into the universe by an overwhelming amount of places all at once. Nobody could keep up with all of it. There were just too many people and too many backstories for fame to exist in the way that it had before. Which meant that this new thing began happening where someone could become an unquestionable star on one part of the internet without ever even rating on a separate part of it. By somewhere around 2014, it had become all but impossible to have one of those monoculture moments, rap included.

But Black Thought's freestyle was so obviously massive and so obviously brilliant and so obviously divine that you didn't need to have any information beyond what you had just watched for those ten minutes. He was so specifically profound that his performance was instantly accessible. And it connected everyone together in this very surprising way that was hard to describe but easy to feel. And that's why I think we all loved it so much.

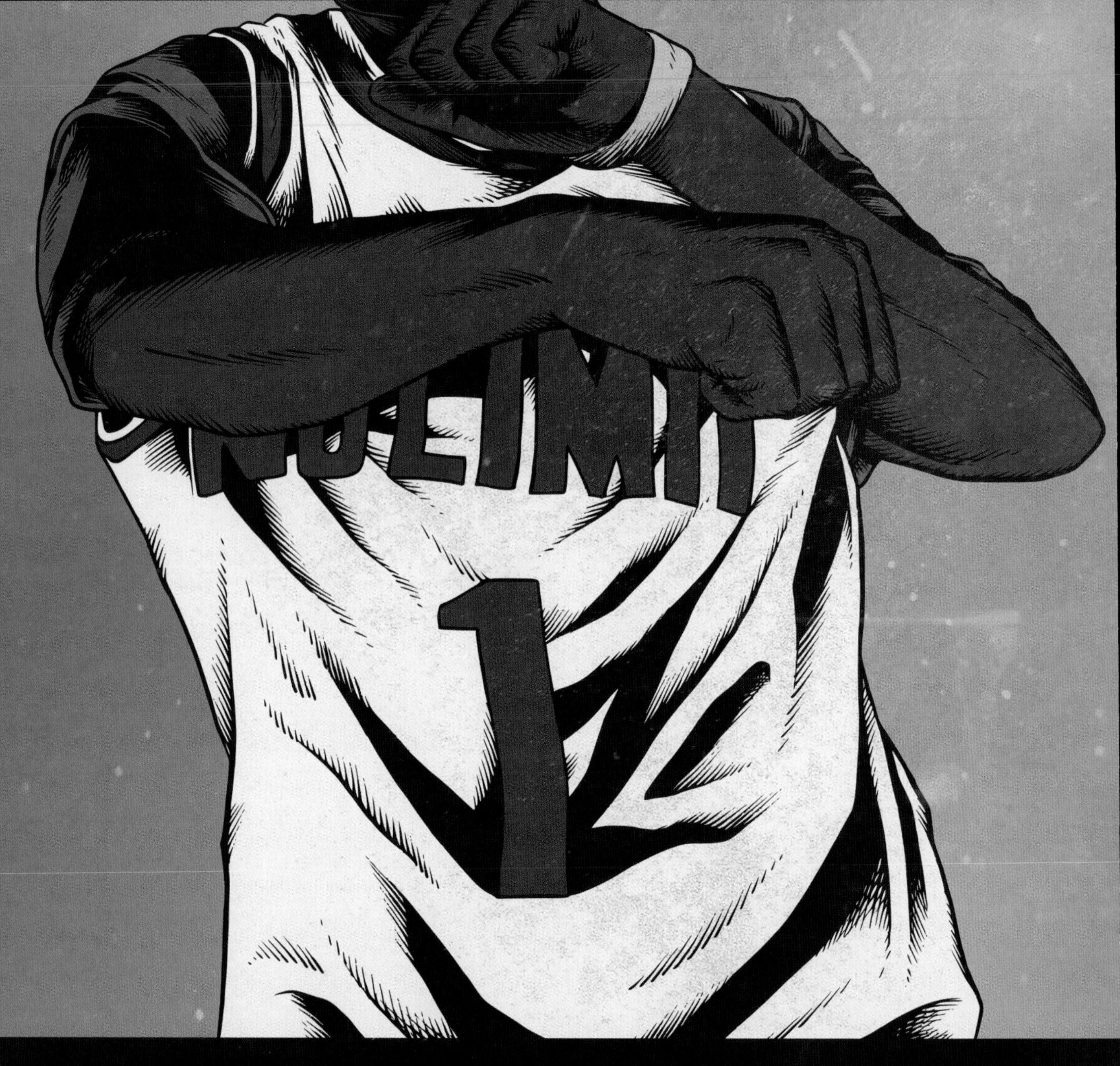

WHICH WAS THE MOST PERFECT DUO IN RAP HISTORY?

THERE ARE TWENTY-FIVE DUOS IN CONTENTION for the title of Most Perfect Duo in Rap History. Here they are, listed alphabetically:

Eightball & MJG, Bad Meets Evil (Eminem and Royce da 5′9″), Big Tymers (Birdman and Mannie Fresh), Birdman and Lil Wayne, Black Star (Mos Def and Talib Kweli), Capone-N-Noreaga, Clipse (Malice and Pusha T), City Girls (Yung Miami and JT), DJ Jazzy Jeff & the Fresh Prince, EPMD (Erick Sermon and PMD), Eric B. & Rakim, Gang Starr (DJ Premier and Guru), Kid 'n Play, Kris Kross (Mac Daddy and Daddy Mac), Method Man & Redman, Mobb Deep (Havoc and Prodigy), Outkast (Big Boi and André 3000), Pete Rock & CL Smooth, Puff and Big, Run the Jewels (Killer Mike and El-P), Salt-n-Pepa, Snoop and Dr. Dre, the Throne (Kanye and Jay-Z), UGK (Bun B and Pimp C), and the Ying Yang Twins (Kaine and D-Roc).

Now, I imagine you read that list and came out of it with a couple questions. You might be saying something to yourself like "Wait. Why are Snoop and Dr. Dre included? And why are Puff and Big included? They were never officially a duo." To which I would say, "You're correct. But, to use Dre and Snoop as an example here, they were inseparable during the biggest and most substantial part of Snoop's career. And Dr. Dre produced literally every track on *Doggystyle*, Snoop's seminal debut album. So, in spirit, I'd argue they were briefly a duo. Same with Puff and Big. There was a period where you never saw one without the other."

To which you might say, "Okay. I guess that's fine. But what about Public Enemy? Why aren't they listed in the group? Couldn't you argue that Public Enemy is just Chuck D and Flavor Flav, which, by definition, makes a duo?" To which I would say, "No. You can't not include Terminator X in Public Enemy. And also don't forget about Professor Griff, who helped found the group. And that's to say nothing of DJ Lord, who took over DJ duties after Terminator X left. Public Enemy was a group. That's how they've always been identified. Same as Run-DMC or N.W.A."

To which you might say, "Well, okay. But if that's the way you're counting things, then shouldn't Salt-n-Pepa be left out of this competition as well? Because they have DJ Spinderella." To which I would say, "Yes, DJ Spinderella is absolutely a part of the group, but Salt-n-Pepa has always been listed in the DUO section of rap rather than the GROUP section. Perhaps it's because the name of their group specifically only identifies two members? I don't know. But that's just how it's always gone. So that's how it'll be here."

To which you might say, "It feels like you're playing a little fast and loose on who is or isn't a duo."

To which I would say, "Duh."[1]

•••••

The Question: Who was the Most Perfect Duo in Rap History?

The Answer: It's very simple. We have a checklist to figure this out. It's made up of ten different requirements.

---

1. Technically, 3rd Bass and Das EFX should also be included among the duos if we're including EPMD and Salt-n-Pepa. And probably also we should have M.O.P. and Nice & Smooth in there as well. But those four groups were never going to outlast any of the duos in the upper tier of the rankings, so I'm just gonna have them in this footnote.

As we go through the requirements, we will lose various duos. The final one left standing at the end of everything is the winner.

1. THE MOST PERFECT DUO IN RAP HISTORY HAS TO BE MADE UP OF TWO PEOPLE WHO ARE KNOWN MORE FOR BEING PART OF A DUO THAN SOLO ARTISTS.

This is foundational, which is why we have to start here. You can't be the Most Perfect Duo in Rap History if your two members aren't identified, before all other things, as part of a duo. It doesn't matter if you've done a bunch of songs together or even a couple projects together: if the first thing that people think of when they hear your name is your career as a solo act and not your career as one half of a duo, then you're out. And that means for this first cut, we're losing the following duos:

- **Bad Meets Evil:** I'm fine with this one.
- **Birdman and Lil Wayne:** I'm fine with this one, too.
- **Big Tymers:** This one hurts a little, but I understand that not everyone feels the same way about Big Tymers as I do.
- **DJ Jazzy Jeff & the Fresh Prince:** Did you know that DJ Jazzy Jeff & the Fresh Prince were actually the first hip-hop act ever to put out a double album? They did it in 1988 with *He's the DJ, I'm the Rapper.* They were also the first hip-hop act to win a Grammy (it happened in 1989; they won the inaugural Best Rap Performance award for "Parents Just Don't Understand"). Neither of those things help prevent them from getting eliminated here, but they're still things that you should know.
- **Kid 'n Play:** They don't violate this rule exactly, but they're more famous for being movie stars than they are for being rappers, so they're gone.
- **Method Man & Redman:** This one stings a lot.
- **Puff and Big:** I hate that we're losing them this early, but I understand.
- **Snoop and Dr. Dre:** [Pretend there's an emoji right here of an arrow pointing up.]
- **The Throne:** Can I tell you very quickly that prior to writing this chapter, I never one time in my life referred to Jay-Z and Kanye West as "the Throne"? I always just called them Jay-Z and Kanye West, as in, "Did you hear *Watch the Throne*, that album that Jay-Z and Kanye West did together?"

That's a very tough first cull.

And truthfully, you could argue that Clipse should be cut this round, too, on account of how most of Pusha T's rap career has been spent as a solo artist, but I just couldn't talk myself into it. He always feels like he's still a part of Clipse for some reason, which is one of those feelings that doesn't really make sense, but also everyone knows what I'm talking about. It's like how Bill Walton is always spiritually connected to the Blazers even though he played there for only four of his ten years in the league. So Clipse stays.

Remaining Duos: Eightball & MJG, Black Star, Capone-N-Noreaga, Clipse, City Girls, EPMD, Eric B. & Rakim, Gang Starr, Kris Kross, Mobb Deep, Outkast, Pete Rock & CL Smooth, Run the Jewels, Salt-n-Pepa, UGK, and the Ying Yang Twins

2. THE MOST PERFECT DUO IN RAP HISTORY HAS TO HAVE RELEASED AT LEAST TWO PROPER ALBUMS TOGETHER.

Longevity has to play some sort of part in all of this. That's why this rule is here. It sucks, because it means we're losing Black Star, but also it's fine, because they probably should've been eliminated during the first one anyway. Everyone else is safe.

Remaining Duos: Eightball & MJG, Capone-N-Noreaga, Clipse, City Girls, EPMD, Eric B. & Rakim, Gang Starr, Kris Kross, Mobb Deep, Outkast, Pete Rock & CL Smooth, Run the Jewels, Salt-n-Pepa, UGK, and the Ying Yang Twins

3. THE MOST PERFECT DUO IN RAP HISTORY HAS TO HAVE BEEN ABLE TO BUY A TICKET TO AN R-RATED MOVIE WHEN THEY WERE AT THEIR MOST FAMOUS.

It's easy to think of Kris Kross as a kind of rap novelty act because (a) they were children when they became stars and (b) they had a gimmick early on where they would wear their clothes backward. But the truth is, they were very good rappers and also very successful. Take "Jump," for example, their smash debut single. It spent eight weeks at the top of the *Billboard* Hot 100 chart, which was longer than any rap song had ever been up there.[2] It sold over two million copies alone as a single. And it helped propel their album *Totally Krossed Out* up past the four-million-copies-sold mark. And for context: The only duo in contention for the Most Perfect Duo in Rap History championship belt to have an album that sold more copies than that is Outkast. No other duo ever even got close.

That being said, rap is for grown-ups. The pick for the Most Perfect Duo in Rap History has to be one whose members could have gone to see *My Cousin Vinny* without adult supervision. So we're losing Kris Kross here.

Remaining Duos: Eightball & MJG, Capone-N-Noreaga, Clipse, City Girls, EPMD, Eric B. & Rakim, Gang Starr, Mobb Deep, Outkast, Pete Rock & CL Smooth, Run the Jewels, Salt-n-Pepa, UGK, and the Ying Yang Twins

4. THIS ONE WILL BE CONTROVERSIAL, BUT THE MOST PERFECT DUO IN RAP HISTORY HAS TO BE MADE UP OF TWO PEOPLE WHO RAP ON OVER 90 PERCENT OF THEIR SONGS.

Both people in the duo have to be known primarily as rappers. That's just what it has to be. We're talking about rap here. We need rappers. I'm sorry.

Now, to be clear, it's fine if one or both of the members of the duo also produce songs, like how Pimp C did for UGK or El-P does for Run the Jewels. But we have to be able to identify both members of the duo as rappers first. Any duo that can't say that for both members has to be cut here. And that means we're saying goodbye to the following duos:

2. It also topped the charts in Australia, Canada, Europe, Finland, Ireland, New Zealand, Switzerland, and Zimbabwe.

- **Eric B. & Rakim:** You should be mad about this. I'm mad about this. Every version of rap that you know today can, in one way or another, be connected back to Rakim. He changed everything when he landed on Earth from whatever galaxy he came from in 1987.
- **Pete Rock & CL Smooth:** I do not like this at all. Pete Rock is one of the six greatest producers ever. (To this day, I still see the opening screen for *NBA Street Vol. 2* whenever I hear the beginning of "T.R.O.Y.") ("T.R.O.Y." is usually everyone's pick for the Best Pete Rock Beat, but I'm more partial to the beat he made for Nas's "The World Is Yours.")
- **Gang Starr:** *Gah.* This loss sucks. It is completely reasonable to argue that DJ Premier is the greatest producer of all time. (The absolute lowest he can be on the list is third place. Anything below that is, to put it plainly, stupid.) Losing him this early is...I mean...I don't even know. You might as well hit me in the forehead with a fucking ax.

Remaining Duos: Eightball & MJG, Capone-N-Noreaga, Clipse, City Girls, EPMD, Mobb Deep, Outkast, Run the Jewels, Salt-n-Pepa, UGK, and the Ying Yang Twins

5. THE MOST PERFECT DUO IN RAP HISTORY CAN'T HAVE MORE THAN ONE SONG THAT CENTERS ON WHISPERS AND/OR WHISTLING.

That means we're losing the Ying Yang Twins here. They put out "Whistle While You Twurk" in 2000 and "Wait (The Whisper Song)" in 2005.

(A sidebar: "Whistle While You Twurk" is a play on "Whistle While You Work" from 1937's *Snow White and the Seven Dwarfs*. I always wondered if the Ying Yang Twins had to get permission from Disney to do that. It just really makes me laugh to think about Mickey Mouse sitting at a boardroom table, fielding sampling requests, reading the lyrics to "Whistle While You Twurk," and being like, "They wanna use one of our premier properties in a song where the phrase 'make that pussy fart' appears multiple times?")

Remaining Duos: Eightball & MJG, Capone-N-Noreaga, Clipse, City Girls, EPMD, Mobb Deep, Outkast, Run the Jewels, Salt-n-Pepa, and UGK

6. ACTUALLY, I CHANGED MY MIND—THE MOST PERFECT DUO IN RAP HISTORY DOES NOT HAVE TO BE MADE UP OF TWO PEOPLE WHO RAP ON OVER 90 PERCENT OF THEIR SONGS.

That was a mistake earlier. You can't have the rapping without the producers and/or the DJs. That's my bad. Let's fix that. That requirement is officially rescinded. We're getting back Eric B. & Rakim, Pete Rock & CL Smooth, and Gang Starr. Celebrate.

Remaining Duos: Eightball & MJG, Capone-N-Noreaga, Clipse, City Girls, EPMD, Eric B. & Rakim, Gang Starr, Mobb Deep, Outkast, Pete Rock & CL Smooth, Run the Jewels, Salt-n-Pepa, and UGK

7. THE MOST PERFECT DUO IN RAP HISTORY HAS TO HAVE AT LEAST TWO ALBUMS THAT WERE CERTIFIED GOLD OR HIGHER BY THE RIAA.

Just as longevity has to play some role in this discussion, so too do record sales. They should never be the end-all-be-all in a rap argument, but they should definitely be something that gets brought into the equation. Of our remaining thirteen duos, only seven are making it past here. We're losing the following:

- **Capone-N-Noreaga:** An underappreciated duo in the rap canon. I'm proud of them for having made it this far in the competition.
- **Clipse:** The Lord was not willin', as it turns out.
- **City Girls:** The only reason they're out here is because we're catching them very early in their duo career. They'd likely last another round or two if this book were written in 2026 instead of 2021.
- **Pete Rock & CL Smooth:** This sucks. Because it also means we're losing . . .
- **Gang Starr:** GOD DAMN IT. I rigged the game with Requirement No. 6 specifically to get them back into the fold, only to see them lose out again. This must be what Juliet felt like at the end of *Romeo + Juliet* when she woke up from her fake death to see that Romeo had just finished drinking the poison that was gonna kill him. This is my least favorite chapter in the book.
- **Run the Jewels:** The most surprising loss in this category.

Remaining Duos: Eightball & MJG, EPMD, Eric B. & Rakim, Mobb Deep, Outkast, Salt-n-Pepa, and UGK

8. THE MOST PERFECT DUO IN RAP HISTORY HAS TO BE ONE WHERE IT CAN REASONABLY BE ARGUED THAT EACH PERSON IS BETTER AND MORE IMPORTANT TO THE DUO'S OVERALL SUCCESS THAN THE OTHER.

This one is very important. You can't be the Most Perfect Duo in Rap History if one member is clearly doing all the heavy lifting. Unfortunately for us, every piece of all of the remaining duos is strong. We're far enough into the conversation now that there aren't any real and true weak points. Eightball and MJG are both essential to their duo, and Erick Sermon and PMD are both essential to theirs, and Eric B. and Rakim are both essential to theirs, and on and on and on. So nobody's getting cut here. And honestly, I can't really think of too many other requirements to throw at the remaining group that would trip any of them up. They're all major league, and they're all historically significant in very specific ways, and they're all interesting pairings. I'm not quite sure how to ge—oh, wait. I know. I know what to do . . .

9. THE MOST PERFECT DUO IN RAP HISTORY HAS TO HAVE BEEN NOMINATED FOR TWO OR MORE GRAMMYS.

We're up in rareified now. The Grammys, as a machine, are imperfect and implicitly biased. And so if any of our duos can clear this particular hurdle, it means they are of such profound importance that not even the mechanisms of a broken cultural measurement system can pin their wings down to the board.

The Only Three Duos Who Get Past This Checkpoint: UGK (two nominations), Salt-n-Pepa (five nominations, one win), and Outkast (seventeen nominations, six wins)

10. HOW MANY ESSENTIAL ALBUMS DOES THE DUO HAVE?

Out of these final three duos, it's UGK who has my favorite album (1996's *Ridin' Dirty*, which I will continue to argue is the best southern rap album of all time). So if it were me just picking which of the remaining duos I liked the most, then UGK would walk away here a winner.

But if we take stock of each duo's essential albums—which is to say, albums that, beyond just being good, changed or advanced rap in a crucial and appreciable way—then here's the tally: Salt-n-Pepa has two (1986's *Hot, Cool & Vicious* and 1993's *Very Necessary*), UGK has two (1992's *Too Hard to Swallow* and 1996's *Ridin' Dirty*), and Outkast has three (1994's *Southernplayalisticadillacmuzik*, 1996's *ATLiens*, and 1998's *Aquemini*). And that means the final overall tally leaves Salt-n-Pepa and UGK tussling for second place on the podium and Outkast emerging victorious.

The Winning Duo: Big Boi and André 3000

"If there is someone like me in the world, and I am at one end of the spectrum, couldn't there be someone else opposite of me at the other end? . . . He probably doesn't even know it. The kind of person these stories are about. A person put here to protect the rest of us. To guard us."

–Elijah Price, November 21, 2000

2PAC WAS MURDERED IN LAS VEGAS in September of 1996. He'd gotten into a car with Suge Knight sometime after attending the Mike Tyson–Bruce Seldon fight at the MGM Grand.[1] Someone pulled up next to them at a stoplight and fired shots into the car. Four of the shots hit 2Pac. Several days later, he died in the intensive care unit of the University Medical Center of Southern Nevada. And so I say again: 2Pac was murdered in Las Vegas in September of 1996.

The eventual rumor, though—at least among teenagers on the southwest side of San Antonio in 1997—was that 2Pac wasn't actually dead. The eventual rumor—at least among teenagers on the southwest side of San Antonio in 1997—was that he'd faked his own death and he'd begun releasing music under the name Makaveli. And the proof was the song "Hail Mary."

"Hail Mary" was released in February of 1997, five months after 2Pac's body had been cremated. It was the second song of his that had been released posthumously,[2] but it was the first song of his that wasn't billed as a 2Pac song. It was billed as a Makaveli song. That's how the DJs were teeing it up on the radio, and also that's how 2Pac introduced himself on the track, and also that's whom the album the song came from belonged to (the album was called *The Don Killuminati: The 7 Day Theory*, and the presenting artist on it was Makaveli).

"Hail Mary" would come on, and someone would be like, "See?! This person has the exact same voice as 2Pac! And the exact same speaking cadence! And the exact same rapping tendencies! And this is a new song! And he's calling himself Makaveli! But it's definitely 2Pac! How can 2Pac put out music if he's dead?! 2Pac is alive!"

Or someone would look at the cover of *The Don Killuminati* and be like, "See! It says Makaveli on there, but clearly that's a painting of 2Pac up on a cross! Look at the bandanna! He's communicating with us! 2Pac is alive!"

Or someone would be like, "If you take the letters in Makaveli and rearrange them, you can form the phrase 'Am alive K'!" And then a second person would be like, "What about the *K*, though? What does that *K* mean?" And the first person would be like, "What?! Who cares?! It's *2Pac*, not *2Pack*! Fuck the letter *K*! 2Pac is alive!"

When Biggie was murdered in March of 1997, it didn't inspire the same kind of anagrammatic speculation that 2Pac's murder had. It did, however, replicate an eerie number of ghastly similarities.

Biggie, like 2Pac, was shot four times. And Biggie, like 2Pac, was sitting in the passenger seat of an automobile when it happened. And Biggie, like 2Pac, was caught unawares at a stoplight following a celebratory night out with his friends when the assaulting party attacked. And Biggie's murder, like 2Pac's, remains still unsolved and shrouded in conspiratorial mystery all these years later. Even small details from their murders seemed to somehow mirror each other. (The shots that killed 2Pac, for

1. You can watch this whole fight on YouTube, by the way. It's less than one round long. Mike Tyson was swinging mailboxes filled with concrete at Seldon's head.

2. The first was "I Ain't Mad at Cha," which came out just two days after he passed.

example, reportedly came from someone in a white car that had pulled up next to them. The shots that killed Biggie reportedly came from someone in a black car.)

And I don't precisely know the larger meaning of all of those things. But I do precisely know that losing two of the greatest rappers ever over the course of a six-month stretch in the mid-'90s was super fucking sucky. It was so overwhelmingly sad, in fact, that coming up with outlandish theories and tenuous ties between the two was one of the ways that some people chose to cope with it then and choose to cope with it now.

•••••

TEN BIGGIE THINGS, EACH OF WHICH ARE THE BEST

- **The Best Biggie Album:** 1994's *Ready to Die.*
- **The Best Biggie Song That Was a Single:** "Big Poppa," followed closely by "Hypnotize," followed closely by "Juicy."
- **The Best Biggie Song That Wasn't a Single:** "Gimme the Loot," followed closely by "Ten Crack Commandments," followed closely by "Suicidal Thoughts."
- **The Best Biggie Guest Verse:** When he showed up on Total's "Can't You See."[3]
- **The Best Biggie Musical Aside to Casually Bring Up in a Conversation to Make It Seem Like You Know a Lot About Music:** They made a biopic about Biggie's life in 2009. It was called *Notorious.* Angela Bassett played his mother. She was in a movie in 1995 called *Waiting to Exhale* that had a soundtrack that featured Toni Braxton, Patti LaBelle, SWV, Whitney Houston, Chanté Moore, Chaka Khan, TLC, and Mary J. Blige, all of whom were mentioned by name in Biggie's song "Just Playing (Dreams)," wherein he imagined having sex with various R&B singers.
- **The Best Biggie Non-Music Pop-Culture Moment:** When he guest appeared as himself on an episode of *Martin,* and Gina and Pam kept trying to sing for him.
- **The Best Biggie Accessory:** Remember the photo of him where he's wearing the crown tilted to the side? That's it. It's the crown. It looks perfect on him. It fits on his head the way Excalibur fit in King Arthur's hand.
- **The Best Surprising Biggie Tidbit:** Per a Puff Daddy interview in 2009, the clip you hear at the end of the song "Respect," where it sounds like a woman is performing oral sex on him, is actually real. That was really happening in the studio, and they just recorded it.
- **The Best Unexpected Word to Describe Biggie's Voice:** "Humid." His voice sounds like it feels like jungle air.
- **The Best Two-Sentence Argument for Biggie Being Picked as the Greatest Rapper of All Time:** Nobody has ever had better control of their words and a better grasp on how to say them than Biggie. In his finest moments, he is a god creating the universe.

---

3. I know that the general consensus here is that his verse on Jay-Z's "Brooklyn's Finest" is his best guest verse, but I prefer Biggie when he's doing his R&B thing over Biggie when he's talking about shooting your daughter in her calf muscle.

.....

Five years after Biggie passed, a movie called *Hardball* came out. It was one of those white-savior movies about a gambling addict (Conor O'Neill, played by Keanu Reeves) who ends up coaching an inner-city youth baseball team because he wants to earn money to pay back some bookies who are looking to bend his legs in the wrong direction.

The coaching thing starts out terrible for him, but then he falls in love with the kids and things start to get better. And the team has their biggest jump forward because of Biggie Smalls. What happens is the shortstop on the team – this extremely nervous but likable kid named Miles – asks if he could pitch one game. And Coach O'Neill is hesitant at first but eventually gives in.

That next game, Miles suits up to pitch. And when he does, he makes sure to include a pair of headphones with his game attire. He walks out onto the mound, looks at the batter, lets the music enter his ears, and then starts dancing. Nobody else can hear the music, so the other team starts laughing. Miles, who can't hear their jeers, shakes himself loose, loads up the ball, and then fires a fucking laser beam to his catcher. The camera cuts to the other team, and they aren't laughing anymore. They're in awe and completely silent, except for one kid, who just mutters, ". . . Damn." They know that only destruction lies ahead now.

Miles sets up again for another pitch, and it's the same thing. Then a third pitch, and that's that. The batter's struck out. Coach O'Neill asks his assistant (G-Baby, the younger brother of one of the players on the team) what Miles is listening to. And the kid says, "Same song over and over. 'Big Poppa' by Notorious B.I.G." Coach O'Neill asks how the song goes, and so G-Baby sings the hook. Coach O'Neill stares at him for a second, then nods his head one time. And that's when "Big Poppa" kicks on for real as the soundtrack for the scene, and then we get a montage of Miles throwing strike after strike after strike. Miles was just a normal baseball player whenever he wasn't listening to "Big Poppa," but as soon as Biggie's voice touched his brain, Miles turned into goddamn Pedro Martinez.

There's a part in the song "Big Poppa" where Biggie says to a woman he's courting that they should watch a movie in a Jacuzzi. I wish Biggie would've lived long enough to have seen that subplot in *Hardball.* He probably would've gotten a big kick out of it.[4]

.....

TEN 2PAC THINGS, EACH OF WHICH ARE THE BEST

- **The Best 2Pac Album:** 1996's *All Eyez on Me.*
- **The Best 2Pac Song That Was a Single:** "California Love," followed closely by "Dear Mama," followed closely by "Keep Ya Head Up."
- **The Best 2Pac Song That Wasn't a Single:** "Picture Me Rollin'," followed closely by "Me Against the World," followed closely by "Me and My Girlfriend."
- **The Best 2Pac Guest Verse:** When he showed up on Scarface's "Smile."

4. He would not have gotten a big kick out of the ending, though. Because the movie ends with G-Baby accidentally getting shot to death during a gang initiation involving a former player who was kicked off the team for being too old. It's probably the most unnecessary movie death in movie history.

- **The Best 2Pac Musical Aside to Casually Bring Up in a Conversation to Make It Seem Like You Know a Lot About Music:** The first forty-five seconds of "Hail Mary" are the best first forty-five seconds of any 2Pac song. You get him speaking in his normal voice, and you get him rapping, and you get him talking shit, and you get him doing that very wonderful 2Pac yell that he would do where it'd feel like the sound was hitting your ears from all directions, and it's all happening on a beat that feels at once contemplative and confrontational and haunted. But "Hail Mary" is not, all in all, the best 2Pac song. It's not even a podium finisher, really.
- **The Best 2Pac Non-Music Pop-Culture Moment:** The obvious answer here is to point out his three-year stretch when he starred in 1992's *Juice*, 1993's *Poetic Justice*, and 1994's *Above the Rim*. It's so extremely easy to look at his acting work during that period and believe that had he been around for as long as he should've been around, he'd have eventually won at least one Oscar. But let's go with something a little more obscure. Let's go with his background cameo in the 1991 dark comedy *Nothing but Trouble*.
- **The Best 2Pac Accessory:** The bandanna. Come on.
- **The Best Surprising 2Pac Tidbit:** His ex-wife said that he auditioned for the part of Bubba in 1994's *Forrest Gump*.
- **The Best Unexpected Word to Describe 2Pac's Voice:** "Symphonic." It comes at you all at once.
- **The Best Two-Sentence Argument for 2Pac Being Picked as the Greatest Rapper of All Time:** Nobody has ever had a stronger grasp on how to pump words full of emotion than 2Pac. He weaponized charisma in a way that we hadn't seen before and we haven't seen since.

•••••

One of my fondest memories from growing up is going to my friend Marco's house and listening to 2Pac's *All Eyez on Me* album while we played *Killer Instinct* on Super Nintendo. I was fifteen at the time, which means I was right at that point where I was excited because I could feel myself stepping further out into the world on my own, but also I wasn't so far out there yet that I had any kind of real understanding of how dangerous and unforgiving of a place it could be. And I think that's why 2Pac was the perfect soundtrack for that moment. Because, for one, it felt like he was talking directly to me about potentially being an adult, and that was very exciting. And then, for two, I'd come to find out later, Marco felt like 2Pac was talking to him about already being an adult, and it was very empowering for him.

Marco had a mom, but he and his sisters lived with his grandparents, neither of whom were in any condition to take care of children. As such, Marco did pretty much whatever he wanted to do whenever he wanted to do it. He didn't have to ask permission to spend the night anywhere, and he didn't have to ask permission to skip school if he didn't feel like going, and he didn't have to ask permission to eat a bag of Cool Ranch Doritos or a handful of Skittles for dinner if that was what he felt like doing on any given night. That was the kind of life he was living. And at fifteen, I thought it was cool as fuck. I thought that he had the life that I wanted. But then I got older. And that was when I realized that the ways in which he was existing that I thought were great were actually pretty bad. All of those situations looked different when I saw them as an adult. He wasn't emancipated and flourishing. He was just a child, and he was alone and untended to and uncared for. And those things all eventually conspired against him, unraveling his life.

•••••

A little over a year after the massive success of M. Night Shyamalan's sci-fi thriller *The Sixth Sense*, his follow-up movie, another sci-fi thriller called *Unbreakable*, was released. It wasn't nearly as gigantic as *The Sixth Sense*, but it proved to be even more ambitious.[5]

In it, a security guard (David Dunn, played by Bruce Willis) survives a grisly train crash that kills all of the other 131 passengers. News of his survival spreads, and that's how we get introduced to Elijah Price, an art-gallery owner (played by Samuel L. Jackson) with a wonderful haircut and an affinity for comic books. Price, who suffers from brittle bone disease, which makes him extremely susceptible to broken bones, arranges a meeting with Dunn, during which he says the quote that I cited at the top of this chapter. Price believes that similar to the way you can't have Light without Dark or Good without Evil, you also can't have Weak without Strong. He says that he knew somebody like Dunn was out there – somebody indestructible – because there had to be someone of incredible physical strength in the world to balance out his own incredible physical weakness.

The twist in the movie ends up being that Price not only caused the train crash but also caused several other similar accidents that resulted in countless deaths. And he did so because he wanted to find this indestructible person, because according to him, if that indestructible person existed, then it meant that Price needed to exist as well. He explains it all in his final monologue of the movie, saying, "Now that we know who you are, I know who I am. I'm not a mistake. It all makes sense. In a comic, you know how you can tell who the archvillain's going to be? He's the exact opposite of the hero. And most times, they're friends, like you and me."

Now, all of the pieces of his argument don't match up perfectly with what I'm about to write next, but they're close enough that I'm certain you're going to get the point. No two solo rappers have ever been as perfectly and inextricably linked as 2Pac and Biggie. No two rappers ever will. They were fated together as a pairing by the cosmos – a perfect union of contrasting styles and contrasting ideologies and contrasting personas and contrasting skill sets.

Individually, they were brilliant masters, obviously. But there's never a way to tell the story of one without also telling the story of the other. Which is why the answer to the question "2Pac or Biggie?" can never be "2Pac" and can never be "Biggie."

The answer to "2Pac or Biggie?" can only ever be 2Pac *and* Biggie.

5. It was also very good. It's my second favorite of his movies. First place is *Signs*.

ACKNOWLEDGMENTS

My first favorite part of writing a book is when the publisher gives me the money for having done so. My second favorite part of writing a book, though, is writing the acknowledgments. It always makes me feel good to write out the names of the people who helped make the book a possibility, and I mean that in both a direct sense (like, for example, the people who literally put the book together) and an indirect sense (like, for example, the people who did things that I used as inspiration at various moments during the book-writing process). And so, let me say some of those names.

Thank you to everyone who has ever made a rap song, first and foremost. What you do is beautiful and important, and I hope you know that the entire world is legitimately a better place because of your work. That's not hyperbole. It's a big truth.

Thank you to Sean Desmond, who (a) was the person who gave me a book contract to write this book; and (b) edited the book. I hope you like the way this turned out. Thanks for flying down to Texas and eating at Olive Garden with me that one time. It was a wonderful date. I hope we work together for many, many books.

Thank you to Arturo Torres, who drew all of the art in the book. It's so wild to look back at the stuff you made for our first book together and measure it up against the work you did for this one.

Thank you to Dart Adams, who (a) helped research information for the book; and (b) fact-checked the book. You're the best. The only time I did not enjoy working with you on this was that one night when the Spurs and the Celtics played, and my beloved Spurs gave up a 32-point lead to your beloved Celtics. Jayson Tatum scored 60 that night. It was miserable. Other than that, though, you were a delight to work with.

Thank you to each of the people who wrote blurbs for the "Ninja Rap" chapter. That's Clover Hope, Rob Markman, Kathy Iandoli, Sean Fennessey, Rembert Browne, Dart Adams, Danyel Smith, Hunter Harris, Van Lathan, and Nadirah Simmons. I consider all ten of you to be better and smarter writers than me, which is why I was (and am) so proud that you each opted to participate in this.

Thank you to Daniel Greenberg, my beautiful book agent. You're a champion. I can't believe I forgot to mention you in the acknowledgment section of *Movies (And Other Things)*. I owe you an extra Thank You in this acknowledgment section to make up for it.

Thank you to each of the people who worked on the book behind the scenes. I appreciate everything you did, be it anything from making sure the design was airtight to making sure that people heard about the book and were excited about the book. That's Jarrod Taylor, Kristen Lemire, Nyamekye Waliyaya, Tareth Mitch, and Janice Lee.

Thank you to Renard Mitchell and Alex Zaragoza, both of whom helped with research for various chapters in this book.

Thank you to everyone who wrote a book on rap that I read while I researched for this. Your work was very inspirational, and I have a great fondness in my chest for you because I know that you care about rap as much as I do. Some (but not all) of those books include: Nelson George's *Hip Hop America*, Clover Hope's *The Motherlode*, Jay-Z and Dream Hampton's *Decoded*, Gucci Mane and Neil Martinez-Belkin's *The Autobiography of Gucci Mane*, Hanif Aburraqib's *Go Ahead in the Rain*, Kathy Iandoli's *God Save the Queens*, Rakim's *Sweat the Technique*, Ben Westhoff's *Original Gangstas*, Raquel Cepeda's *And It Don't Stop*, Soren Baker's *The History of Gangsta Rap*, Joan Morgan's *When Chickenheads Come Home to Roost*, Joan Morgan's *She Begat This*, The RZA's *The Tao of Wu*, Jeff Chang's *Can't Stop, Won't Stop*, Queen Latifah's *Ladies First*,

Michael Diamond and Adam Horovitz's *Beastie Boys Book*, Dan Charnas's *The Big Payback*, Brian Coleman's *Check the Technique*, Questlove's *Mo' Meta Blues*, and a whole bunch more that I won't remember until after this book has been published and then I'm gonna feel like an asshole for having left them out.

Thank you to everyone who made a documentary on rap that I watched while I researched for this. Your work was very inspirational, and I have a great fondness in my chest for you because I know that you care about rap as much as I do. Some (but not all) of those documentaries include: *Something From Nothing*; *The Art of Rap*; *Hip-Hop Evolution*; *Can't Stop, Won't Stop—A Bad Boy Story*; *Tupac: Resurrection*; *Before Anything: The Cash Money Story*; *Fade to Black*; *Time Is ILLmatic*; *Dave Chappelle's Block Party*; *The Defiant Ones*; *Biggie: I Got a Story to Tell*; *Style Wars*; *Rhyme & Reason*; *Bears, Rhymes & Life: The Travels of a Tribe Called Quest*; *Backstage*; *G Funk*; *Biggie & Tupac*; *Beef; And You Don't Stop: 30 Years of Hip-Hop*; *My Mic Sounds Nice: A Truth About Women and Hip-Hop*; *Stretch and Bobbito: Radio That Changed Lives*; and a whole bunch more that I won't remember until after this book has been published and then I'm gonna feel like an asshole for having left them out.

Thank you to Larami, the love of my life. Thanks for telling me about Mos Def when we met in college. There's nobody I like listening to rap music with more than you. (Actually, all things measured, there's nobody I like doing *anything* with more than you. You remain the top level.)

Thank you to Parker, Braxton, and Caleb. I love you three so, so much, and would absolutely fistfight one of those aliens from *A Quiet Place* to protect you.

Thank you to Jada and Jasara, both of whom told me to make sure I mentioned them in the acknowledgment section of whatever book it was that I wrote next. I hope you two see this and I hope you two smile because of it. And thank you to Roman and Sofia, neither of whom told me to make sure I mentioned them but both of whom I hope see this and know that their uncle is always thinking about them.

Thank you to my mom and my dad for never discouraging me from listening to rap. That was a real cool move by y'all.

Thank you to my sisters, Yasminda, Nastasja, and Marie. I love you. And I would happily run someone over with my car if you needed me to.

Thank you to my grandma, who bought me DMX's *It's Dark and Hell Is Hot* album for my birthday in 1998. I miss you a lot all the time. I wish you'd have gotten the chance to stick around awhile longer to see how monumental of a moment that ended up being in my life.

Thank you again to Daniel Greenberg, my beautiful book agent. You're a champion. This is your second Thank You. Now we're even.

Thank you to The FOH. None of this shit works without y'all. It's like I have several hundred thousand big brothers and big sisters that I can dial up whenever I need help with something. It's very empowering. Let's keep causing trouble on the internet together.

Thank you to the late night weirdos on Twitter for always being awake whenever I finished a marathon writing session and wanted someone to talk to at 3:30 in the morning.

And thank you to every rap music video that was regularly played on MTV between 1994 and 1999, including but not limited to Biggie's "Big Poppa," Missy Elliott's "The Rain," DMX's "Ruff Ryders' Anthem," Juvenile's "Ha," Master P's "Make 'Em Say Uhh!," Da Brat's "Funkdafied," Lauryn Hill's "Ex-Factor," Wyclef's "Gone Till November," Busta Rhymes's "Dangerous," Busta Rhymes and Janet Jackson's "What's It Gonna Be?!," Will Smith's "Men in Black," Puff Daddy's "Been Around the World," 2Pac's "California Love," and Lil' Kim's "Crush On You."